Scott Foresman SCIENCE for Texas

Series Authors

Dr. Timothy Cooney
*Professor of Earth Science and
  Science Education*
Earth Science Department
University of Northern Iowa
Cedar Falls, Iowa

Michael Anthony DiSpezio
Science Education Specialist
Cape Cod Children's Museum
Falmouth, Massachusetts

Barbara K. Foots
Science Education Consultant
Houston, Texas

Dr. Angie L. Matamoros
Science Curriculum Specialist
Broward County Schools
Ft. Lauderdale, Florida

Kate Boehm Nyquist
Science Writer and Curriculum Specialist
Mount Pleasant, South Carolina

Dr. Karen L. Ostlund
Professor
Science Education Center
The University of Texas at Austin
Austin, Texas

Contributing Authors

Dr. Anna Uhl Chamot
*Associate Professor and
  ESL Faculty Advisor*
Department of Teacher Preparation
  and Special Education
Graduate School of Education
  and Human Development
The George Washington University
Washington, DC

Dr. Jim Cummins
Professor
Modern Language Centre and
  Curriculum Department
Ontario Institute for Studies in Education
Toronto, Canada

Gale Philips Kahn
Lecturer, Science and Math Education
Elementary Education Department
California State University, Fullerton
Fullerton, California

Vincent Sipkovich
Teacher
Irvine Unified School District
Irvine, California

Steve Weinberg
Science Consultant
Connecticut State
  Department of Education
Hartford, Connecticut

Scott Foresman

Editorial Offices: Glenview, Illinois; New York, New York
Sales Offices: Reading, Massachusetts; Duluth, Georgia;
Glenview, Illinois; Carrollton, Texas; Menlo Park, California
www.sfscience.com

Content Consultants

Dr. J. Scott Cairns
National Institutes of Health
Bethesda, Maryland

Jackie Cleveland
Elementary Resource Specialist
Mesa Public School District
Mesa, Arizona

Robert L. Kolenda
Science Lead Teacher, K-12
Neshaminy School District
Langhorne, Pennsylvania

David P. Lopath
Teacher
The Consolidated School District
of New Britain
New Britain, Connecticut

Sammantha Lane Magsino
Science Coordinator
Institute of Geophysics
University of Texas at Austin
Austin, Texas

Kathleen Middleton
Director, Health Education
ToucanEd
Soquel, California

Irwin Slesnick
Professor of Biology
Western Washington University
Bellingham, Washington

Dr. James C. Walters
Professor of Geology
University of Northern Iowa
Cedar Falls, Iowa

Multicultural Consultants

Dr. Shirley Gholston Key
Assistant Professor
University of Houston-Downtown
Houston, Texas

Damon L. Mitchell
Quality Auditor
Louisiana-Pacific Corporation
Conroe, Texas

Classroom Reviewers

Kathleen Avery
Teacher
Kellogg Science/Technology
Magnet
Wichita, Kansas

Margaret S. Brown
Teacher
Cedar Grove Primary
Williamston, South Carolina

Deborah Browne
Teacher
Whitesville Elementary School
Moncks Corner, South Carolina

Wendy Capron
Teacher
Corlears School
New York, New York

Jiwon Choi
Teacher
Corlears School
New York, New York

John Cirrincione
Teacher
West Seneca Central Schools
West Seneca, New York

Jacqueline Colander
Teacher
Norfolk Public Schools
Norfolk, Virginia

Dr. Terry Contant
Teacher
Conroe Independent
School District
The Woodlands, Texas

Susan Crowley-Walsh
Teacher
Meadowbrook Elementary School
Gladstone, Missouri

Charlene K. Dindo
Teacher
Fairhope K-1 Center/Pelican's
Nest Science Lab
Fairhope, Alabama

Laurie Duffee
Teacher
Barnard Elementary
Tulsa, Oklahoma

Beth Anne Ebler
Teacher
Newark Public Schools
Newark, New Jersey

Karen P. Farrell
Teacher
Rondout Elementary School District
#72
Lake Forest, Illinois

Anna M. Gaiter
Teacher
Los Angeles Unified School District
Los Angeles Systemic Initiative
Los Angeles, California

Federica M. Gallegos
Teacher
Highland Park Elementary
Salt Lake School District
Salt Lake City, Utah

Janet E. Gray
Teacher
Anderson Elementary - Conroe ISD
Conroe, Texas

Karen Guinn
Teacher
Ehrhardt Elementary School - KISD
Spring, Texas

Denis John Hagerty
Teacher
Al Ittihad Private Schools
Dubai, United Arab Emirates

Judith Halpern
Teacher
Bannockburn School
Deerfield, Illinois

Debra D. Harper
Teacher
Community School District 9
Bronx, New York

Gretchen Harr
Teacher
Denver Public Schools - Doull School
Denver, Colorado

Bonnie L. Hawthorne
Teacher
Jim Darcy School
School Dist #1
Helena, Montana

Marselle Heywood-Julian
Teacher
Community School District 6
New York, New York

Scott Klene
Teacher
Bannockburn School 106
Bannockburn, Illinois

Thomas Kranz
Teacher
Livonia Primary School
Livonia, New York

Tom Leahy
Teacher
Coos Bay School District
Coos Bay, Oregon

Mary Littig
Teacher
Kellogg Science/Technology
Magnet
Wichita, Kansas

Patricia Marin
Teacher
Corlears School
New York, New York

Susan Maki
Teacher
Cotton Creek CUSD 118
Island Lake, Illinois

Efraín Meléndez
Teacher
East LA Mathematics Science
Center LAUSD
Los Angeles, California

Becky Mojalid
Teacher
Manarat Jeddah Girls' School
Jeddah, Saudi Arabia

Susan Nations
Teacher
Sulphur Springs Elementary
Tampa, Florida

Brooke Palmer
Teacher
Whitesville Elementary
Moncks Corner, South Carolina

Jayne Pedersen
Teacher
Laura B. Sprague
School District 103
Lincolnshire, Illinois

Shirley Pfingston
Teacher
Orland School Dist 135
Orland Park, Illinois

Teresa Gayle Rountree
Teacher
Box Elder School District
Brigham City, Utah

Helen C. Smith
Teacher
Schultz Elementary
Klein Independent School District
Tomball, Texas

Denette Smith-Gibson
Teacher
Mitchell Intermediate, CISD
The Woodlands, Texas

Mary Jean Syrek
Teacher
Dr. Charles R. Drew Science
Magnet
Buffalo, New York

Rosemary Troxel
Teacher
Libertyville School District 70
Libertyville, Illinois

Susan D. Vani
Teacher
Laura B. Sprague School
School District 103
Lincolnshire, Illinois

Debra Worman
Teacher
Bryant Elementary
Tulsa, Oklahoma

Dr. Gayla Wright
Teacher
Edmond Public School
Edmond, Oklahoma

ISBN: 0-673-59357-6
Copyright © 2000, Addison-Wesley Educational Publishers Inc.
All Rights Reserved. Printed in the United States of America.

4567890 DOW 03 02 01 00

⚠ Activity and Safety Consultants

Laura Adams
Teacher
Holley-Navarre Intermediate
Navarre, Florida

Dr. Charlie Ashman
Teacher
Carl Sandburg Middle School
Mundelein District #75
Mundelein, Illinois

Christopher Atlee
Teacher
Horace Mann Elementary
Wichita Public Schools
Wichita, Kansas

David Bachman
Consultant
Chicago, Illinois

Sherry Baldwin
Teacher
Shady Brook
Bedford ISD
Euless, Texas

Pam Bazis
Teacher
Richardson ISD
  Classical Magnet School
Richardson, Texas

Angela Boese
Teacher
McCollom Elementary
Wichita Public Schools USD #259
Wichita, Kansas

Jan Buckelew
Teacher
Taylor Ranch Elementary
Venice, Florida

Shonie Castaneda
Teacher
Carman Elementary, PSJA
Pharr, Texas

Donna Coffey
Teacher
Melrose Elementary - Pinellas
St. Petersburg, Florida

Diamantina Contreras
Teacher
J.T. Brackenridge Elementary
San Antonio ISD
San Antonio, Texas

Susanna Curtis
Teacher
Lake Bluff Middle School
Lake Bluff, Illinois

Karen Farrell
Teacher
Rondout Elementary School,
  Dist. #72
Lake Forest, Illinois

Paul Gannon
Teacher
El Paso ISD
El Paso, Texas

Nancy Garman
Teacher
Jefferson Elementary School
Charleston, Illinois

Susan Graves
Teacher
Beech Elementary
Wichita Public Schools USD #259
Wichita, Kansas

Jo Anna Harrison
Teacher
Cornelius Elementary
Houston ISD
Houston, Texas

Monica Hartman
Teacher
Richard Elementary
Detroit Public Schools
Detroit, Michigan

Kelly Howard
Teacher
Sarasota, Florida

Kelly Kimborough
Teacher
Richardson ISD
  Classical Magnet School
Richardson, Texas

Mary Leveron
Teacher
Velasco Elementary
Brazosport ISD
Freeport, Texas

Becky McClendon
Teacher
A.P. Beutel Elementary
Brazosport ISD
Freeport, Texas

Suzanne Milstead
Teacher
Liestman Elementary
Alief ISD
Houston, Texas

Debbie Oliver
Teacher
School Board of Broward County
Ft. Lauderdale, Florida

Sharon Pearthree
Teacher
School Board of Broward County
Ft. Lauderdale, Florida

Jayne Pedersen
Teacher
Laura B. Sprague School
District 103
Lincolnshire, Illinois

Sharon Pedroja
Teacher
Riverside Cultural
  Arts/History Magnet
Wichita Public Schools USD #259
Wichita, Kansas

Marcia Percell
Teacher
Pharr, San Juan, Alamo ISD
Pharr, Texas

Shirley Pfingston
Teacher
Orland School Dist #135
Orland Park, Illinois

Sharon S. Placko
Teacher
District 26, Mt. Prospect
Mt. Prospect, IL

Glenda Rall
Teacher
Seltzer Elementary
USD #259
Wichita, Kansas

Nelda Requenez
Teacher
Canterbury Elementary
Edinburg, Texas

Dr. Beth Rice
Teacher
Loxahatchee Groves
  Elementary School
Loxahatchee, Florida

Martha Salom Romero
Teacher
El Paso ISD
El Paso, Texas

Paula Sanders
Teacher
Welleby Elementary School
Sunrise, Florida

Lynn Setchell
Teacher
Sigsbee Elementary School
Key West, Florida

Rhonda Shook
Teacher
Mueller Elementary
Wichita Public Schools USD #259
Wichita, Kansas

Anna Marie Smith
Teacher
Orland School Dist. # 135
Orland Park, Illinois

Nancy Ann Varneke
Teacher
Seltzer Elementary
Wichita Public Schools USD #259
Wichita, Kansas

Aimee Walsh
Teacher
Rolling Meadows, Illinois

Ilene Wagner
Teacher
O.A. Thorp Scholastic Acacemy
Chicago Public Schools
Chicago, Illinois

Brian Warren
Teacher
Riley Community Consolidated
  School District 18
Marengo, Illinois

Tammie White
Teacher
Holley-Navarre
  Intermediate School
Navarre, Florida

Dr. Mychael Willon
Principal
Horace Mann Elementary
Wichita Public Schools
Wichita, Kansas

- -

Inclusion Consultants

Dr. Eric J. Pyle, Ph.D.
*Assistant Professor, Science
  Education*
Department of Educational Theory
  and Practice
West Virginia University
Morgantown, West Virginia

Dr. Gretchen Butera, Ph.D.
*Associate Professor, Special
  Education*
Department of Education Theory
  and Practice
West Virginia University
Morgantown, West Virginia

Bilingual Consultant

Irma Gomez-Torres
Dalindo Elementary
Austin ISD
Austin, Texas

Bilingual Reviewers

Mary E. Morales
E.A. Jones Elementary
Fort Bend ISD
Missouri City, Texas

Gabriela T. Nolasco
Pebble Hills Elementary
Ysleta ISD
El Paso, Texas

Maribel B. Tanguma
Reed and Mock Elementary
San Juan, Texas

Yesenia Garza
Reed and Mock Elementary
San Juan, Texas

Teri Gallegos
St. Andrew's School
Austin, Texas

iii

Unit A
Life Science

Unit B
Physical Science

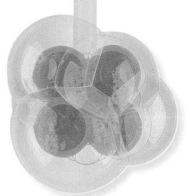

Unit C
Earth Science

Unit D
Human Body

Your Science Handbook

Using Scientific Methods for Science Inquiry

Scientists use scientific methods to find answers to questions. Scientific methods have the steps shown on these pages. Scientists sometimes use the steps in different order. You can use these steps for your own science inquiries.

Problem

The problem is the question you want to answer. Inquiry has led to many discoveries in science. Ask your question.

Do seeds grow better in soil or in sand?

Give your hypothesis.

Tell what you think the answer is to the problem.

If you plant seeds in soil, they will grow better than seeds planted in sand. ▶

Control the variables.

Change one thing when you test your hypothesis. Keep everything else the same.

I will put the same amount of water in each cup.

Test your hypothesis.

Do experiments to test your hypothesis. You may need to do experiments more than one time to see if the results are the same each time.

◀ Observe the seeds and compare how they grow.

Collect your data.

Collect data about the problem. Record your data on a chart. You might make drawings or write words or sentences.

Tell your conclusion.

Compare your results and hypothesis. Decide if your hypothesis is right or wrong. Tell what you decide.

Seeds planted in soil grow better than seeds planted in sand.

? Inquire Further

Use what you learn to answer other problems or questions. You may want to do your experiment again or change your experiment.

Does the amount of water affect how plants grow? ▶

Using Process Skills for Science Inquiry

Scientists use process skills to do research. You will use process skills when you do the activities in this book.

When you test something, you use process skills. When you collect data, you use process skills. When you make conclusions and tell what you learn, you use process skills.

I hear a high sound

Observing
Your senses are seeing, hearing, smelling, touching, and tasting. Use your senses to find out about objects or things that happen.

Communicating
Use words, pictures, charts, or graphs to share what you learn.

Classifying
Sort or group objects by their properties.

Estimating and Measuring
Estimate means to tell what you think an object's measurement is. Make an estimate. Then measure the object.

Inferring
Make a conclusion or a guess from what you observe or from what you already know.

Predicting
Tell what you think will happen.

Making Definitions
Use what you already know to describe something or tell what it means.

Making and Using Models
Make a model to show what you know about something.

Giving Hypotheses
Make a statement you can test to answer a problem or question.

Collecting Data
Record what you observe and measure. Use graphs, charts, pictures, or words. Use what you learned to answer problems or questions.

Controlling Variables
Change one thing that may affect what happens. Keep everything else the same.

Experimenting
Plan and do an investigation to test a hypothesis or to answer a problem. Then make conclusions.

? Science Inquiry

As you use your science book, you will ask questions, do investigations, answer your questions, and then tell others what you learned. This is called science inquiry. You can use science inquiry to do this science project.

What objects are lighter than an apple?

1 **Ask a question about living things, objects, or things that happen.**

What objects are lighter than an apple?

2 **Plan and do a simple investigation to answer your question.**

Put an apple on one side of a pan balance. Put another object on the other side. Observe to see which object is lighter.

3 **Use some simple materials and tools to help you.**

Use a pan balance to compare the weight of the objects. Use a chart to show which objects are lighter than the apple.

4 **Use what you observed to answer your question.**

Which objects are lighter than an apple?

5 **Share your information with your class.**

You can use a chart, words, or pictures.

Unit A
Life
Science

Science and Technology
In Your World!

Why do some zoos have fake trees?

Branches pop out of the trunks of the fake trees. Giraffes get the exercise they need by walking from tree to tree to eat real food from the fake branches.

Chapter 1
Plants

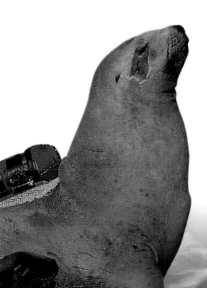

Can animals make movies?

Yes! This seal wears a video camera on its back. It takes pictures that show scientists what animals do under water.

Chapter 2
Animals

What is a virtual aquarium?

It is a fish tank you can design on a computer. A website lets you choose fish and a habitat. Then your aquarium shows up on the screen.

Chapter 3
Where Plants and Animals Live

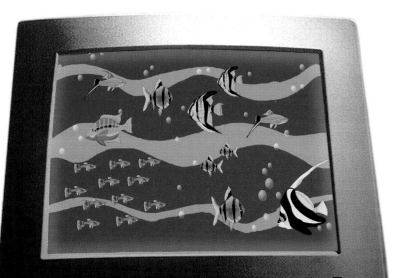

Chapter 1
Plants

Plant a Little Seed

Sing to the tune of *I've Been Working on the Railroad*.

Plant a seed and see what happens.
You will be surprised.

In the ground, the roots are growing,
But they're hidden from your eyes.

A stem will soon be growing upward
Reaching for the sky.

From the stem the leaves are growing.
Soon a flower may catch your eye.

First there's a seed.

Then there are roots.

Then come a stem, leaves and a flower.

Plant a little seed.

Plant a little seed.

Plant a seed and watch it grow!

Original lyrics by Gerri Brioso and Richard Freitas.
Produced by Children's Television Workshop.

Learning Science Words

Find the word on this page with yellow behind it. This is a special science word.

Now read the sentence. The sentence tells you what the science word means.

Roots hold the plant in the ground.

Look at page A8. What special science words do you see?

roots

When you see a science word in this book, write it on a card. Draw a picture to show the word. Keep the word cards in your desk or in a special folder.

roots

Turn the page to learn more science words.

Turn the page.

What do the roots and stem do?

It is a windy day. Hold onto your hat, or it might blow away! What keeps a plant from blowing away?

Plants have roots. **Roots** hold the plant in the ground. Find the roots in the picture. How does the root of the carrot look different from the other roots?

Roots take in water, too. Where does the water go? It goes to the stem. The **stem** takes the water to other parts of the plant.

Observe roots.

Materials

plant   cup of water   foil

crayon   tape

Process Skills

• observing

Process Skills

Steps

1 Put a plant in the cup.

2 Add water to cover the roots.

3 Cover the top of the jar with the foil.

4 Mark how high the water is.

5 Observe the jar every day.

Share. Draw the plant and water when you start and after five days.

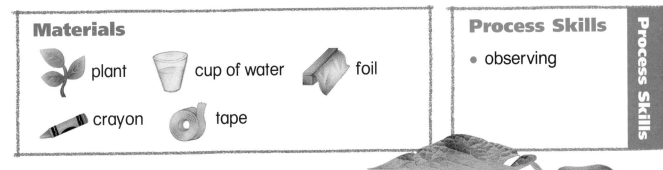

Lesson Review

1. What do the roots do?

2. What does the stem do?

3. **Tell** what happened to the water in the cup.

How does water move through plants?

Process Skills

- predicting
- observing

Materials

cup of water food color celery

paper towel

Steps

1 Put a little water in a cup.

2 Add 10 drops of food color.

3 Put the celery into the cup. Stir.

4 Draw what you predict will happen.

5 Observe the celery the next day. Break the celery. Draw what happened.

Draw what you predict will happen.

Draw what happened.

Think About Your Results

1. What happened to the water?

2. How does the colored water get to the leaves?

? Inquire Further

With what other plants could you try this activity?

What do leaves do?

It is a sunny summer day. You can sit under a shady tree. Look up and see all the leaves!

Leaves are an important part of a plant. Leaves use sunlight, air, and water to make food for the plant.

Leaves come in many shapes and sizes. Some are pointed. Others are round. Some are smaller than your fingernail. Others are bigger than your hand. What kinds of leaves have you seen?

Make a leaf rubbing.

Materials

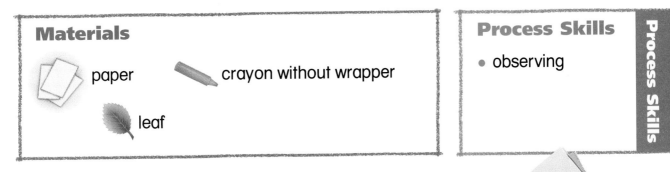

paper

crayon without wrapper

leaf

Process Skills

- observing

Steps

1 Put a leaf between two pieces of paper.

2 Rub the side of the crayon over the leaf.

3 Observe the leaf rubbing.

Share. See if a friend can guess which leaf you used for your rubbing.

Lesson Review

1. What do the leaves do?

2. What are some leaf shapes?

3. Tell what your leaf rubbing looks like.

How does a seed grow into a plant?

Dig a hole. Plant a seed. What happens to the seed in the ground?

A **seed** can grow into a new plant. This picture shows a bean seed. Water in the soil helps the seed coat come off. Next, a root grows down. A stem grows up. Leaves grow.

The seed has grown into a bean plant. The new plant needs sunlight, air, and water to grow.

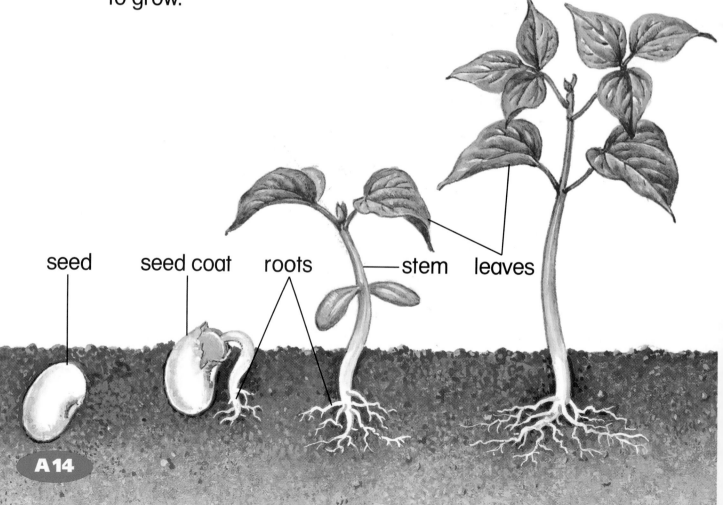

seed   seed coat   roots   stem   leaves

Grow a plant.

Materials

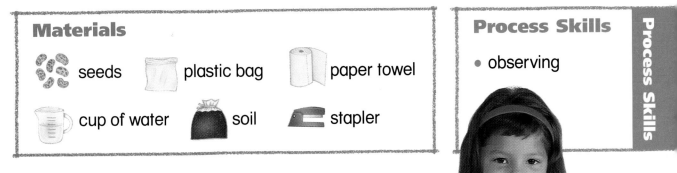

seeds   plastic bag   paper towel

cup of water   soil   stapler

Process Skills

• observing

Steps

1. Put 3 seeds in the bag.

2. Put a little water in the bag.

3. Close the bag.

4. **Observe** the seeds as they grow.

5. When the seeds grow roots, choose one plant. Put it in a cup of soil.

Share. Draw your plant as it grows.

Lesson Review

1. Does the root grow up or down?

2. What does a plant need to grow?

3. **Show** how a plant grows from a seed. Act it out.

How does an apple grow?

Mmm! Bite into a juicy apple. Did you know the apple started as a flower?

In spring, the apple tree is covered with green leaves and flowers.

The petals fall off the flower. An apple begins to form.

Can you find the tiny apple? The apple is a **fruit**. The fruit grows all summer.

In the fall the apple is ripe. It is ready to eat! Look at the cut apple. Find the seeds inside.

Lesson Review

1. What is an apple?

2. What is inside an apple?

3. **Draw** pictures to show how an apple grows.

Experiment with plant growth.

Process Skills

Process Skills

- experimenting
- observing

Materials

2 plants in containers water

index cards

Problem

How does water affect how plants grow?

Give Your Hypothesis

If you water one plant but not the other, what will happen? Tell what you think.

water

no water

Control the Variables

Put both plants in the same place.

Test Your Hypothesis

Follow these steps to do the experiment.

1. Label one plant **water.** Water this plant when the soil feels dry.

2. Label the other plant **no water.** Do not water this plant.

3. Observe the plants every day.

Collect Your Data

Use a chart like this one. Draw pictures to show the plants on each day.

Tell Your Conclusion

Compare your results and hypothesis. How does water affect how plants grow?

Inquire Further

What will happen if you give a plant too much water?

Day ——

water   no water

What parts of plants do you eat?

Would you like to eat leaves for lunch? When you eat lettuce or spinach, you are eating leaves!

People eat parts of plants. When you eat a carrot, you are eating a root. Part of the broccoli you eat is a stem. Asparagus is a stem too. Peas, corn, and nuts are seeds. Apples and oranges are fruits.

What plant parts do you see in this picture?

Classify the plants you eat.

Materials

pictures of foods   paper

glue

Process Skills

- classifying

Process Skills

Steps

1 Write the word **roots** on one paper. Do the same thing for **stems, leaves, fruit,** and **seeds.**

2 Gather pictures of foods. Decide what plant part each picture shows.

3 Classify the pictures. Glue them onto the correct papers.

Share. Tell what plant parts you like to eat.

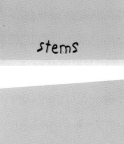

roots

stems

leaves

fruit

seeds

Lesson Review

1. What roots can you eat?

2. What leaves can you eat?

3. **Draw** a picture of your lunch. Tell if it has a root, stem, leaf, fruit, or seed.

How do people use plants?

Think about your favorite jeans. They are made of cotton. Did you know cotton comes from a plant?

Rope and straw baskets come from plants too. People use wood from trees to make furniture and other things. What do you know that is made of wood?

This forester is planting new trees. When they are big, some will be cut down and made into paper or other things.

Classify objects made from plants.

Materials

classroom objects

two cards

Process Skills

• classifying

Process Skills

Steps

1. Write **from plants** on one card.
   Write **not from plants** on another card.

2. Gather some objects. Which are from plants? Which are not from plants?

3. **Classify** the objects into the two groups.

Share. What did you use today that is from a plant?

Lesson Review

1. What is paper made from?

2. What plant do people use to make jeans?

3. **Draw** an object that comes from a plant. Draw an object that does not come from a plant.

Chapter 1 Review

Reviewing Science Words

1. What do the **roots** do?
2. What does the **stem** do?
3. What do **leaves** do?
4. Tell how a **seed** grows into a plant.
5. Name one kind of **fruit**.

Reviewing Science Ideas

1. What root, stem, leaf, seed, and fruit can you eat? Make a list.
2. Name three things people make from plants.

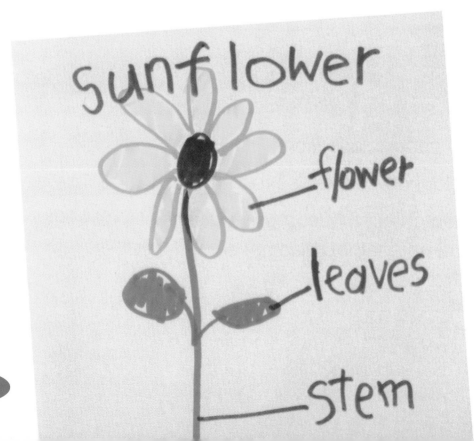

Make a poster of a plant.

Materials

 drawing paper

 crayons or markers

1 Draw a plant. Label the parts.

2 Name your plant.

3 Tell what your plant needs to stay alive.

4 Tell how people might use your plant.

5 Share your poster with others.

Chapter 2
Animals

All Kinds of Animals

♪ Sing to the tune of *Oh, Susanna.*

There are animals of many kinds,
They can be short or tall.
Most animals have legs that bend
But some have none at all.

Hippopotami have short fat legs
Giraffes' are tall and thin.
And if they run a race today,
Who do you think would win?

Animals are travelers.
There are lots of reasons why.
With feathers, fins or scales or feet,
They walk, slither, swim, or fly.

Original lyrics by Gerri Brioso and Richard Freitas.
Produced by Children's Television Workshop.
Copyright ©1999 Sesame Street, Inc.

Reading a Science Activity

Look at the activity about animals. Point to the title. Look at the picture. What materials do you need? Do the steps in order.

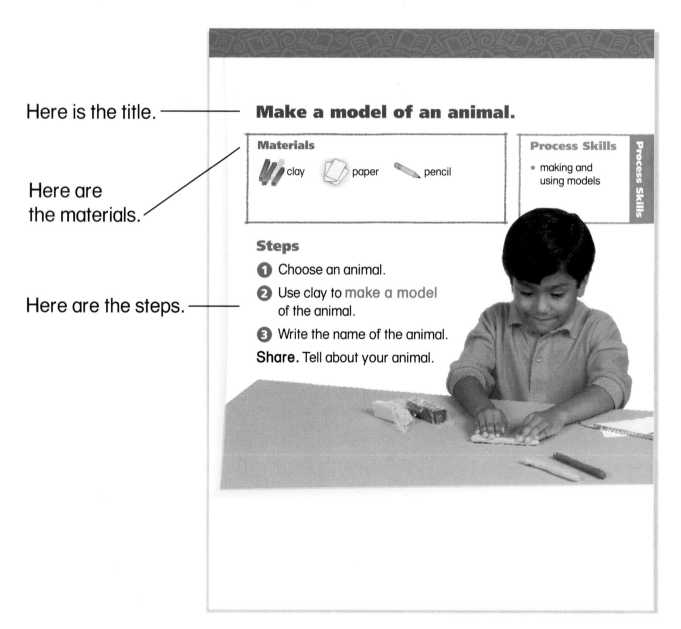

Here is the title. ——

Make a model of an animal.

Here are the materials. —

Materials

clay   paper   pencil

Process Skills

• making and using models

Steps

Here are the steps. ——

1. Choose an animal.
2. Use clay to make a model of the animal.
3. Write the name of the animal.

Share. Tell about your animal.

Make a model of an animal.

Materials

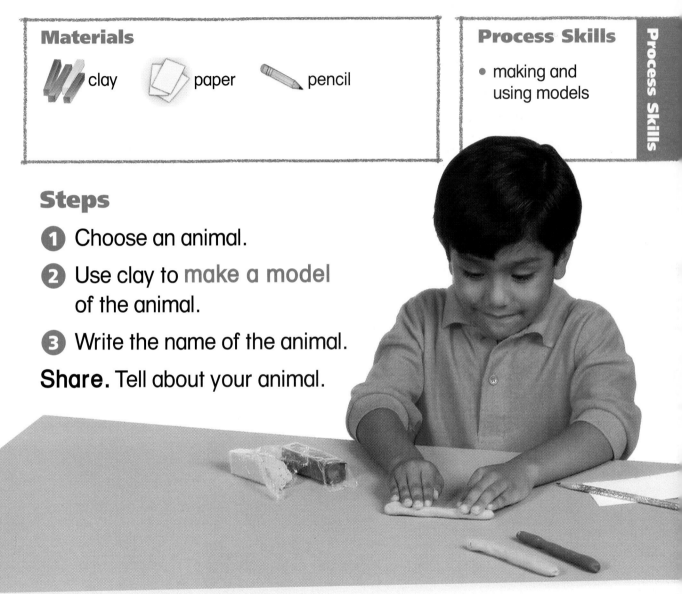

clay   paper   pencil

Process Skills

- making and using models

Steps

1 Choose an animal.

2 Use clay to make a model of the animal.

3 Write the name of the animal.

Share. Tell about your animal.

Turn the page to read a lesson and an activity.

Turn the page.

What kinds of animals are there?

Look up! A bird is flying. Look down! A frog is hopping by. Animals are everywhere!

Animals come in many sizes. What is the biggest animal you can think of? What is the smallest?

Animals come in many shapes and colors. Tell about the shape of the fish. Find an animal that has bright colors. What else can you tell about animals?

Classify animals.

Materials

animal pictures

2 pieces of paper

Process Skills

- classifying
- communicating (tell)

Process Skills

Steps

1 Classify the pictures into two groups.

2 Have a friend tell how you grouped the pictures.

3 Take turns. Do it again.

Share. Tell how you classified the pictures.

Lesson Review

1. Name a big animal.

2. Name a small animal.

3. Tell another way to classify the animal pictures.

How do animals move?

Do you like to skip or run? Do you like to jump or crawl?

Animals move in many ways too. A dog uses legs to walk or run. A monkey uses arms and legs to climb and swing in trees.

Snakes and fish have no legs. A snake slithers on the ground. A fish uses fins to swim. What does a duck use to swim?

How does this frog move? Can you move in that way?

Move like an animal.

Materials	Process Skills
animal cards	• observing

Steps

① Work with a group.

② Choose an animal card.

③ Move like the animal.

④ Have the group **observe** and guess the animal.

Share. Name an animal that can move in more than one way.

Lesson Review

1. Name four ways animals move.

2. What parts of animals help them move?

3. **Draw** a picture that shows an animal moving.

What coverings do animals have?

Brrr! It is a cold day. How do you stay warm?

A tiger is covered with fur. Fur keeps the tiger warm. A bird's feathers keep heat in and water out.

Coverings help animals in other ways. The scales on a fish are slippery. They help the fish swim. How do you think a shell helps a turtle?

Find fur, feathers, scales, and a shell in the pictures. Which animal matches each covering?

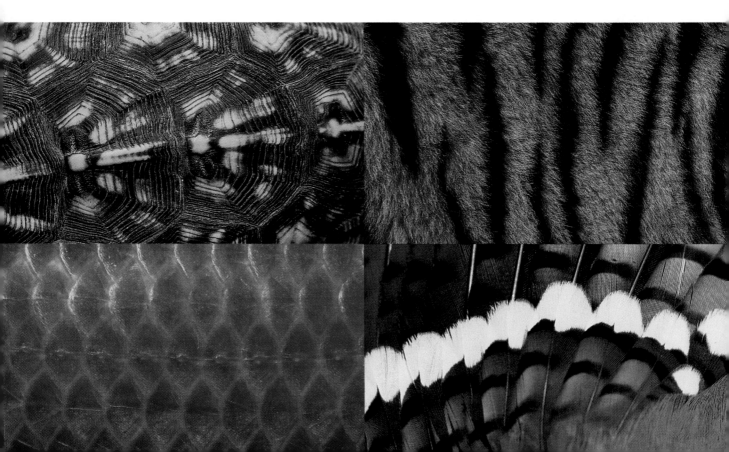

Observe a feather.

Materials

feather   hand lens

Process Skills

- communicating (write)
- observing

Steps

1 Touch the feather. Feel all the parts.

2 **Write** how the feather feels.

3 Use a hand lens. **Observe** the feather.

4 Draw the feather.

Share. Tell how parts of the feather are different.

Lesson Review

1. Name four animal coverings.

2. How can fur help animals?

3. **Tell** how feathers help birds.

What is an insect?

They creep! They crawl! They fly! What do you think they are? They are insects.

beetle

An **insect** is an animal. All insects have three main body parts. These body parts are called the **head** , **thorax** , and **abdomen** . Find the body parts of the ant.

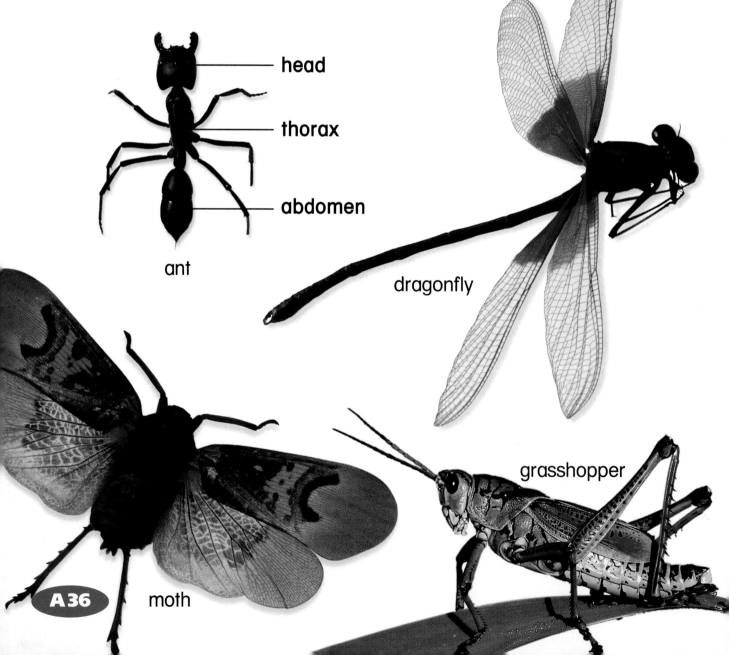

head

thorax

abdomen

ant

dragonfly

grasshopper

moth

butterfly

mantis

wasp

Find the picture of the wasp. How many legs does it have? All insects have six legs.

Lesson Review

1. Name the three main body parts of an insect.

2. How many legs does an insect have?

3. **Tell** the names of some insects.

What are the parts of an ant?

Process Skills

- observing
- making and using models

Materials

safety goggles

clay

pipe cleaners

Steps

1. Put on your safety goggles.

2. **Observe** the picture of the ant.

3. **Make a model.** Shape clay into three main body parts.

4. Stick the parts together.

5. Add pipe cleaners for legs.

6. Add other body parts.

Think About Your Results

1. How is your model like a real ant?

2. How is your model different from a real ant?

? Inquire Further

What are some other insect body parts?

What do animals need?

A snake, a skunk, a snail, and a spider all need the same things. What do they need?

All animals need food and water. This bird gets food and water by eating berries. Where else can it find water?

The spider catches insects in a web. The spider gets food and water by eating insects.

Animals also need air and a place to live. Pets live with people. The spider lives in a web. Where else do animals live?

Lesson Review

1. What four things do animals need?
2. Where do some animals live?
3. **Tell** how a spider gets food and water.

What are baby animals like?

A baby leopard is called a cub. How does a leopard take care of its cub?

Some baby animals need care from their parents. A **parent** is a mother or father. The leopard licks its baby to keep it clean. The bird brings food to its babies. How do other animals care for their babies?

A tadpole is a baby frog. A tadpole does not need care from its parents. Find the picture of the tadpole. How does it look different from its parent?

Lesson Review

1. Name an animal that does not need care from its parents.

2. List two ways that animals take care of their babies.

3. **Draw** a baby animal and a parent that look different from each other.

Chapter 2 Review

Reviewing Science Words

1. How many legs does an **insect** have?
2. Draw a picture of an insect. Point to the **head** , **thorax** , and **abdomen** .
3. What is a **parent** ?

Reviewing Science Ideas

1. Name four ways that animals move.
2. Name two animal coverings.
3. Name four things that animals need.
4. What are some ways that animals take care of their babies?

Make an animal mask.

Materials

crayons　　scissors　　paper

yarn　　glue　　paper plates

1. Make an animal face on your paper plate.
2. Wear your mask. Move like your animal.
3. Make the sounds your animal makes.
4. Tell what your animal needs.

Chapter 3
Where Plants and Animals Live

The Right Habitat

♪ Sing to the tune of *My Bonnie Lies over the Ocean.*

The lizard lives out in the desert.
Around him the cacti grow tall.
It's sunny and dry every day there,
A habitat fit for them all.

The octopus lives in the ocean.

It finds things on which it can dine.

Shrimp, clams, crabs, mussels,

and sea snails,

That habitat suits it just fine.

Habitats, habitats,

Habitats have what they need to live.

Habitats, habitats,

Habitats have what they need.

Tallying

| This is a tally mark. It means 1.

||||| These tally marks mean 5.

This chart shows how many animals are in the tree.

Animals	Tally	Total
Squirrel	|	1
Bird	|||||	5

How many squirrels are in the tree?

How many birds are in the tree?

This chart shows how many apples are in the basket.

Apples	Tally	Total
Red	THT THT	
Yellow	THT II	

What is the total number of red apples?

What is the total number of yellow apples?

Turn the page to learn about more things to tally.

Turn the page.

What are living things?

How do you think a bee, a flower, and a frog are alike?

Plants and animals are **living things**. Living things can grow and change. This flower grew from a seed.

Some living things move on their own. This frog can jump. Living things can be parents. Find the picture of the parent.

Nonliving things cannot move on their own. They cannot grow. Find the pictures of nonliving things.

Tally living and nonliving things.

Materials

paper   pencil

Process Skills

- observing
- classifying

Process Skills

Steps

1. Make a chart like the one in the picture.

2. **Observe** things around you.

3. **Classify** the things as living or nonliving.

4. Make a tally mark for each living and nonliving thing.

Share. Tell if you tallied more living or more nonliving things.

Lesson Review

1. Name three living things.

2. How can you tell that a rock is a nonliving thing?

3. **Draw** a living and a nonliving thing.

What is a habitat?

Tomatoes are growing in the garden. What other living things do you see?

A **habitat** is a place where plants and animals live. A habitat has everything a plant or animal needs.

This garden is a habitat for many living things. There is food, water, and air for the animals. There is sunlight, water, and air for the plants.

What animals live in this garden? What do they eat? Where do they find water?

Make a model of a garden habitat.

Materials

tagboard crayons glue

craft stick scissors

Process Skills

- making and using models

Process Skills

Steps

1 Draw and cut out an animal picture.

2 Glue the picture to a craft stick.

3 Draw a garden that has plants, water, and animals.

4 Put your animal puppet in the model of the garden. Show it finding food and water.

Share. Name some other living things that might live in the garden.

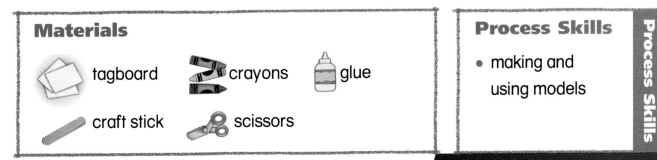

Lesson Review

1. What is a habitat?

2. What living things might you find in a garden?

3. **Tell** what living things need.

What lives in the ocean?

Did you ever wonder what lives in the ocean? You might be surprised!

Some animals have special body parts that help them live in the ocean.

The sea turtle has flippers that help it swim. The sea urchin has sharp spines that help protect it.

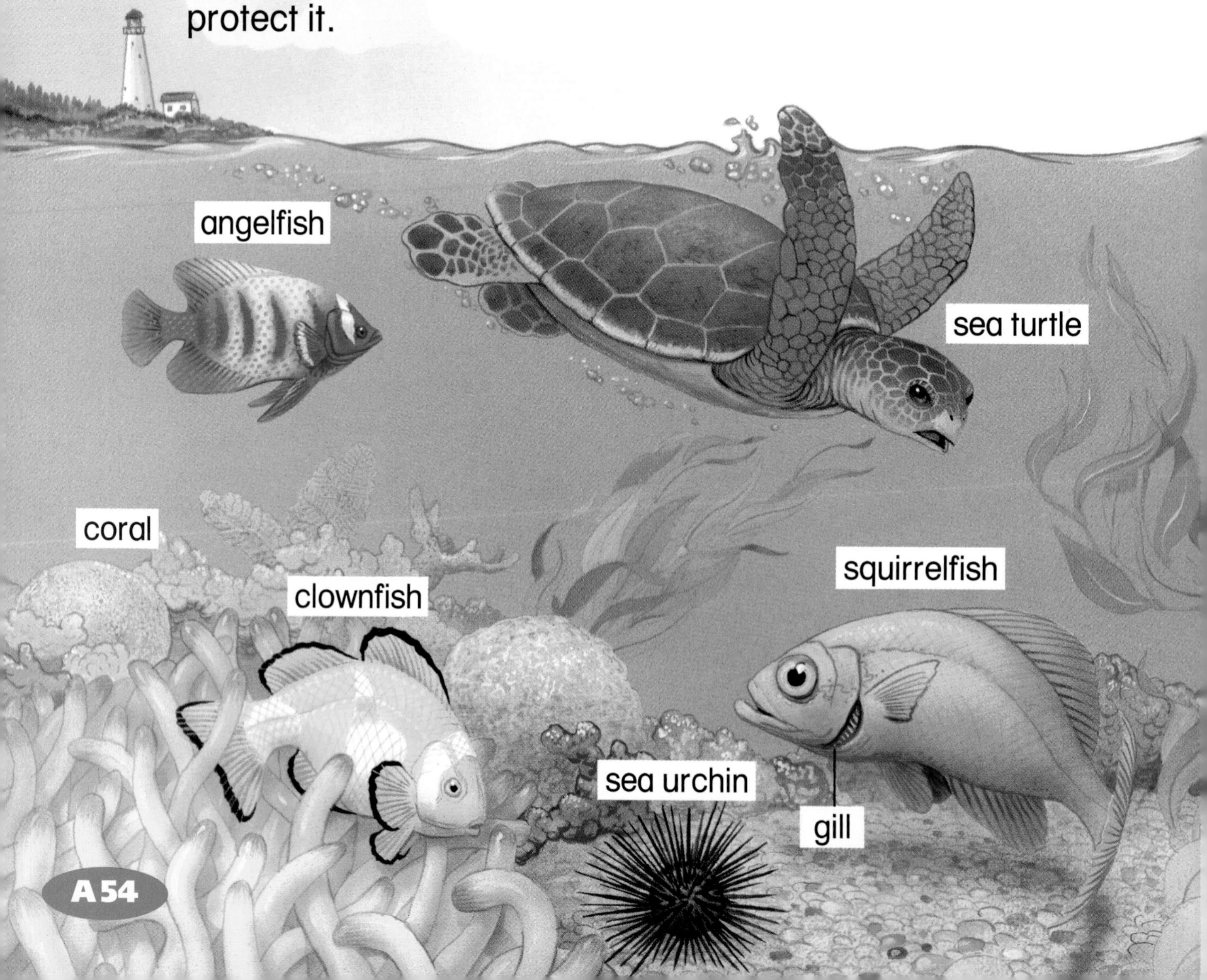

angelfish

sea turtle

coral

squirrelfish

clownfish

sea urchin

gill

Dolphins use a blowhole on top of their heads to breathe air. Fish use gills to breathe in the water. What other animals live in the ocean?

blowhole

dolphins

Lesson Review

1. Name some animals that live in the ocean.

2. What special body parts help some animals live in the ocean?

3. **Draw** an ocean habitat. Show living things that live there.

eel

ray

starfish

What lives in the forest and desert?

Pretend you are walking in a forest or a desert. What do you see and hear?

The forest is a habitat for living things. Trees grow in a forest. Animals use the trees in different ways. The squirrel makes a nest in the tree. The woodpecker finds insects under the bark. The newt lives in the shade of the trees.

The desert is a dry habitat. The kit fox, the elf owl, and the gila monster are some desert animals. Cactuses are desert plants that can live for a long time without water. You can find different kinds of cactuses in this picture.

Lesson Review

1. How do woodpeckers use trees?

2. What are some animals and plants that live in the desert?

3. **Write** about a trip you might take to a forest or desert.

How can you make a habitat?

Process Skills

- observing

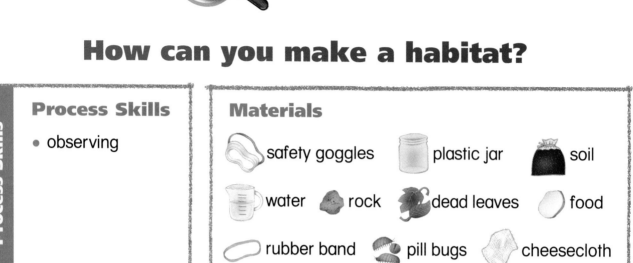

Materials

safety goggles · plastic jar · soil · water · rock · dead leaves · food · rubber band · pill bugs · cheesecloth

Steps

1. Put on your safety goggles.

2. Put soil in the jar. Add a little water.

3. Put a rock, dead leaves, sticks, and food in the jar.

4. Put pill bugs in the jar. Cover the jar.

5. **Observe** the pill bugs.

Think About Your Results

1. What did the pill bugs do after you put them in their new home?

2. What do pill bugs need in their home to stay alive?

? Inquire Further

Suppose you wanted to have more pill bugs. What changes would you make to the jar?

Chapter 3 Review

Reviewing Science Words

1. What can **living things** do?

2. How do you know that a book is a **nonliving thing**?

3. What might you find in a forest **habitat**?

Reviewing Science Ideas

1. Name a living and a nonliving thing.

2. Name a habitat. Tell what plants or animals might live there.

3. What are some things that an animal needs?

Make a model of a habitat.

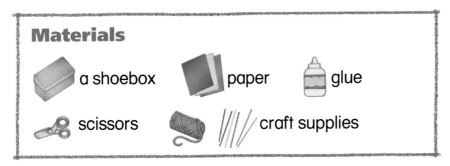
1 Choose a habitat.

2 Find out what living and nonliving things are in that habitat.

3 Make a model of the habitat. Show plants and animals. Show nonliving things.

4 Tell about the living and nonliving things in the habitat.

Unit A
Performance Review

You have learned many things about plants and animals. To celebrate what you know, you can have a party!

Plan your party.

1. Pick a project you will do for the party.

2. Decide what you will need.

3. Share your project with your friends.

Have a parade.

Choose an animal. Draw a picture of the animal and write its name on a sign. Use yarn to hang the sign around your neck. Have an animal parade. Try to make yourself look, move, and sound like your animal.

Play a game.

Write clues about a plant or animal. Read the clues. After each clue, give your partner a chance to guess the plant or animal.

Put on a puppet show.

Think of a story to tell about a plant or animal. Use a big box to make a puppet stage. Decorate it to look like a habitat for your plant or animal. Make puppets out of paper bags. Put on your show for the class.

Writing About Habitats

When you explain how things are alike and different, you are comparing. You can write sentences to compare and contrast things.

1. **Prewrite** Choose two habitats. Make a chart that tells about each habitat. List animals, plants, and nonliving things in your chart.

2. **Draft** Use the words in your chart to write sentences about each habitat. Tell how the habitats are alike and different.

3. **Revise** Read what you wrote. Do you like it?

4. **Edit** Check your writing to make sure it is correct. Make a neat copy.

5. **Publish** Share your chart and your writing with others. You can draw pictures of the habitats.

Unit B
Physical Science

Science and Technology
In Your World!

How does a blimp fly?

A blimp is a huge airship. A blimp floats in the sky because the gas inside is lighter than air. Blimps usually fly slowly and low. People flying in it get a good look at the earth.

Chapter 1
Grouping Objects

How can a vest help a firefighter?

This firefighter's special vest has sensors in it. When the air nearby gets too hot, the sensors tell a tiny computer. Then the vest sounds an alarm.

Chapter 2
Sound, Light, and Heat

What is a water escalator?

It is a large tube filled with water. The water moves around and around. It takes riders to the top of the water slide.

Chapter 3
Moving and Working

Chapter 1
Grouping Objects

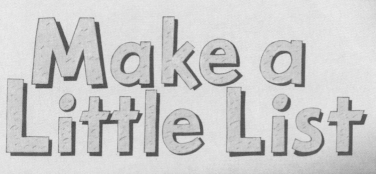

Make a Little List

Sing to the tune of *This Old Man*.

Water and juice
Can be poured.
But can you name any more?
Sit right down and make a little list.
Ask your friends what you have missed.

Keys will sink.

Pencils will float.

What else will sink? What else will float?

Sit right down and make a little list.

Ask your friends what you have missed.

Here's a riddle just for you.

How many things can water do?

Sit right down and make a little list.

Ask your friends what you have missed.

How can you group objects?

It is round. It is green and orange. It is smooth. It can float on water. You can see it on this page. What is it?

An **object** is a thing you can see or touch. Tell about the objects in the picture. What colors and shapes do you see? Which objects might feel smooth? Which might feel heavy?

You can learn about objects by sorting them into groups. How could you group these objects?

Float and sink objects.

Materials

 large container   water

classroom objects

Process Skills

- predicting
- observing

Process Skills

Steps

1. Choose an object.

2. **Predict.** Will it sink or float?

3. Put the object in water. **Observe.** Does it sink or float?

4. Try some other objects.

Share. Why do you think some objects sink and others float?

Lesson Review

1. What objects do you see around you? List five.

2. Look at the objects in your desk. How could you group these objects?

3. **Draw** a picture of two objects that sink and two objects that float.

How are solids and liquids different?

Would you put a book in a fishbowl? How silly! Would you put orange juice in your desk? What a mess!

The book and the blocks are solids. **Solids** have their own shape. They do not change shape when they are moved from place to place.

Water and orange juice are liquids. **Liquids** can change shape. If you pour a liquid from a tall pitcher into a round bowl, what shape will it be?

Solids and liquids both take up space and have a certain size. Which of these pictures shows a solid? Which shows a liquid? How do you know?

Lesson Review

1. How can you tell if an object is a solid?

2. If you pour a liquid into a tall glass, what shape will it be?

3. **Draw** a solid and a liquid. Write an **S** under the solid. Write an **L** under the liquid.

What are gases like?

Suppose you pop a balloon. Can you see, hear, or feel what is inside?

Gas takes up space. A gas has no shape of its own. It can change shape and size.

Air is made of gases. Air has no color. It has no taste. It is all around, but you cannot even see it!

There is air inside the balloons. Look at the bubbles. There is air inside bubbles, too. How does the air get inside?

Use objects to make bubbles.

Materials

safety goggles   soapy water

objects for making bubbles

Steps

1. Put on safety goggles.

2. Use different objects to make bubbles.

3. **Observe** the size and shape of the bubbles.

Share. Tell how bubbles made with different objects are alike and different.

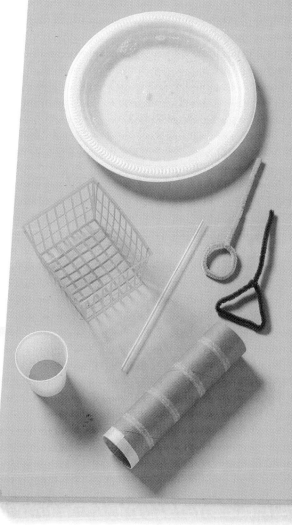

Lesson Review

1. Tell what a gas is like.

2. Where can you find air?

3. **Draw** an object you used to make bubbles. Draw the bubbles it made.

Predicting

When you predict, you tell what you think will happen. Look at the pictures. Predict what will happen next.

What might happen instead? Predict again.

What do you think is more likely to happen?

Look at the pictures. Predict what will happen next. Why do you think that will happen?

Turn the page to predict what will happen to bubbles.

Turn the page.

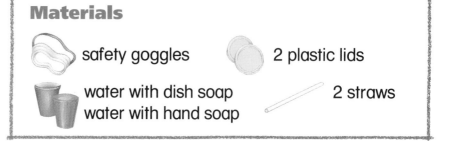

Experiment with bubbles.

Process Skills

Process Skills

- experimenting
- predicting

Materials

- safety goggles
- water with dish soap
- water with hand soap
- 2 plastic lids
- 2 straws

Problem

Does hand soap or dish soap make bubbles that last longer?

Give Your Hypothesis

Will bubbles made with hand soap or dish soap last longer? Tell what you think.

Control the Variables

Make the bubbles the same size.

Test Your Hypothesis

Follow these steps to do the experiment.

1 Put on your safety goggles.

2 Work with a partner. Use hand soap and dish soap.

3 Predict. Will bubbles made with hand soap or dish soap last longer?

4 Spread a little soapy water on each lid.

5 Blow a bubble on one lid. At the same time, your partner blows a bubble on the other lid.

6 Which bubble lasted longer? Tally.

7 Do it ten times. Tally each time.

Collect Your Data

Use a chart like this one. Tally to show which bubble lasted longer.

Tell Your Conclusion

Compare your results and hypothesis. Which bubbles lasted longer?

Inquire Further

What kind of soap makes bigger bubbles?

How can water change?

Put water into a freezer. Will you find water inside when you open the freezer the next day?

You know that water is a liquid. Water can change to a solid. This solid is called ice. Water changes to ice when it is so cold that it freezes. When the ice is heated, it changes back into a liquid. Look at the picture. Name the solid and the liquid.

before school   after school

Water can also change into a gas. When water changes to a gas, it **evaporates**. It goes into the air. You cannot see it.

Look at the pictures. What happened to the water in the puddle? It evaporated.

Lesson Review

1. What happens to water when it is very cold?

2. What happens to ice when it is heated?

3. Tell where water goes when it evaporates.

What happens when water evaporates?

Process Skills

- observing
- predicting

Materials

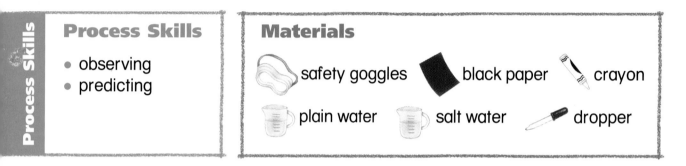

safety goggles   black paper   crayon
plain water   salt water   dropper

Steps

1. Put on your safety goggles.

2. Use a crayon to label one half of the paper **P** for plain water. Label the other half **S** for salt water.

3 Put a few drops of plain water on the **P** side.

4 Put a few drops of salt water on the **S** side.

5 Observe. Draw what you see.

6 Predict. Tell a friend what you think will happen the next day.

7 The next day, observe and draw what you see.

Think About the Results

1. What did you observe on the second day?

2. What happened to the water?

 Inquire Further

What would happen if you used sugar water?

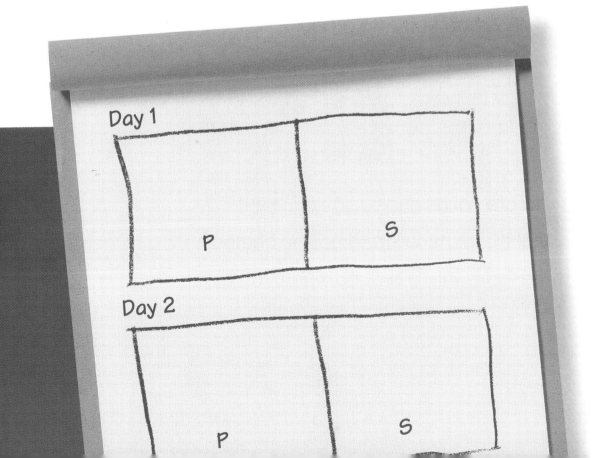

Chapter 1 Review

Reviewing Science Words

1. List three **objects** in your desk.

2. Find a picture of a **solid**, a **liquid**, and a **gas**.

3. Where can you find **air**?

4. Where does water go when it **evaporates**?

Reviewing Science Ideas

1. Put these objects into groups.
   Name each group.

2. How are solids and liquids different?

3. What happens to ice when it is heated?

4. What goes into a balloon when you blow
   it up?

Write a recipe for a drink.

Materials

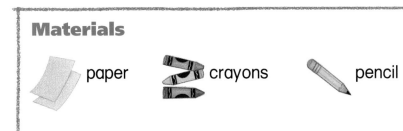

paper   crayons   pencil

1. Choose a solid for your drink.

2. Choose a liquid for your drink.

3. Write a recipe that tells what to do with the solid and liquid.

4. Tell what might happen if your drink gets too cold or too hot.

5. Name your drink.

Sound, Light, and Heat

Dark, Cool, and Quiet

♪ Sing to the tune of *Cockles and Mussels*.

The room that you stand in
is dark, cool, and quiet.
You want a big change
so now what can you do?

You open the shades.
Let the sun pour in brightly.
Then let in the puppy
who barks at your shoe.

Original lyrics by Gerri Brioso and Richard Freitas.
Produced by Children's Television Workshop.
Copyright ©1999 Sesame Street, Inc.

You might feel a bit silly,
the room is still chilly.
So drink some hot cocoa
and you'll warm up fast.

Things are much different,
More light, heat, and sounds.
It's brighter! It's louder!
You've warmed up at last!

What kinds of sounds are there?

A fire truck rushes down the street. A dog barks at cars. What a noisy corner!

Some sounds are loud. Loud sounds can warn you of danger. The siren on a fire truck warns people to get out of the way. What loud sounds have you heard?

Some sounds are soft. A whisper is a soft sound. What is the softest sound you can make?

If you were on this corner, what loud and soft sounds might you hear?

Make a drum.

Materials

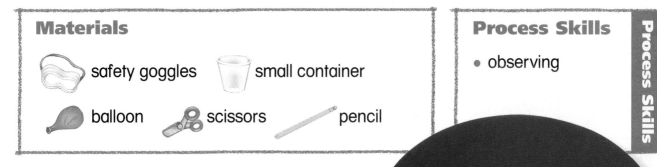

safety goggles   small container

balloon   scissors   pencil

Process Skills

- observing

Steps

1. Put on your safety goggles.

2. Cut the end off of a balloon.

3. Stretch the balloon over the container.

4. Use a pencil to beat the drum.

5. Observe the sounds. Make loud sounds. Make soft sounds.

Share. Tell how you made loud and soft sounds.

Lesson Review

1. What can make a loud sound?

2. What can make a soft sound?

3. **Show** how you can make loud and soft sounds with your drum.

How are sounds made?

Quietly hum your favorite song. Listen to the tune. How do the sounds change?

Some sounds are high. This triangle makes a high sound. Some sounds are low. This drum makes a low sound. When you sing or play a keyboard, you can make high and low sounds.

All sounds are made when something vibrates. **Vibrate** means to move back and forth very fast. When you beat a drum, parts of the drum vibrate to make sound.

Use a ruler to make sounds.

Materials

safety goggles   ruler

Process Skills

- observing

Process Skills

Steps

1. Put on your safety goggles.

2. Hold one end of the ruler on your desk.

3. Snap the other end of the ruler.

4. **Observe.** What do you hear? What do you see?

Share. Tell what you heard and saw when you snapped the ruler.

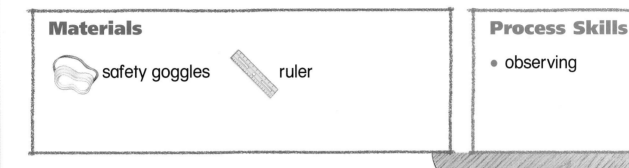

Lesson Review

1. What happens when something vibrates?

2. Name something that can make a high sound and something that can make a low sound.

3. **Show** how a ruler vibrates to make sound.

Does sound travel through things?

Process Skills

- observing

Materials

book

bag filled with water

bag filled with air

pencil

Steps

1 Put the book on a table. Put one ear on the book. Put your hand over your other ear.

2 Have your partner tap the pencil on the table. Observe what you hear.

3 Do it again with the bag of water and a bag with air inside.

4 Use a chart like the one in the picture. Write how well you hear the tapping sound.

Think About Your Results

1. When was the tapping sound loudest?

2. When was the tapping sound softest?

Inquire Further

Suppose you were trying to hear footsteps. Would you put your ear next to the ground or hold your head up in the air?

What is the sound traveling through?	How well do you hear?
Book	
Water	
Air	

How is a shadow made?

Think of a time when you saw a shadow. What shape did it have? What made the shadow?

Light comes from the sun, fire, or a light bulb. A shadow is made when something blocks the light. Light cannot go through this toy boat. The toy blocks the light and makes a **shadow**. Observe how the shape of the shadow is like the shape of the toy.

You can see shadows outside on a sunny day. What do you think is making the shadow in the picture below?

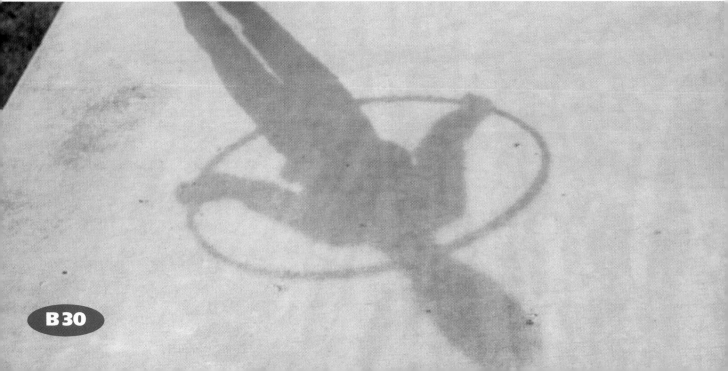

Observe shadows.

Materials

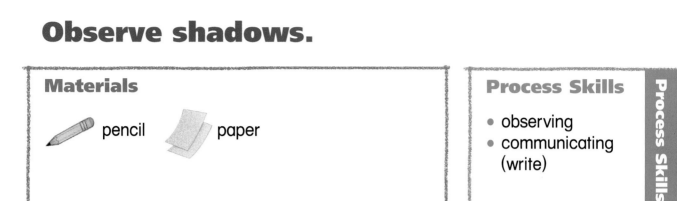 pencil   paper

Process Skills

- observing
- communicating (write)

Steps

1. Use a chart like this one.
2. **Observe** some shadows.
3. Draw the shadow.
4. **Write** what object made the shadow.

Share. Tell about one of the shadows you found.

Draw the shadow.	What made the shadow?

Lesson Review

1. Where does light come from?
2. How is a shadow made?
3. **Draw** a picture of a shadow.

Telling Time

A clock has numbers and hands. The long hand is called the minute hand. It is pointing to 12.

The short hand is called the hour hand. It is pointing to 9. It is 9 o'clock.

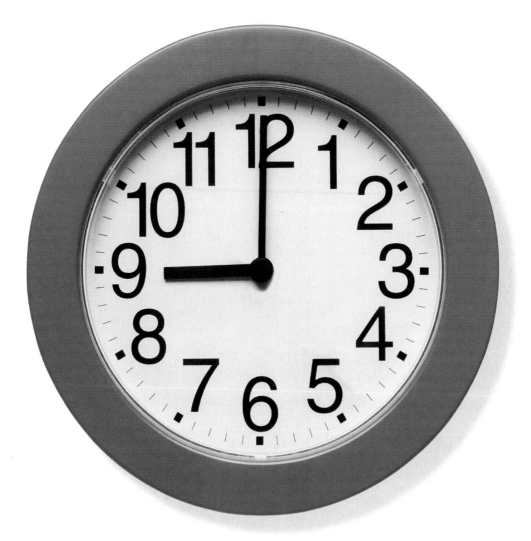

What time is it? What is happening at each time?

Turn the page for an activity
about time and shadows.

Turn the
page.

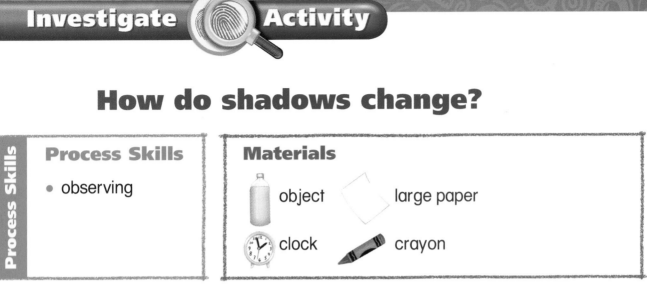

How do shadows change?

Process Skills

Process Skills

- observing

Materials

object   large paper

clock   crayon

Steps

1 Start this activity in the morning.

2 Choose an object.

3 Find a sunny place.

4 Put your object on the paper.
Trace its shadow.

5 Write what time it is.

6 Do it again near lunchtime. Observe how the shadow has changed.

7 Do it again before going home. Observe again.

Think About Your Results

1. When was the shadow the longest?

2. When was the shadow the shortest?

Inquire Further

How does the shadow under a tree change during the day?

What gives off heat?

On a hot summer day, would you like to play in the sun or in the shade of a tree?

Heat comes from the light of the sun. The sun shines on the land and water. It can also shine on you! When you are outside, you may feel warmer in a sunny place than in the shade.

Fire gives off heat. This picture shows a fire cooking marshmallows.

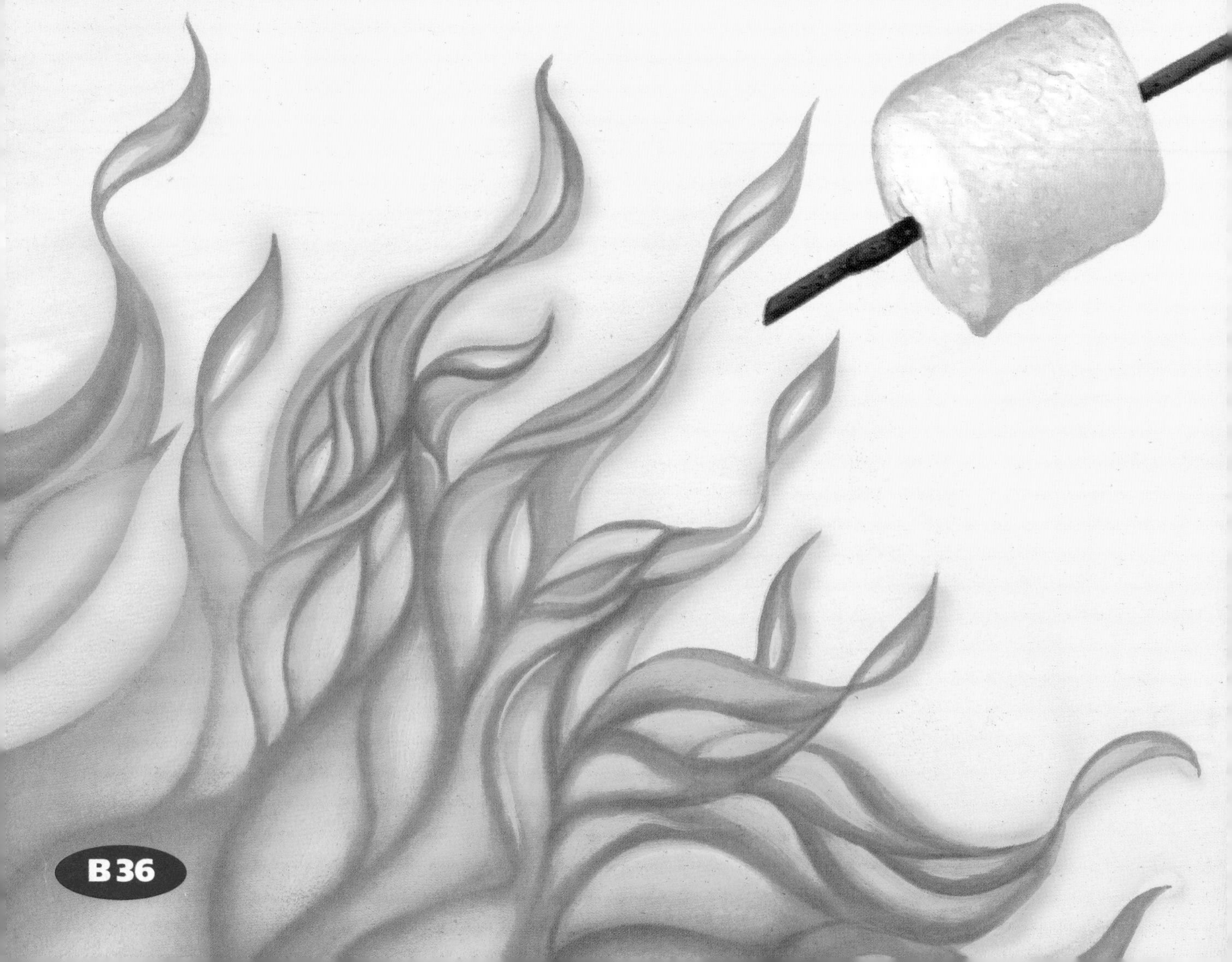

Heat comes from other things too. Rubbing things together can give off heat. Lamps, stoves, and toasters give off heat. What else do you know about that gives off heat?

Lesson Review

1. What comes from the light of the sun?

2. What can you feel when you rub your hands together?

3. **Draw** three things that give off heat.

What feels hot?

Mmm! Here is some hot cocoa to drink! Be careful, the pan is very hot!

This pan is made of metal. Heat moves easily through metal. Heat does not move easily through wood and cloth. The wood keeps the counter from getting hot. What could you use to protect your hands from the heat?

If you put hot cocoa in this metal cup it would feel hot. This foam cup does not feel hot. Heat does not move easily through foam.

Lesson Review

1. Name something that heat moves through easily.

2. Name something that heat does not move through easily.

3. Would you put a hot drink in a metal cup or a foam cup? Why?

How can you keep an ice cube frozen?

Process Skills

- observing

Materials

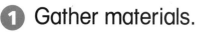

ice cube   plastic bag   twist tie

other materials

Steps

1. Gather materials.

2. Use the materials to make a container that keeps an ice cube frozen.

3. Put the ice cube in a plastic bag. Put it in your container.

4 When your teacher tells you, take the plastic bag out of the container. Observe. How much ice is still frozen?

5 Compare your ice cube with others in your class.

Think About Your Results

1. Which containers kept ice frozen longer?

2. Why do you think ice stayed frozen longer in some containers than in others?

 **Inquire Further**

How could you change your container to keep ice frozen longer?

Chapter 2 Review

Reviewing Science Words

1. What can **vibrate** to make sound?
2. Tell how you could make a **shadow** .

Reviewing Science Ideas

1. What loud and soft sounds have you heard?
2. What happens when something vibrates?
3. How does a shadow change during the day?
4. Name three things that give off heat.
5. Why is a foam cup sometimes used for hot cocoa?

Tell a story.

Materials

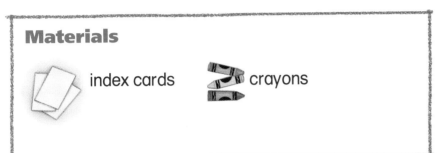

index cards   crayons

1. Use 3 cards. Draw a picture that shows sound, a picture that shows light or a shadow, and a picture that shows heat.

2. Put each picture into the class pile of sound, light, or heat cards.

3. Choose a card from each pile.

4. Tell a story that uses 2 of the 3 cards.

Sound

Light

Chapter 3

Moving and Working

On the Move

🎵 Sing to the tune of *Turkey in the Straw*.

If you want to move a ball
from here to over there,

You can kick it with your foot
and send it through the air.

If the ball's too heavy,
don't you despair.

Make a ramp, send it rolling.
It will get over there.

Push it or pull it.
Move it everywhere.

Roll it down, throw it up,
high into the air.

What else can you do
to make things move?

Try a magnet or a lever
and your moving will improve.

Original lyrics by Gerri Brioso and Richard Freitas.
Produced by Children's Television Workshop.

How can you move things?

It is fun to ride in a wagon. How are these children making the wagon move?

You can **push** or **pull** to make things move. The girl holding the handle is pulling the wagon. Her sister is pushing from behind.

When you put clothes away, you pull to open a drawer. To close the drawer, you push it shut. What else can you pull or push?

Push and pull a boat.

Materials

 aluminum foil

bowl of water

Process Skills

- making and using models
- classifying

Steps

1 Use foil to **make a model** of a boat.

2 Set the boat on the water.

3 Find ways to make the boat move.

4 **Classify** the ways. Each time you make the boat move, tell if you are using a push or a pull.

Share. Show two ways you can move your boat.

Lesson Review

1. What are two ways you can move things?

2. Tell about something you moved today. Did you push or pull?

3. **Tell** how you used a push and a pull to make your boat move.

Using a Map

A map shows how to get from place to place. This map shows how to get from a home to the park.

How can the car get from the blue house to the school? Use your finger to show how the car can go.

Turn the page to learn more about how things move.

Turn the page.

What ways do things move?

Would you rather bounce a ball or toss a bean bag? Would you rather twirl a jump rope or spin a top?

You can make things move in many ways. You can throw a ball up and watch it fall back to the ground. You can roll a ball far. You can tap it so it hardly moves.

Find the two marbles in this picture. Tell about how they move. What might make them go fast, slow, or change direction?

Make a maze.

Materials

 blocks   ◯ table tennis ball

⟋ straw

Process Skills

- observing

Steps

1 Build a maze.

2 Put the ball at one end of the maze.

3 Blow the ball with the straw. Observe how the ball moves, stops, and changes direction.

4 Move the ball through the maze. Then move it back again.

Share. Draw a map of your maze. Draw a line to show where the ball went.

Lesson Review

1. Name different ways that you can make things move.

2. What can make a marble go fast?

3. **Tell** how you changed the direction of the ball.

What does a magnet attract?

Some are round. Some are fancy. One is shaped like a horseshoe. Where have you seen magnets?

This picture shows many kinds of **magnets**. A magnet pulls some things toward it. It **attracts** these things. How can you find out what a magnet attracts?

A magnet can **repel** another magnet. When a magnet repels another magnet, it pushes it away.

Find out what a magnet attracts.

Materials

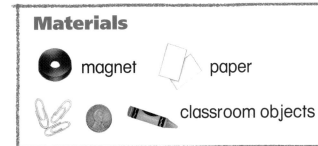

magnet   paper

classroom objects

Process Skills

- classifying

Steps

1 Write **attracts** on one paper.
Write **does not attract** on the other paper.

2 Test things with a magnet.

3 Classify the things. Put them on the correct paper.

Share. Tell what other things you would like to test with the magnet.

Lesson Review

1. What can a magnet attract?

2. List three things that are not attracted to a magnet.

3. **Tell** what you observed about things that the magnet attracted.

B 53

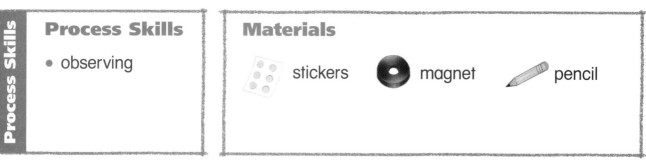
Can magnets push and pull?

Process Skills	Materials
• observing	stickers magnet pencil

Steps

1. Put a sticker on each side of a magnet. Draw a car on each sticker.

2. Use your car to pull your partner's car. Observe.

3. Use your car to push your partner's car. Observe. When your car pushes, it must not touch your partner's car.

4. Use a map like the one shown. Push your partner's car along the road to the store.

5 Pull your partner's car back to the garage.

Think About Your Results

1. Tell how you pulled your partner's car.

2. Tell how you pushed your partner's car.

Inquire Further

What else can your car pull along the road?

How do people use machines?

A tractor and a car are both machines. Did you know that a hammer and a can opener are machines, too?

These workers use some kinds of **simple machines** to build a house. Simple machines make work easier.

A **wheel** helps to move a heavy load.

A **ramp** makes it easier to move things up or down.

A **pulley** is used to lift a big box.

A **lever** can be used to take a lid off a box.

Lesson Review

1. What do simple machines do?

2. How could you use a ramp?

3. **Draw** a machine you use that has a wheel.

How does a lever work?

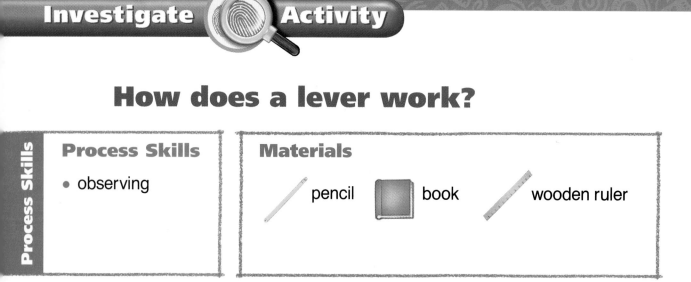

Process Skills

- observing

Materials

pencil   book   wooden ruler

Steps

1. Set up a book, pencil, and ruler as shown in the picture. The pencil is under the 20 centimeter mark. The book is on the 5.

2. Push down on the end of the ruler to lift the book.

3. Do it again with the pencil under the 15.

4. Do it again with the pencil under the 10.

5 Observe each time. Which time was it easiest to lift the book?

6 Draw a picture of the ruler, book, and pencil. Show where the pencil is when it is easiest to lift the book.

Think About Your Results

1. Was it easiest to lift the book with the pencil under the 10, 15, or 20?

2. Would it be easier to lift the book with the pencil under the 12 or 18 centimeter mark?

Inquire Further

A ruler makes a good lever. What else could you as a lever?

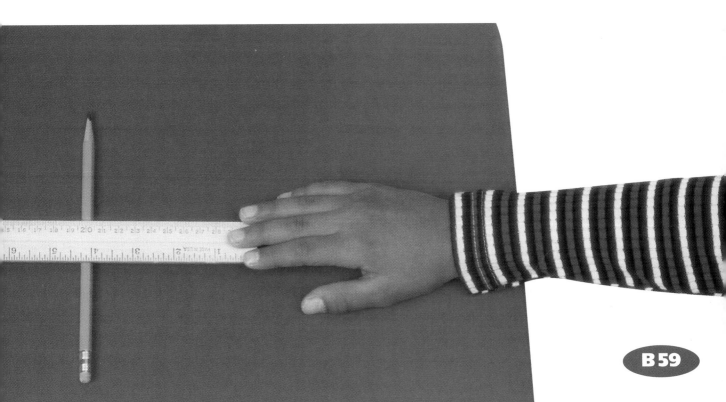

Chapter 3 Review

Reviewing Science Words

1. Name something that you can **push**.
2. Name something that you can **pull**.
3. What can a **magnet** do?
4. Name something that a magnet can **attract**.
5. What happens when a magnet **repels**?
6. Match the picture of each **simple machine** to the word.

ramp

pulley

lever

wheel

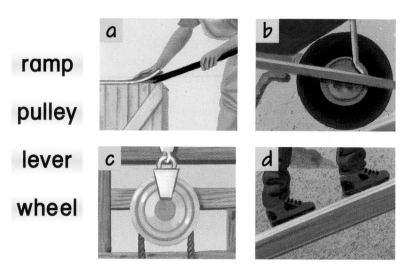

Reviewing Science Ideas

1. How can you change the way a ball moves?
2. What can you do with a lever?

Design a toy.

Materials

drawing paper

crayons

pencil

1. Make a poster of your toy.

2. Name your toy.

3. Label the parts.

4. Tell how to use your toy. Use science words such as push, pull, wheel, lever, ramp, pulley, and magnet.

Push Pull Train

rope to pull with

magnets

wheel

Unit B
Performance Review

There are solids, liquids, and gases all around you. There is sound, light, and heat. People are moving and working. Show what you know about all these things in a class museum.

Plan a museum.

1. Choose a project to do.

2. Think about what you need to make your project.

3. What will you do first?

Make an exhibit.

Label one side of your exhibit **push** and the other side **pull**. Look for objects that you move by pushing or pulling. Put the objects in the exhibit. Tell how you push or pull to make them move.

Tape record sounds.

Think of different ways to make sounds. Record the sounds on a tape recorder. Play your recording. Have your friends tell about the sounds and guess how you made them.

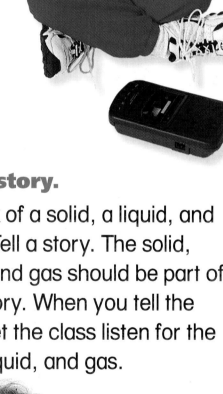

Tell a story.

Think of a solid, a liquid, and a gas. Tell a story. The solid, liquid, and gas should be part of your story. When you tell the story, let the class listen for the solid, liquid, and gas.

Writing Clues to Describe an Object

You can describe something without telling what it is. When you do this, you give a clue about it. You can describe how it looks, sounds, feels, smells, or tastes. You can tell what it is made of or what it is used for.

1. **Prewrite** Choose an object. Observe the object. Think of clues to describe it.

2. **Draft** Write clues that describe the object.

3. **Revise** Read the clues. Will others be able to guess the object? Make changes if you want to.

4. **Edit** Check your writing to make sure it is correct. Make a neat copy.

5. **Publish** Share your clues with others. See if they can guess the object.

It is long and thin.
It is made of wood.
You can write with it

Unit C
Earth Science

Your Science Handbook

Science and Technology
In Your World!

How can an old tire help a cow?

This cow is standing on a special mat made from recycled tires. The cow can rest on the mat and be comfortable.

Chapter 1
The Earth

What is the weather like?

Is it cold in Canada? Is it sunny in Spain? Find out what the weather is like around the world. Use the Internet.

Chapter 2
Weather

Back Forward Reload Home Search Guides Images Print Security Stop

Locations http://www.weather_on_net.com

Welcome to WWW Weather Foreca

Weather Maps

Forecast

Storm Prediction

Warnings

for current

What is the Hubble Space Telescope?

It is a very strong telescope that moves through space and takes pictures. The Hubble Space Telescope helps scientists see things they cannot see from Earth.

Chapter 3
The Sky

Chapter 1
The Earth

On Top of a Mountain

♫ Sing to the tune of *On Top of Old Smokey*.

Climb up on a mountain
Sit under a tree
And look at Earth's wonders.
So many to see.

You'll see rocks and soil
As you look here and there.
All sizes and colors.
It's fun to compare.

There's clear sparkling water
In rivers and lakes.
With fresh air for breathing
A fine home Earth makes.

C5

Using a Bar Graph

A bar graph helps you compare groups.
This bar graph shows what colors children like.

My Favorite Color

1 2 3 4 5 6 7 8 9 10

This bar graph shows that 5 children like
blue. It shows that 7 children like red. Do more
children like blue or red?

What does this bar graph show?

Snacks We Like

1 2 3 4 5 6 7 8 9 10

How many carrots are there?

How many pretzels are there?

How many orange slices are there?

How many more pretzels are
there than carrots?

Turn the page for an activity
that uses bar graphs.

Turn the
page.

C7

What are rocks like?

Looking for rocks is fun. You can find them in dirt and in water. Some houses and roads are made of rocks. Rocks are everywhere!

Rocks come in many sizes, colors, and shapes. Rocks can be shiny or dull. They can be rough or smooth.

Air, water, and ice can change rocks. This is called **weathering** . Rough rocks can become smooth. Big rocks can break into smaller pieces. Tiny bits of sand were once parts of rocks!

Graph rocks.

Materials

 rocks

Process Skills

- observing
- classifying

Process Skills

Steps

1 Observe the rocks. How are they alike and different?

2 Use a graph like this one. Classify the rocks into two groups

3 Label the graph.

Share. Tell about your graph.

Lesson Review

1. What words can you use to tell about rocks?

2. How can weathering change rocks?

3. **Show** another way to sort and graph the rocks.

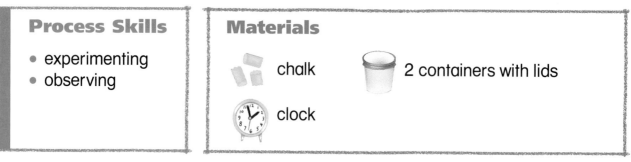
Experiment with weathering.

Process Skills

Process Skills
- experimenting
- observing

Materials

chalk

clock

2 containers with lids

Problem

How can weathering change chalk?

Give Your Hypothesis

If you shake chalk, will it weather?
Tell what you think.

Control the Variables

Put chalk into each container. You will shake one container. You will not shake the other.

Test Your Hypothesis

Follow these steps to do the experiment.

1. Observe the pieces of chalk. Draw how they look.

2. Put chalk into each container. Put on the lids.

3. Shake one container for one minute.

4. Open the containers and observe the pieces of chalk again. Draw how they look now.

Collect Your Data

Use a chart like this to draw the chalk.

Tell Your Conclusion

Compare the results to your hypothesis. How did the chalk change?

? Inquire Further

What will happen if you put water and chalk in the container?

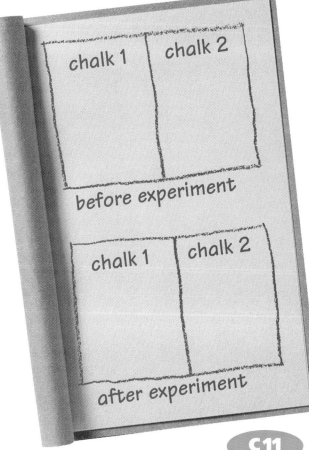

chalk 1 | chalk 2

before experiment

chalk 1 | chalk 2

after experiment

What is soil?

Did you ever dig a hole in the ground?
What did you see?

   Soil is made of tiny bits of rock. Some soil
also has clay, sand, or parts of living things that
have died.

   Living things use soil in many ways. Some
animals find food in the soil. Others live under
the ground.

People use soil to grow food. Roots of plants and trees grow in soil. What can you see in this picture of soil?

Lesson Review

1. What is soil made of?

2. How do living things use soil?

3. Draw some soil. Show what you might find in the soil.

What kinds of soils are there?

Process Skills

- observing

Materials

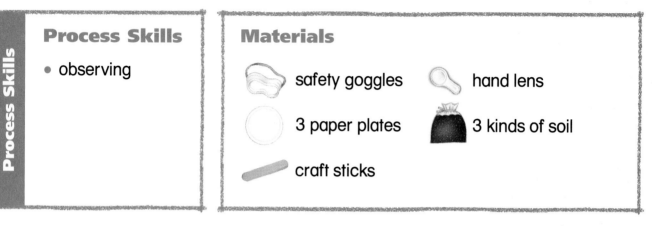

safety goggles

hand lens

3 paper plates

3 kinds of soil

craft sticks

Steps

1. Put on your safety goggles.

2. Number the plates 1, 2, and 3.

3. Put a different soil on each plate.

4. Observe each soil.

5. Draw what you observe.
   Use a chart like this one.

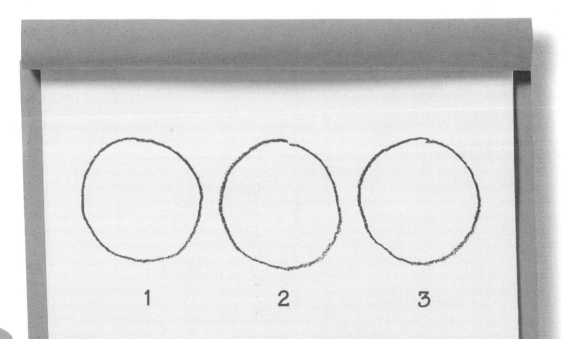

1   2   3

Think About Your Results

1. Tell how the soils are alike or different.

2. What did you find in the soils?

? Inquire Further

In which soil would seeds grow the fastest?

What is the earth like?

Choose a hill or a desert, a lake or a mountain. Where would you like to go on the earth?

The earth has air all around it. The earth has land and water. Look at the land and water in these pictures. In some places, the land is flat. In other places, there are mountains. What is the land like where you live?

Most of the water on the earth is in the oceans. There is water in rivers, streams, and lakes too. Do you live near water?

The globe shows the shape of the earth. It is shaped like a ball. The blue places on the globe show water. The rest is land. Do you see more water or land on the globe?

Lesson Review

1. What is all around the earth?

2. What is the shape of the earth?

3. **Show** where there is water and land on the globe.

How do people use air, land, and water?

Living things need air to stay alive. Plants need air to grow. People need clean air to breathe. People have been working together to keep air clean.

People can keep the land clean too. The girl in this picture is throwing away trash. How can you help keep the land clean?

People need clean water to stay alive and healthy. People use water for drinking, cooking, and washing. How are people in the picture using water?

You can help keep water clean. You can try not to use more water than you need.

Lesson Review

1. How can you help keep the land clean?

2. Name three ways people use water.

3. **Draw** a picture that shows one way to use water.

What can you reuse and recycle?

Find the metal, plastic, glass, and paper in the picture. What can you do with these things?

When you **reuse** something, you use it again. Think before you throw away a box or a toy. Can you use the box in a different way? Could someone play with the toy?

Another way to use something again is to **recycle**. Plastic can be recycled. It can be melted and made into new things. Plastic bottles might become a new chair!

Reuse a container.

Materials

container   art supplies

scissors

Process Skills

- communicating (tell)

Steps

1. Think of a way to reuse your container.

2. Use art supplies to make your idea.

Share. Tell what you made.

Lesson Review

1. Name something you can reuse.

2. Name one thing that can be recycled.

3. **Tell** what would happen if people reused more things.

Chapter 1 Review

Reviewing Science Words

1. How can **weathering** change rocks?

2. What might you find in **soil**?

3. Tell how you could **reuse** a shoe box.

4. What are some things you can **recycle**?

Reviewing Science Ideas

1. What words can you use to tell about rocks?

2. How can rocks change?

3. Where is there water on the earth?

4. What are some ways people use water?

Make an earth book.

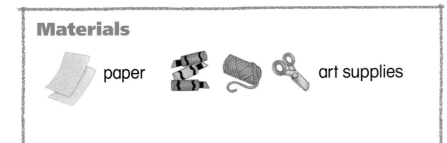
1. Make a round book.
2. Draw the earth on the cover.
3. Draw or write one thing about the earth on each page.
4. Share your book. Read the words. Show the pictures.

Weather

The Weather Changed

♫ Sing to the tune of *Bingo*.

The weather changed from yesterday,
And will it change tomorrow?
Will there be sun or rain?
Will the wind blow or not?
Will it be hot or cold?
We'll only know tomorrow.

The weather changes month to month,
And also with the seasons.
Which season's very cold?
Which season's very warm?
Which season makes leaves fall?
What is your favorite season?

Original lyrics by Gerri Brioso and Richard Freitas.
Produced by Children's Television Workshop.

Using a Chart

You can use a chart to find information. A chart has columns and rows. Columns go up and down. Rows go across.

Weather

Day	Weather	Temperature
Monday	☁	hot
Tuesday	○	warm
Wednesday	🌧	cool

This chart tells about the weather. Point to the first column. This column tells the name of the day.

Point to the second and third columns. What do these columns tell about?

Our Favorite Weather

Name	Weather	Temperature
Tom	❄	cold
Anna	☁	warm
Lee	○	hot

What does this chart tell about?

What does each column show?

What is Tom's favorite weather?

What is Anna's favorite temperature?

Turn the page to learn more about using a chart.

Turn the page.

What can you tell about weather?

Look out a window. What is it like outside? Do you need a raincoat and an umbrella?

It might be sunny, cloudy, or rainy. It might be still or windy. All of these words tell about the weather. **Temperature** is how hot or cold it is. What is the temperature outside today?

Weather is always changing. Think of what the weather was like yesterday. Is the weather different today?

Chart the weather.

Materials

 paper ⟩⟩ crayons

Process Skills

- observing

Process Skills

Steps

1 Observe the weather.

2 Use a chart like this one. Draw a sun, rain, snow, or clouds to show the weather.

3 Tell about the temperature.

4 Do this for 5 days.

Share. Tell how the weather changed this week.

Weather Chart

Day	weather	temperature
Monday	☁	cool
Tuesday		
Wednesday		
Thursday		
Friday		

Lesson Review

1. What words can you use to tell about the temperature?

2. Tell what the weather is like today.

3. **Draw** a picture of yourself in your favorite kind of weather.

How can you observe wind?

Process Skills

- observing

Materials

8 streamers   paper plate

glue   yarn

Steps

1 Turn the paper plate upside down.
Glue streamers to the plate.

2 Tie yarn through holes in the plate.

3 Blow gently on the streamers.
Observe and draw the results.

4 Now blow hard on the streamers.
Observe and draw the results.

5 Go outside. **Observe** and draw the streamers blowing in the wind.

Think About Your Results

1. What happened when you blew gently on the streamers?

2. What happened when you blew hard on the streamers?

Inquire Further

What kinds of things might happen on a very windy day?

How can you measure temperature?

On a hot day, you can wear shorts outside. If it is cold, you might need a coat. How do you know how hot or cold it is?

A **thermometer** measures the temperature. The red line in a thermometer shows how hot or cold it is.

It is a hot day. The red line in this thermometer is high.

It is a cold day. The red line in this thermometer is low.

Use a thermometer.

Materials

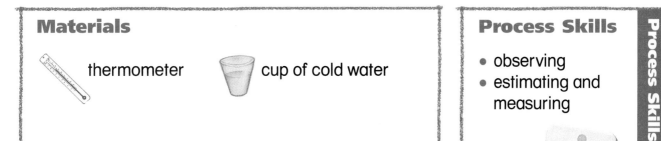

thermometer   cup of cold water

Process Skills

- observing
- estimating and measuring

Process Skills

Steps

1 Observe the red line in your thermometer.

2 Put your thumb over the round end of the thermometer. Observe what happens to the red line.

3 Put the thermometer in cold water.

4 Observe the red line again.

Share. Tell which time the thermometer measured the lowest temperature.

Lesson Review

1. What does a thermometer tell about the weather?

2. Tell where the red line in a thermometer might be on a hot day.

3. Tell what happened to the red line when you put the thermometer in cold water.

How do clouds form?

Are there clouds in the sky today? What do they look like? How did they get there?

There is water in the air. You cannot see it. It is called **water vapor** . When the air cools, the water vapor in it forms clouds.

Clouds are made of tiny drops of water or ice. The water or ice can fall from clouds as rain, snow, or hail.

Fog is a cloud that is near the ground. It is hard to see through fog. ▼

▲ These white, puffy clouds look like cotton balls.

You might see a cloud like this before a storm. ▼

These wispy clouds are very high in the sky. ▲

Lesson Review

1. What is water vapor?

2. What are clouds made of?

3. **Draw** a cloud. Tell what you know about the kind of cloud you drew.

How can you make a cloud?

Process Skills

- observing

Materials

jar · metal lid · ice cubes · warm water

Steps

1. Rinse the jar in warm water.
2. Put a little warm water in the jar.
3. Place the lid upside down on top of the jar.
4. Put ice cubes on the lid.
5. **Observe** what happens inside the jar.

Think About Your Results

1. What happened inside the jar?

2. Draw what happened.

? Inquire Further

What would happen if you did not put ice on the lid?

How can you stay safe in bad weather?

A storm is coming! You need to stay safe. What should you do?

Stormy weather can be dangerous. Strong wind and heavy rain can harm houses and cause floods. During bad weather, listen to a weather report. The report will tell your family how to stay safe.

During a lightning storm, stay away from trees. Go inside. ▼

▲ During a tornado, go to the safest part of your home. Stay away from windows.

▲ During a blizzard, stay inside and keep warm.

Lesson Review

1. Why should you listen to a weather report during a storm?

2. Where is a safe place to be during a lightning storm?

3. **Draw** a picture showing what you and your family might do during a storm.

What are seasons like?

Do you have a favorite time of the year?
What do you like about that time?

A **season** is a time of the year. The seasons are winter, spring, summer, and fall. The temperature changes from season to season. What changes do you see in these pictures?

Winter

Spring

Summer

Fall

Dress for the seasons.

Materials

 crayons  paper

Process Skills

- classifying

Steps

1. Choose a season.

2. Draw yourself doing an outdoor activity in that season. Show what clothes you would wear.

3. Work in a group. Classify your pictures as summer, fall, winter, and spring.

Share. Tell how the clothes you drew are right for the season.

Lesson Review

1. Name the four seasons.

2. What is the coldest season of the year?

3. **Tell** what you might do during each season.

What do animals do in winter?

Brrr! It is a cold winter day. You need a coat and hat to stay warm when you play outside.

Animals find ways to stay warm in winter too. Some animals **migrate**, or move to a warmer place. These geese are flying south where the winter is warmer. Whales, butterflies, and other animals also migrate.

Some animals **hibernate**, or have a long, deep sleep. Woodchucks hibernate all winter in a hole in the ground. In spring, they come out and look for food.

These pictures show the same arctic fox. In summer, the fox's fur is brown. In winter, the fur is white. White fur helps the fox hide in snow.

Lesson Review

1. Why do some animals migrate?

2. Tell about an animal that hibernates.

3. **Tell** how white fur helps the fox in winter.

Chapter 2 Review

Reviewing Science Words

1. What words can you use to tell about the **temperature**?

2. What does a **thermometer** tell you?

3. Where is **water vapor**?

4. List the four **seasons**.

5. Why do some animals **migrate**?

6. What do animals do when they **hibernate**?

Reviewing Science Ideas

1. What words can you use to tell about weather?

2. What are clouds made of?

3. What should you do when a storm is coming?

4. Tell what clothing you might wear in cold weather.

Today is cloudy and rainy.

Report the weather.

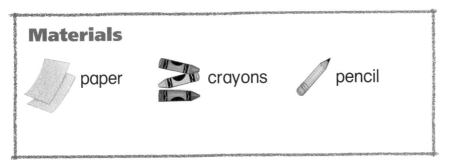

Materials

paper   crayons   pencil

1 Write a weather report.

2 Use words to tell about the weather. Is it hot or cold? Is it sunny or rainy? What season is it?

3 Draw a picture that shows what to wear outside.

4 Tell what you think the weather will be like tomorrow.

Chapter 3
The Sky

Up in the Sky

♪ Sing to the tune of *Take Me Out to the Ballgame.*

In the sky is a bright light.

A light that we call the sun.

It gives us daylight and warmth and heat.

Play in the sun, it just cannot be beat!

But at night,

We can't see the sunshine.

We often can see the moon.

Did you know,

That,

Moonlight is sunlight,

That shines on the moon!

Original lyrics by Gerri Brioso and Richard Freitas.
Produced by Children's Television Workshop.

How are day and night different?

The sun is shining. It is time to get up.
A new day is beginning!

Earth is always turning. The sun shines on part of Earth. Where the sun shines, it is day. Where do you see the sun in the morning? Where do you see it at noon? Where do you see it in the evening?

Part of Earth is turned away from the sun. It is night on this part of Earth. It is dark. You might see stars or the moon. Sometimes you can see the moon during the day too!

Compare the day and night sky.

Materials

 crayons

 construction paper

art supplies

Process Skills

- observing

Steps

1 **Observe** the day sky.

2 Make a picture of the day sky.

3 Think about what you might **observe** in the night sky.

4 Make a picture of the night sky.

Share. Tell how the day and night sky are alike and different.

Lesson Review

1. How do you know when it is day?

2. How do you know when it is night?

3. **Tell** what you might see in the night sky and in the day sky.

Why do we need the sun?

Find the sun in the picture. Does it look bigger or smaller than the tractor?

The sun may look smaller than the tractor, but it is really very big. It is much, much bigger than Earth. The sun looks small because it is so far away.

Plants and animals need the sun. You need the sun. Almost all living things need the sun. Without the sun, there would be almost no life on Earth.

Find out why the sun looks small.

Materials

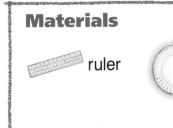 ruler   paper plate

- estimating and measuring

Steps

1 Measure across a paper plate.

2 Have your partner hold the plate. Move 5 steps away from your partner.

3 Hold up the ruler in front of you. Measure how big the plate looks now.

Share. Tell how the size of the plate looked different.

Lesson Review

1. Why does the sun look small?

2. Name two living things that need the sun.

3. Tell how you can make the plate look smaller.

What is the moon like?

It is nighttime. Look up in the sky. You might see the moon!

A **telescope** can help you see things that are far away. This girl is using a telescope to look at the moon.

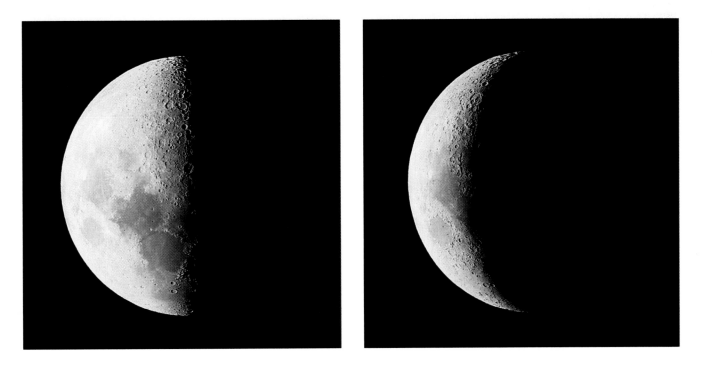

Look at the different shapes of the moon. The shapes of the moon are called **phases**. On some nights, the moon looks round. This is called a full moon. At other times, you see smaller parts of the moon. Sometimes, you cannot see the moon at all.

The moon does not make its own light. Light from the sun shines on the moon. You only see the part of the moon that has light shining on it.

Lesson Review

1. What does a telescope do?

2. What makes the moon look like it is shining?

3. **Draw** three phases of the moon.

Real and Imaginary

Some things are real. Some things are imaginary.

Which child is telling about something real? Which child is telling about something imaginary?

The clouds are white.

There is a rabbit in the sky.

Look at the pictures. Tell about the picture that shows something real. Tell about the picture that shows something imaginary.

Turn the page to learn about something real and something imaginary.

Turn the page.

What are stars like?

Guess how many stars are in the sky? There are too many to count!

Stars are made of hot gases that glow. Stars give off their own light. Our sun is a star. It is the star closest to Earth.

Long ago, people imagined that lines connected groups of stars. The lines and stars looked like pictures in the night sky.

Big Dipper

Look at these pictures. Find a cup with a long handle. Look at the man. Find the stars that make his belt. What is the name of each group of stars?

Orion

Lesson Review

1. What is a star made of?

2. What star is closest to Earth?

3. **Draw** a picture of a group of stars. Write its name.

What star picture can you make?

Process Skills

Process Skills

- making and using models

Materials

construction paper   white crayon

dots   glue

Steps

1. Use dots to make a picture. The dots are a model of stars in the sky.

2. Glue the dots to the paper.

3. Use a crayon to connect the dots.

4. Give your star picture a name.

Think About Your Results

1. Are stars in the sky really joined together?

2. What star pictures have you seen in the night sky?

Inquire Further

What other star pictures can you make?

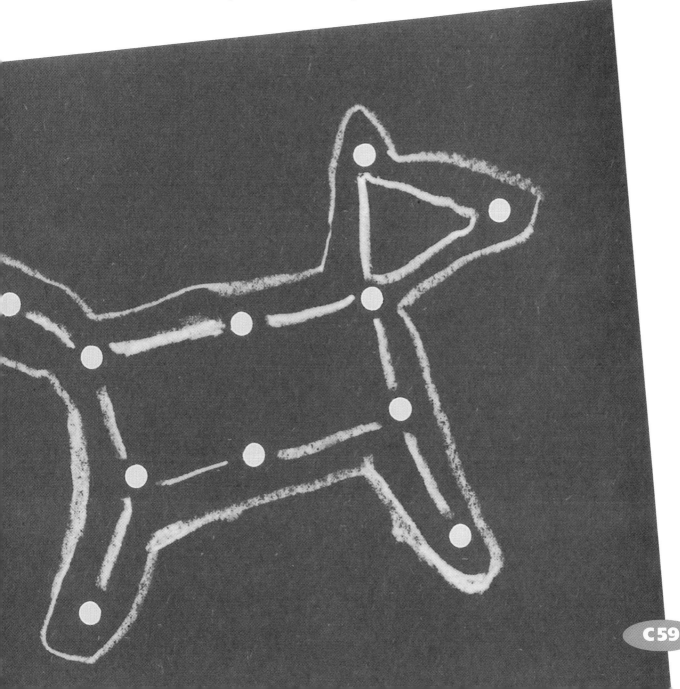

Chapter 3 Review

Reviewing Science Words

1. What can you use a **telescope** for?
2. Tell about one **phase** of the moon.

Reviewing Science Ideas

1. What might you see in the day sky?
2. What might you see in the night sky?
3. Tell why the sun looks small.
4. Name a group of stars that makes a picture.

Make a mural.

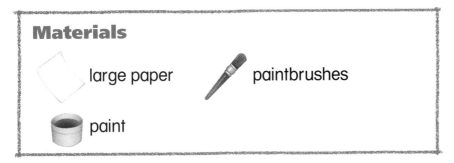

Materials

large paper

paintbrushes

paint

1 Choose day or night.

2 Think about what you might see in the day sky or night sky.

3 Make a mural.

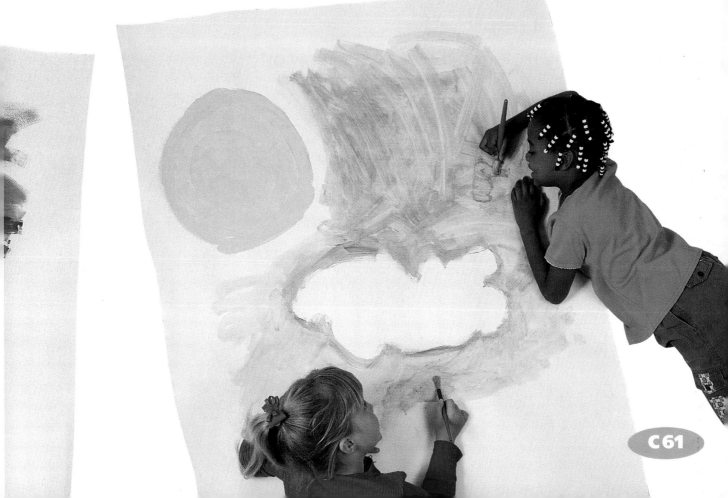

Unit C
Performance Review

There are many places on the earth to visit. Pretend you took an imaginary trip. Where did you go? What was the weather like there? What was it like during the day and at night?

Plan your imaginary trip.

1. Choose a project.

2. Think of what you need to do your project.

3. How will your project tell others about the earth, weather, and the sky?

Make a photo album.

Draw pictures of places you saw on your imaginary trip. Pretend they are pictures that you took with a camera. Put the pictures in a book about your trip.

Write a weather report.

Make a chart that shows what the weather was like in the place that you visited. Show the weather for each day. Tell others what to wear if they go to the same place.

Pretend you are a reporter.

Ask your friends questions about their imaginary trip. Ask where they went and what they saw. Think of more questions to ask.

Writing a Story

A story tells about something that happened. When you write a story, you can tell about where it happened. You can also tell who was there. A story can be real or imaginary.

1. **Prewrite** Choose a place. It can be a mountain, beach, waterfall, or other place on the earth. Draw a picture of it. Think about taking a trip to that place.

2. **Draft** Write a story about the trip. Tell what you did and what you saw.

3. **Revise** Read your story. Do you like it? Make changes if you want to.

4. **Edit** Check your writing to make sure it is correct. Make a neat copy.

5. **Publish** Share your story and picture with others.

Unit D
Human Body

Science and Technology
In Your World!

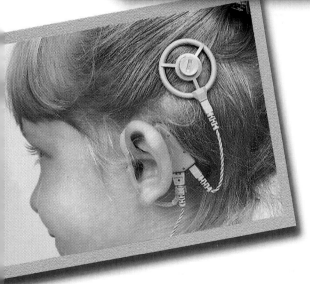

What can a bionic ear do?

It can help children who have impaired hearing. When the children hear how words sound they can learn to talk.

Chapter 1
The Senses

How can light help your teeth?

A laser is a special light. Dentists can use a laser to get rid of cavities that hurt teeth.

Chapter 2
Growing and Changing

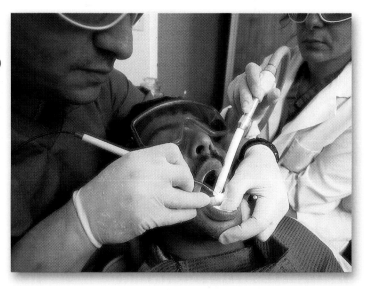

How does a bicycle helmet protect you?

Most helmets have foam inside. The foam is covered with strong plastic. The foam and plastic protect your head in case you fall.

Chapter 3
Taking Care of Your Health

Chapter 1

The Senses

Sing to the tune of *If You're Happy and You Know It, Clap Your Hands.*

You can smell there's something cooking,
Use your nose.
You can see they're apple muffins,
Use your eyes.
With your nose, you smell what's cooking.
With your eyes you see they're muffins.
All your senses let you know what's going on.

With your ears you hear the timer,
When they're done.
With your fingers you can touch them.
Are they cool?
With your ears you hear the timer,
With your fingers you can touch them.
All your senses let you know what's going on.

Take a muffin, take a bite.
Mmm, it's good!
With your tongue, you taste the muffin.
Mmm, it's good!
When you bite into a muffin,
It's your tongue that helps you taste it.
All your senses let you know what's going on.

What can you observe?

Look at all the soap bubbles. Is the water warm enough? It's bath time for this dog!

What do you do when you observe? When you **observe**, you notice many things. Observing helps you learn about things.

What do these people see? What do they hear? What else might they observe?

Tell what is in the bag.

Materials

classroom objects

paper bag

Process Skills

- observing
- inferring

Steps

1 Take turns with a partner.

2 Close your eyes. Have your partner put an object in the bag.

3 Without looking, reach into the bag and **observe** how the object feels.

4 **Infer.** What is the object?

Share. Draw what you think is in the bag. Then look in the bag.

Lesson Review

1. If you were washing a dog, what might you observe?

2. Tell about something you observe in the classroom.

3. **Tell** what you observed about the object in the bag.

Reading Captions

A caption is a sentence that tells about a picture. An arrow points to the picture that goes with the caption.

Find the caption for the picture of the dog. What does it say?

▲ This dog uses its nose to follow a squirrel.

Read the caption for each picture.

▲ Big ears help this deer hear.

An eagle uses its eyes to
see a fish from very far away. ▶

Turn the page to read
more captions.

Turn the
page.

What are the five senses?

What can you use to observe all the things around you?

You can use your **senses** to observe. You have five senses. Your senses are seeing, hearing, smelling, touching, and tasting.

Your ears help you **hear** . ▼

▲ Your eyes help you **see** .

Your nose helps you **smell** . ▼

▲ Your tongue helps you **taste** .

▲ You **touch** things with your skin.

Lesson Review

1. What are the five senses?

2. What part of your body helps you hear?

3. **Draw** a picture of yourself using one of your senses.

What sounds do you hear?

Process Skills

- observing
- inferring

Materials

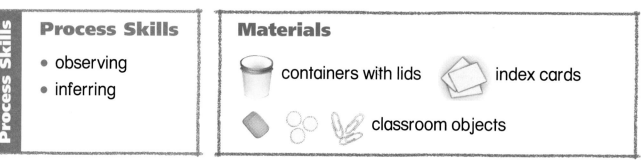

containers with lids   index cards

classroom objects

Steps

1 Shake a container. Observe the sound.

2 Infer. Find the card that tells what you think is in the container.

3 Use a chart like the one in the picture. Record what you think is in the container.

4 Open the container. Record.

5 Do it again.

What sounds do you hear?		
Container Number	Infer what is in the container.	What is in the container?

Think About Your Results

1. How could you tell what was in the containers?

2. Which sounds were hard to identify?

Inquire Further

What could you put in a container that makes a loud sound? What could you put in that makes a soft sound?

chalk

paper clips

3

4

2

Experiment with sight.

Process Skills	Materials
Process Skills • experimenting • collecting and interpreting data (record)	**Materials** safety goggles with one side covered ball

Problem

Can you see better with one eye or two eyes?

Give Your Hypothesis

If you cover one eye, will you catch more or fewer balls? Tell what you think.

Control the Variables

Make sure your partner tosses the ball from the same place each time.

Test Your Hypothesis

Follow these steps to do the experiment.

① Work with a partner.

② Have your partner toss the ball to you 10 times. Count the number of times you catch it.

3 Now put on the safety goggles with one side covered.

4 Have your partner toss the ball to you 10 times. Count the number of times you catch it.

Collect Your Data

Record the number of times you caught the ball using one eye and two eyes.

	Number of Catches
Two Eyes	
One Eye	

Tell Your Conclusion

Compare your results and hypothesis. Can you see better with one eye or two eyes?

Inquire Further

Is it easier to catch the ball with the left or the right eye covered?

Chapter 1 Review

Reviewing Science Words

1. Tell about something you **observe** in your classroom.

2. How can your **senses** help you?

3. Match the picture to the word.

see

hear

touch

smell

taste

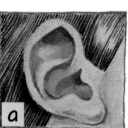
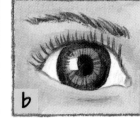
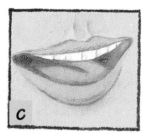
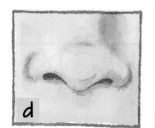
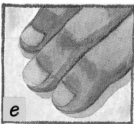

Reviewing Science Ideas

1. What senses do you use when you eat a meal?

2. Pretend you are about to cross the street. Tell what senses might help you.

Put on a play.

Materials

 sense cards

1 Work with a group.

2 Make up a play. Your play must show all the senses.

3 Perform your play for the class.

4 Have the class hold up sense cards to tell which senses you act out in your play.

Growing and Changing

Could It Be Me?

♪ Sing to the tune of *Hush Little Baby.*

I'm looking at a photo and could it be,
That this little baby grew up to be me!
There's not much hair on this baby's head
But mine's long and curly and very red.

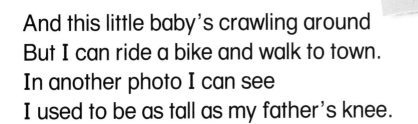

And this little baby's crawling around
But I can ride a bike and walk to town.
In another photo I can see
I used to be as tall as my father's knee.

But now when I stand up next to Dad
My head's at his elbow, that makes me glad.
And if I keep growing in every way
Will I be bigger than Dad some day?

Original lyrics by Gerri Brioso and Richard Freitas.
Produced by Children's Television Workshop.

How have you grown?

Think about how you looked when you were a baby. How big were you? What did you do?

When you were a baby, you could not talk or walk. You crawled from place to place. You may have cried a lot and slept a lot.

You have grown and changed in many ways. You are taller. You can walk, run, and jump. In what other ways have you changed?

See how you have grown.

Materials

 baby picture

 recent picture

Process Skills

- observing
- predicting

Steps

1. **Observe** your baby picture.
2. **Observe** how you look now.
3. Think about how you have grown.
4. **Predict** how you might change as you grow older.

Share. Write about how you have grown.

Lesson Review

1. What are some things that babies do?
2. Tell two ways you might change as you grow older.
3. **Draw** something you can do now that you could not do when you were younger.

Estimating and Measuring

You can measure to find out how long something is. This crayon is about 9 centimeters long.

About how long are the eraser and pencil? Measure to find out.

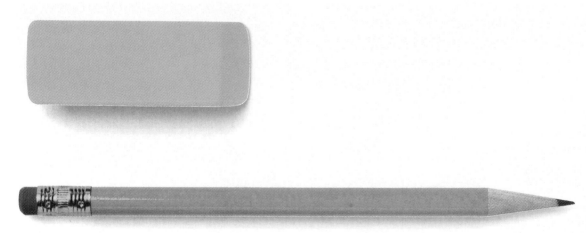

You can estimate before you measure. When you estimate, you tell how long you think something is. About how long do you think the marker is? Estimate. Then measure to find out.

Estimate then measure the paper clip and the scissors.

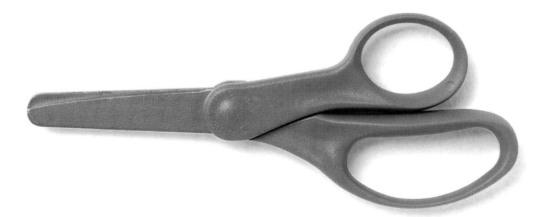

Turn the page for an activity about estimating and measuring.

Turn the page.

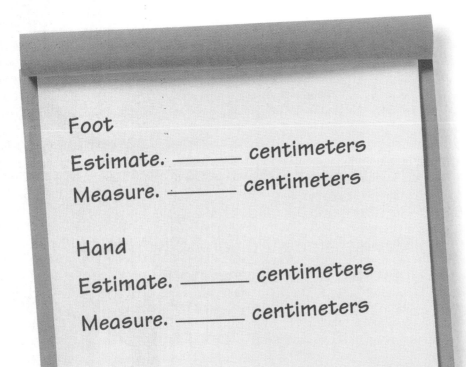
How can you measure your body?

Process Skills

- estimating and measuring

Materials

tape measure

Steps

1. **Estimate** the length of your foot. Record on a chart like this one.

2. **Measure** the length of your foot. Record.

3. Estimate and then measure the length of your hand, arm, and other body parts. Record.

Foot

Estimate. ——— centimeters

Measure. ——— centimeters

Hand

Estimate. ——— centimeters

Measure. ——— centimeters

Think About Your Results

1. Which is longer, your hand or your foot?

2. What can you measure on your body that is less than 5 centimeters long?

 Inquire Further

Which is longer, your arm span or your height?

How do teeth grow and change?

You see them when you smile. You use them when you chew. Sometimes you lose them. What are they?

A baby is born with no teeth showing. Soon, first teeth begin to grow.

This girl has many first teeth. Permanent teeth grow and push out first teeth. Have you lost your front teeth like the girl in the picture?

You see permanent teeth in this boy's smile. If you take care of permanent teeth, they can last your whole life.

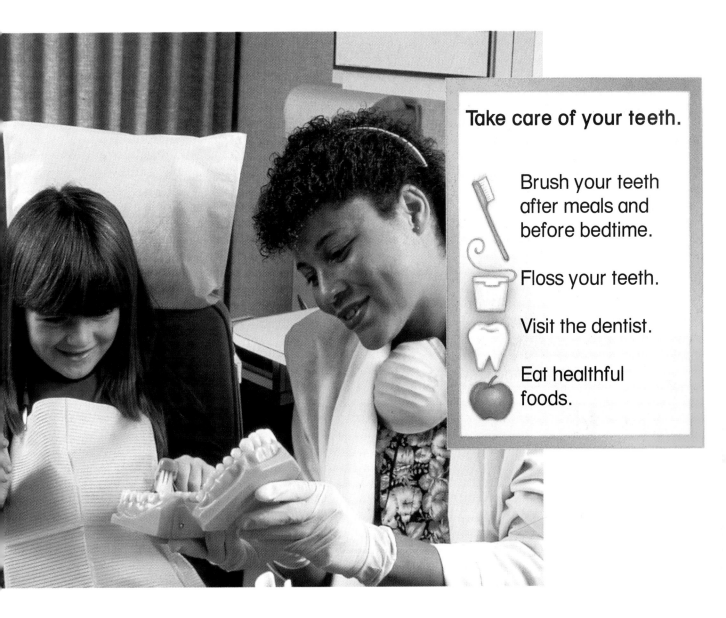

Take care of your teeth.

Brush your teeth after meals and before bedtime.

Floss your teeth.

Visit the dentist.

Eat healthful foods.

Lesson Review

1. How many first teeth have you lost?

2. What pushes out first teeth?

3. **Write** a list of ways to take care of your teeth.

What do bones and muscles do?

Stand up. Turn around. Touch your nose. Sit down. What makes your body move?

Your body has many muscles. **Muscles** help your body move. You use muscles in your arms and hands when you catch a ball. Muscles also help you smile. Put your hands on your cheeks. Smile. You can feel the muscles in your face move!

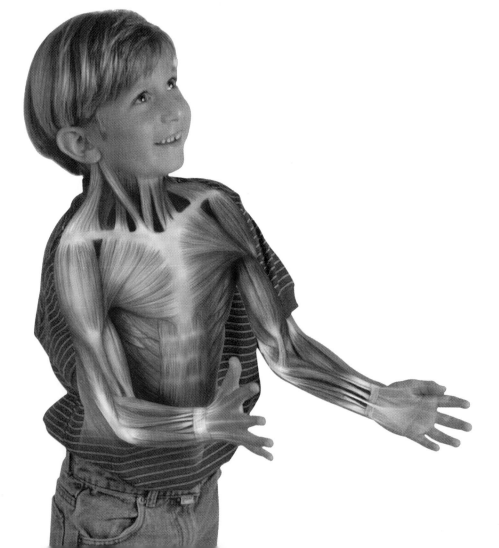

Your body also has many bones. **Bones** hold your body up. Feel the long bones in your legs. Feel the short bones in your fingers. Your bones and muscles work together to help you move.

Lesson Review

1. How can you use your muscles?

2. What do your bones do?

3. **Show** one way to use the muscles in your arm.

Chapter 2 Review

Reviewing Science Words

1. What do your **muscles** do?

2. What do your **bones** do?

Reviewing Science Ideas

1. Tell how you have changed since you were a baby.

2. What four things can you do to take care of your teeth?

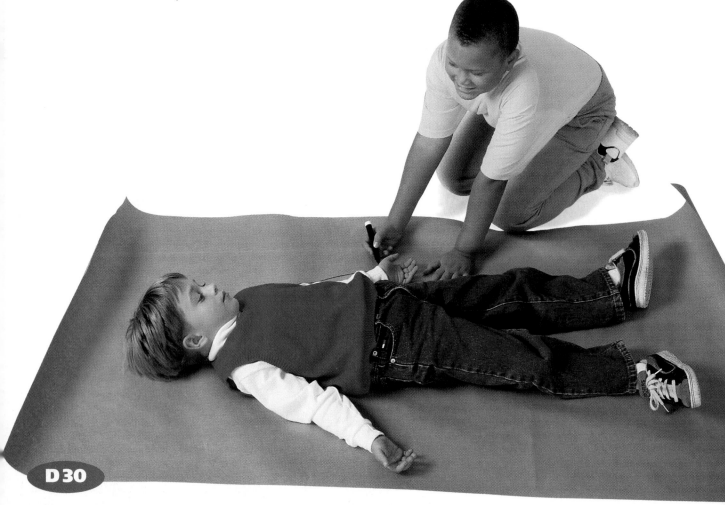

Trace and draw your body.

Materials

large paper   crayons

1 Lie on a large piece of paper.

2 Have your partner trace around your body.

3 Draw teeth in your mouth.

4 Draw your bones.

5 Draw muscles in your arms.

Chapter 3
Taking Care of Your Health

Growing Stronger

♪ Sing to the tune of *Found a Peanut*.

Exercising,
Keeping clean,
And resting when you should,
Is all part of
Keeping healthy.
Try it out,
And you'll feel good.

Eat some good food.
Choose it wisely,
From the healthy foods we know,
Rice and milk, meat,
Fruit and vegetables,
Are some foods
That help you grow.

It's important,
To keep healthy,
If you want to run and play.
Keeping healthy,
Keeps your body,
Growing stronger everyday.

Original lyrics by Gerri Brioso and Richard Freitas.
Produced by Children's Television Workshop.
Copyright ©1999 Sesame Street, Inc.

What foods help you grow?

You need food to grow. Which foods will help you stay healthy?

The **Food Guide Pyramid** shows groups of food. There are six groups in the Food Guide Pyramid. What kinds of foods are in each group?

You need to eat more food from the bottom of the Food Guide Pyramid. You need to eat less food from the top.

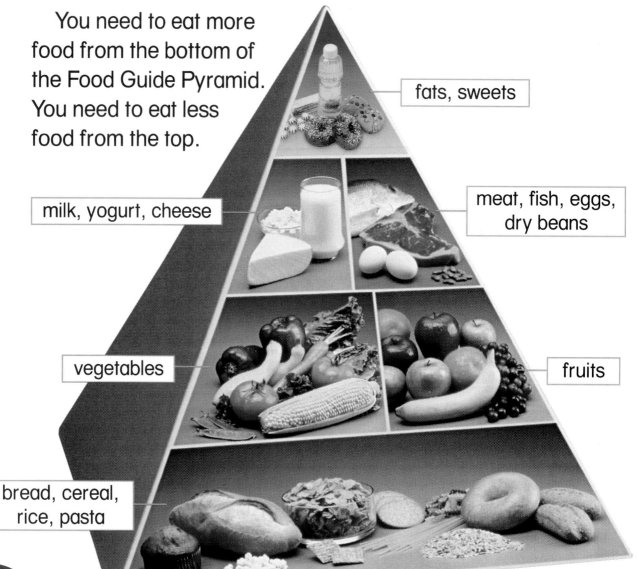

fats, sweets

meat, fish, eggs, dry beans

milk, yogurt, cheese

vegetables

fruits

bread, cereal, rice, pasta

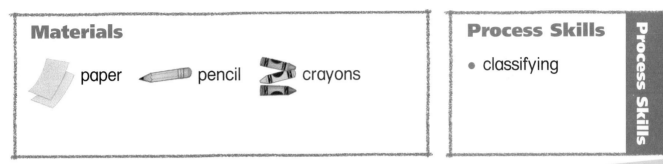
Classify foods.

Materials

paper — pencil — crayons

Process Skills

- classifying

Process Skills

Steps

1 Make a Food Guide Pyramid.

2 Label each food group.

3 Think of foods to classify. Draw one food for each group.

Share. Name a favorite food from each group in the Food Guide Pyramid.

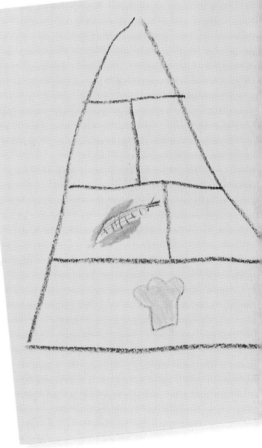

Lesson Review

1. What part of the Food Guide Pyramid shows food you should eat most?

2. What part of the Food Guide Pyramid shows food you should eat least?

3. Tell how you can eat healthier foods.

How can you stay healthy?

Do you like to play tag or balance on one foot? Do you like to fly through the air on a swing or go down a slide?

Playing and moving are ways to **exercise** . Exercise helps you stay healthy. When you jump rope or do a somersault you are exercising. What other ways can you play that give you exercise?

Staying clean also keeps you healthy. Germs can get on your hands. Wash your hands before you eat. Wash them after you touch a pet or use a restroom.

You also need sleep to keep healthy. Sleep helps you work and play. You need eight to ten hours of sleep every night.

Lesson Review

1. What are some things you can do to stay healthy?

2. When should you wash your hands?

3. **Draw** a picture that shows your favorite way to get exercise.

Is it easier to balance with eyes open or closed?

Process Skills

Process Skills

- predicting
- observing
- making definitions

Materials

pencil   paper

Steps

1 Predict. When you stand on one foot, is it easier to balance with your eyes open or closed? Record.

2 Stand on one foot. Observe. How easy is it?

3 Now close your eyes. Stand on one foot. Observe. How easy is it? Record.

4 Predict again. When you stand on your toes, is it easier to balance with your eyes open or closed? Record.

5 Stand on your toes. Observe. How easy is it?

6 Now close your eyes. Stand on your toes. Observe. How easy is it? Record.

Which is easier?

Stand on one foot.

I predict	
I observe	

Stand on toes.

I predict	
I observe	

Think About Your Results

1. Make a definition. Tell what the word **balance** means.

2. Do you balance better with your eyes open or closed?

 Inquire Further

How can you improve your balance?

Using Pictures

You can learn a lot from looking at pictures.
This picture shows a playground that is safe.

Tell how this playground is different from the playground on the other page. What would you do to make this playground more safe?

Turn the page to learn more about staying safe.

Turn the page.

How can you stay safe?

Imagine you are at a busy corner. How can you cross the street safely?

When you cross the street, make sure no cars are coming. Look left, right, and left again. Cross when it is safe. A traffic light or crossing guard can help you.

The children in this picture are waiting to cross the street. White lines on the street show the safest place to walk. This place is called the **crosswalk** .

Find other ways people in this picture are staying safe. What do you observe about the girl with the bicycle or the person in the car? Tell about other ways to stay safe outdoors, at home, and at school.

Lesson Review

1. What should you do before you cross the street?

2. Where is a safe place to cross the street?

3. **Draw** a picture that shows how to stay safe outdoors, at home, or at school.

Chapter 3 Review

Reviewing Science Words

1. What does the **Food Guide Pyramid** show?
2. Name three ways to **exercise**.
3. What is a **crosswalk**?

Reviewing Science Ideas ·

1. From which group in the Food Guide Pyramid do you need to eat the most food?
2. When should you wash your hands?
3. Tell how to cross the street safely.

Make a mobile.

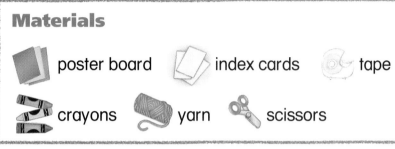

Materials

poster board   index cards   tape

crayons   yarn   scissors

1. Draw a big picture of yourself.

2. Use cards. Draw healthy foods. Draw ways to exercise, rest, and stay clean. Draw ways to stay safe.

3. Tape yarn to each card. Tape the cards to the big picture.

Unit D
Performance Review

You have learned why your senses are important and how to take care of your health. You have learned about growing and changing, too. Have a health fair to show others what you have learned.

Plan your health fair.

1. Pick a project you would like to do.

2. Decide how you will do your project.

3. How will your project tell others about the senses, growing, and health?

Write a poem.

Write a poem about the five senses. Use all five senses in your poem. You can use the words see, hear, touch, taste, and smell.

Play charades.

Think of words that tell about the senses, growing, and health. Write each word on a card. Put the cards into a bag. Choose a card. Act out the word. See if others can guess the word. Take turns.

Play a game.

Listen to your teacher or a classmate tell a safety rule. Then repeat that rule and tell another one. See how many safety rules your class can think of.

Writing About How to Stay Healthy

When you get people to do something, you persuade them. You can also persuade people that something is important. You can make a poster to persuade people. You can draw pictures and write sentences on your poster.

1. **Prewrite** Think of something you can do to stay healthy. Draw a picture on your poster.

2. **Draft** How can you persuade others to follow your idea? Write sentences that tell why your idea a good one.

3. **Revise** Read what you wrote. Will it persuade others to follow your idea?

4. **Edit** Check your writing to make sure it is correct. Copy it onto your poster.

5. **Publish** Share your poster with others. Ask what they think about your idea. Did you persuade them to follow your idea?

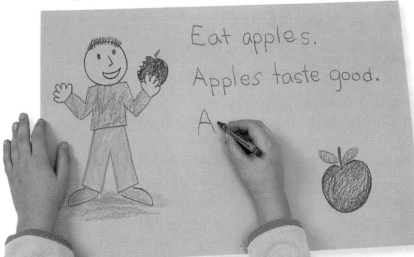

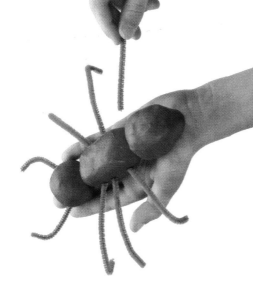

Your Science Handbook

 Safety in Science

Scientists do their experiments safely. You need to be careful when doing experiments too. The next page includes some safety tips to remember.

- Read each experiment carefully.
- Wear safety goggles when needed.
- Clean up spills right away.
- Never taste or smell materials unless your teacher tells you to.
- Tape sharp edges of materials.
- Put things away when you finish an experiment.
- Wash your hands after each experiment.

Using the Metric System

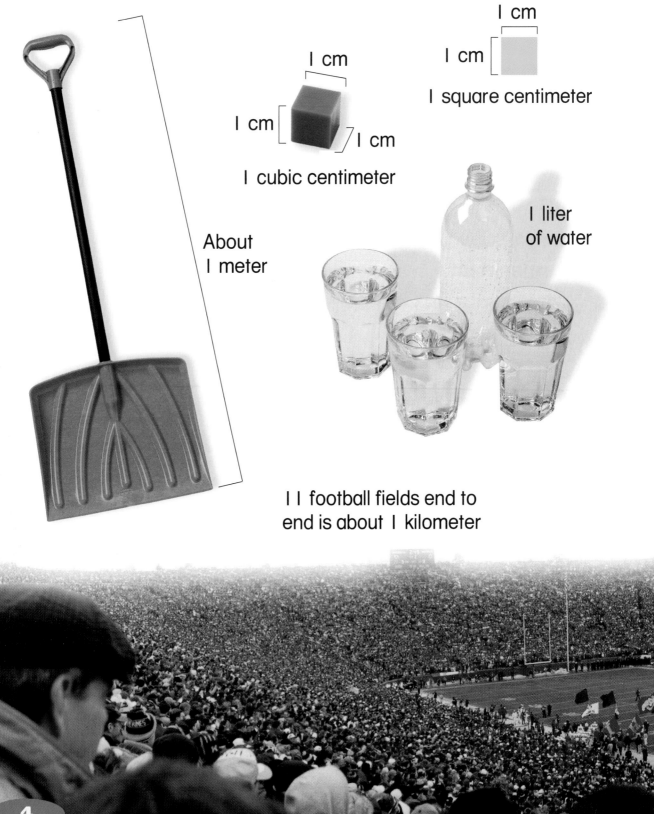

1 cm

1 cm 1 square centimeter

1 cm

1 cm 1 cm

1 cubic centimeter

1 liter
of water

About
1 meter

11 football fields end to
end is about 1 kilometer

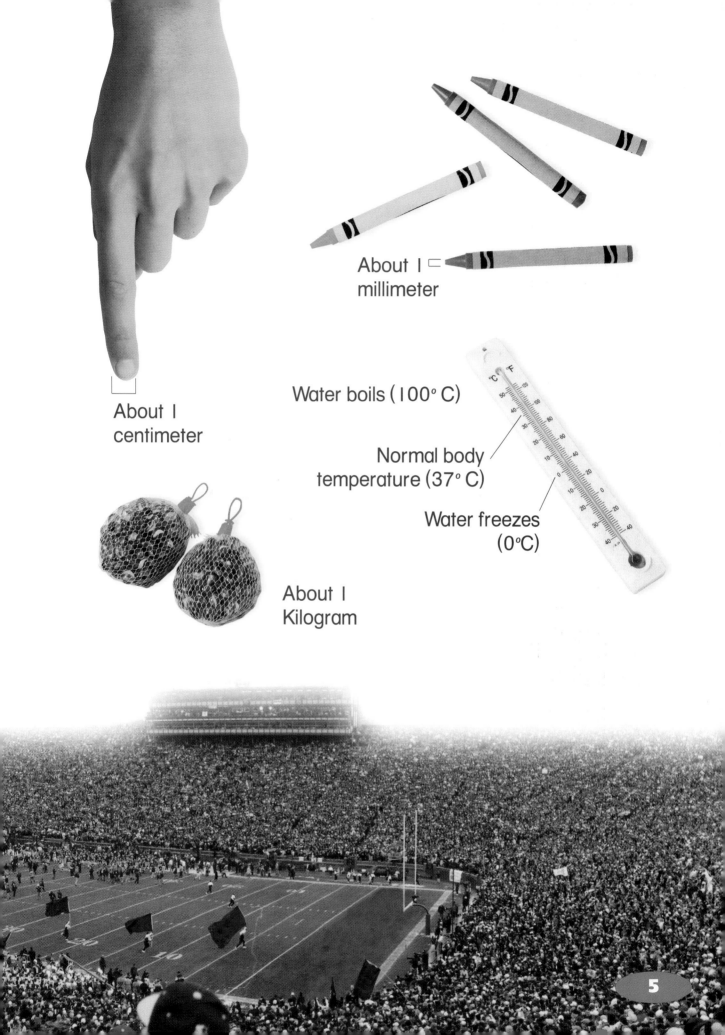

About 1
millimeter

About 1
centimeter

Water boils (100° C)

Normal body
temperature (37° C)

Water freezes
(0°C)

About 1
Kilogram

Observing

How do you observe?

You observe with your five senses. You observe when your eyes see and when your ears hear. You observe when your fingers and body touch things. You observe when your nose smells and your tongue tastes. Only foods should go in your mouth!

Practice Observing

Materials

 hand lens   4 walnuts

Follow these steps

1 Make a chart like this one.

walnuts	

2 Put one walnut in each box of the chart.

3 Observe each walnut with the hand lens.

4 Write what you observe in the box.

5 Draw a picture of each walnut.

6 Take the walnuts out of each box.

Thinking About Your Thinking

Is each walnut a little different from the others? How are they different? Have a friend try to put each walnut in the right box. Have your friend tell how they are different.

Communicating

How do you communicate?

You communicate when you talk. You also communicate when you draw a picture, write a story, act something out, make a graph, or even sing a song.

Practice Communicating

Materials

 paper    crayons

Follow these steps

1 Look at pictures of a stream, river, lake, and ocean.

2 Draw your own picture of a stream, river, lake and ocean.

3 Share your pictures with your class.

4 Describe each picture.

Thinking About Your Thinking

What other ways could you communicate to your classmates about what a stream, river, lake, or ocean is.

Classifying

What does it mean to classify things?

You classify things when you group them by what they have in common. Shape, color, and texture are some ways to classify things. There are often different ways to classify the same things.

Practice Classifying

Materials

 colored blocks of different sizes

Follow these steps

1 Work with a partner.

2 Classify the blocks by color.

3 Classify the blocks again. This time classify by shape.

4 Think of another way to classify the blocks.

Thinking About Your Thinking

Choose some objects. Think of new ways to classify them.

Estimating and Measuring

What is estimating and measuring?

You can estimate before you measure. When you estimate you tell how long, tall, wide, or heavy you think something is. After you make an estimate, you can check it by measuring the object.

Practice Estimating and Measuring

Materials

 Snap Cubes   ruler

Follow these steps

1 Make a chart like the one below.

How many Snap Cubes long?		
Object	Estimate	Measure

2 Choose an object. About how many Snap Cubes long does it look? Make an estimate. Measure the object. Record.

3 Make a chart like this one.

How many centimeters long?		
Object	Estimate	Measure

4 About how many centimeters long does your object look?

5 Repeat the activity with other objects.

Thinking About Your Thinking

How is measuring length with centimeters like measuring length with cubes? How is it different?

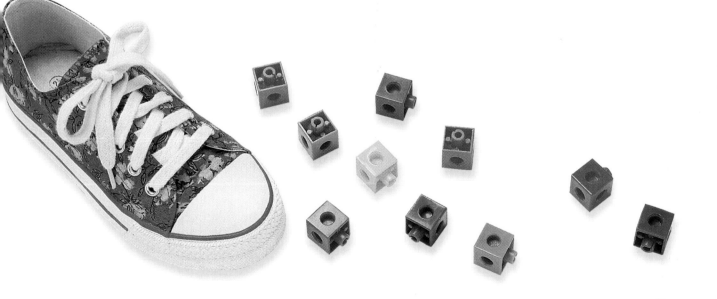

Inferring

What does it mean to infer?

You infer when you make a conclusion or a guess from what you observe or from what you already know. You can infer from what you observe with your five senses.

Practice Inferring

Materials

 16 pinto beans   3 containers with lids

Follow these steps

1 Put 1 bean in a container. Put 5 beans in another container. Put 10 beans in another container.

2 Have your partner shake each container.

3 Ask your partner to infer which container has 1 bean, 5 beans, and 10 beans.

4 Have your partner put the containers in order from the least beans to the most beans.

5 Mix up the containers. Trade places and do the activity again.

Thinking About Your Thinking

Which senses did you use to infer which container had the fewest and most beans?

Predicting

How do you predict?

When you predict, you tell what you think will happen. If you observe something carefully first, it will help you to make better predictions.

Practice Predicting

Materials

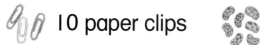 10 paper clips   10 lima beans

Follow these steps

1 Make a chart like the one below.

Patterns				

2 Use the paper clips and lima beans.

3 Make a pattern that fills 4 boxes in a row.

4 Have your partner predict what goes in the next box.

5 Have your partner start a pattern. Predict how to complete the pattern.

Thinking About Your Thinking

What process skill can
help you finish the pattern?

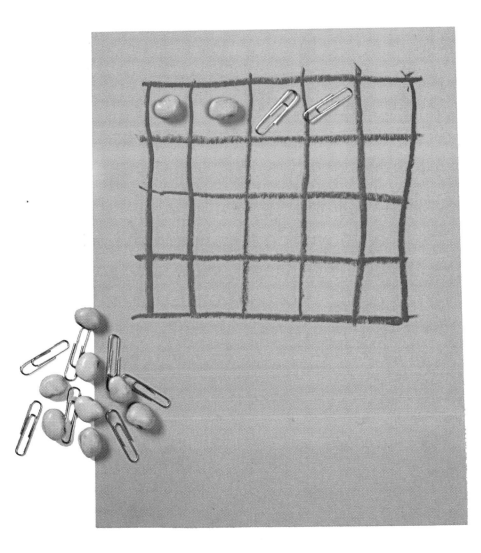

Making Definitions

How can you make a definition?

A definition tells what something means. You can use something you know or something you do to make a definition for a word.

Practice Making Definitions

Materials

 books   ruler

small block

Follow these steps

1 Build a ramp with books and a ruler.

2 Tell what you notice about the ramp. Is it smooth? Is it level? How have you seen ramps used? How can you use a ramp?

3 Put the block at the top of the ramp. Let the block slide down the ramp.

4 Make a definition for the word **ramp**.

5 Find the definition of **ramp** in the dictionary. Write it down.

Thinking About Your Thinking

Compare your definition with the dictionary definition. How were they alike? How were they different? Do you think the block would move if it was on a flat ruler rather than the ramp? Why or why not?

Making and Using Models

What can you do with a model?

You can use a model to show what you know about something. A model can also help others learn about the thing that the model represents.

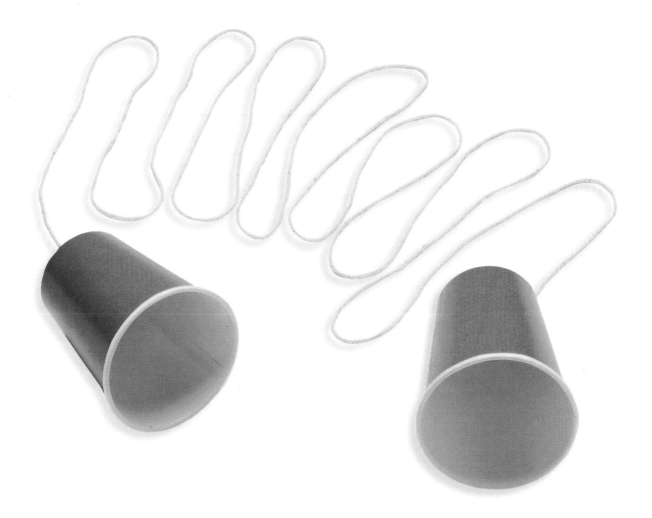

Practice Making and Using Models

Materials

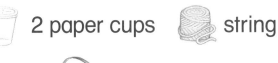 2 paper cups    string

safety goggles

2 paper clips   pencil

Follow these steps

1. Put on your safety goggles.

2. Use the tip of your pencil to poke a small hole in the bottom of each cup.

3. Put the ends of the string through each cup.

4. Tie a paper clip to the end of each string.

5. Have your partner hold one cup as you hold the other cup. Step back until the string is tight.

6. Have your partner talk into the cup. Can you hear what your partner is saying? Take turns talking and listening.

Thinking About Your Thinking

How is your model like a telephone?
How is it different?

Giving Hypotheses

Why do you ask questions and give hypotheses?

You can ask questions to try to understand something. When you give a hypothesis, you make a statement. Then you can test it to see if it is correct.

Practice Giving Hypotheses

Materials

○ cotton ball wooden block

Follow these steps

1 If you blow on a cotton ball and a wooden block with the same force, which will move farther? Tell what you think. This is your hypothesis.

2 Test the hypothesis. Place the cotton ball and the block on your desk.

3 Do the experiment. Blow on the cotton ball. Blow on the block.

Thinking About Your Thinking

Which object went further, the cotton ball or wooden block? Did your results match your hypothesis? What other questions do you have?

Collecting Data

How do you collect and interpret data?

You collect data when you record what you observe. You can use pictures, words, graphs, or charts to display data.

You interpret data when you use what you have learned to explain something or answer a question.

Practice Collecting Data

Materials

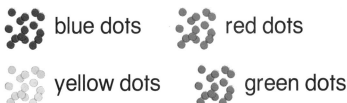

blue	red	yellow	green

blue dots   red dots

yellow dots   green dots

Follow these steps

1. Make a bar graph like this one.

2. Choose a different number of dots for each color.

3. Put blue dots in the column marked **blue**. Put red dots in the column marked **red**.

4. Do the same with your yellow and green dots.

5. Count the dots in each column. Write the number in the circle below each column.

Thinking About Your Thinking

How many of each color dot did you put in your bar graph? Which column had the most dots? Which column had the fewest?

Controlling Variables

What does it mean to control variables?

You control variables when you do an activity and change just one thing. The thing you change is called the variable.

A variable can be almost anything. It can be distance, or light, or temperature. Only one variable changes at a time.

Practice Identifying and Controlling Variables

Materials

 safety goggles   shoe box

3 rubber bands of different thicknesses

Follow these steps

1 Put on your safety goggles.

2 Stretch 1 rubber band over the shoebox. Pluck the rubber band. Was the sound high or low?

3 Stretch another rubber band over the shoe box. Pluck the rubber band. How did the sound compare to the first rubber band?

4 Repeat step 2 with the third rubber band. How did this sound compare with the others?

Thinking About Your Thinking

What is the variable in this activity? What things did not change?

Experimenting

How do you experiment?

When you do an experiment, you follow a plan to answer a question. When you are finished, you make conclusions about what you have learned.

Practice Experimenting

Materials

2 cups of water   salt   sand

plastic spoon

Follow these steps

Problem

What happens to the salt and sand when they are put in water?

Give Your Hypothesis

If you put salt in water and sand in water, which will dissolve? Tell what you think.

Control the Variables

Use the same amount of water and the same temperature of water in both cups.

Test Your Hypothesis

Follow these steps to do the experiment.

1 Label one cup **salt** and the other **sand**.

2 Add water to both cups.

3 Add 2 spoonfuls of salt to the water. Predict. What will happen to the salt? Stir the saltwater for 30 seconds.

4 Add 2 spoonfuls of sand to the other cup. Predict. What will happen the sand? Stir the sand and water for 30 seconds.

Collect Your Data

Draw two pictures. Draw the sand and salt before the experiment. Draw the sand and salt after you stirred them in the water.

Tell Your Conclusion

Compare your results and hypothesis. What happened to the salt and the sand when you added them to the water?

Thinking About Your Thinking

Was your hypothesis correct?
Why or why not?

Endangered Plants and Animals

Some plants and animals are endangered. That means that very few of them are living. People all over the world are working to protect many endangered plants and animals.

Endangered Plants

▶ Eureka Valley Evening Primrose California, U.S.A.

▲ Western Lily Oregon, U.S.A.

▼ Davis Green Pitaya Texas, U.S.A

Endangered Animals

▲ Snow Leopard
Tibet

Orangutan
Borneo and Sumatra ▲

Green Sea Turtle
Hawaii, U.S.A. ▼

Terrariums

A terrarium is a container with soil in it. It has plants in it. It can also have animals, such as lizards, toads, salamanders, and snakes. A lid on top keeps enough water inside. A terrarium is a habitat that has everything the plants and animals need.

Aquariums

Aquariums have water in them. Fish can live in an aquarium. People take care of the fish by feeding them and keeping the water clean. Snails and plants can live in an aquarium too. An aquarium is a habitat that has everything they need.

The thermometer shows how warm the water is.

The heater keeps the water warm.

The filter keeps the water clean.

The air pump puts air into the water.

Using Graphs

Are there more black, orange, or striped fish in the tank? A graph can help you compare the groups. These pages show three kinds of graphs.

Picture Graph

This graph uses pictures. How many fish are in each group?

Fish

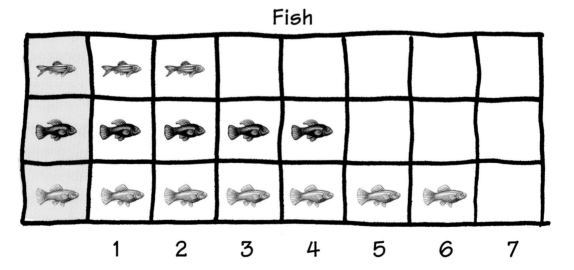

1   2   3   4   5   6   7

Bar Graph

In this bar graph, one box is filled for each fish. How many more orange fish are there than striped fish?

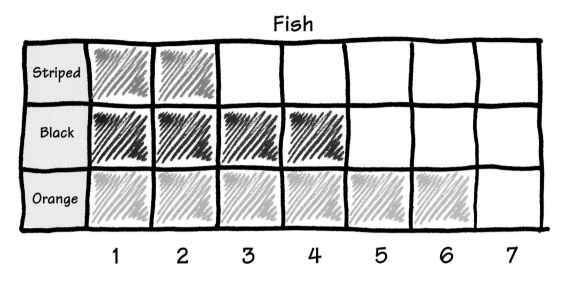

Fish

Striped | Black | Orange

1   2   3   4   5   6   7

Circle Graph

This circle graph shows that there are 2 striped fish and 4 black fish. How many orange fish are there?

Fish

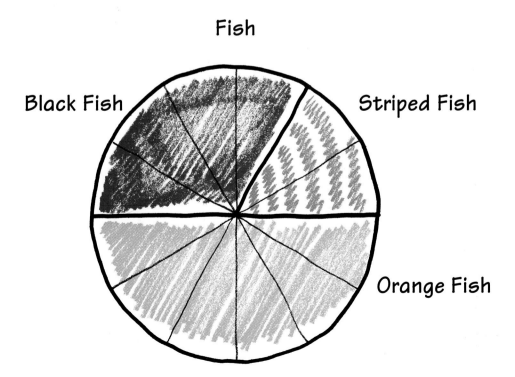

Black Fish

Striped Fish

Orange Fish

Fossils

The pictures on this page show three different fossils. A fossil is a part of or a print of a plant or animal that lived long ago.

Stegosaurus

Tyrannosaurus rex

fern

Dinosaurs

Scientists have learned about many kinds of dinosaurs by studying fossils. They know that some dinosaurs ate plants and others ate meat. Read to find out what these dinosaurs ate.

Triceratops ate plants.

Stegosaurus ate plants.

Compsognathus ate meat.

Tyrannosaurus ate meat.

Electricity

All objects have tiny bits of electricity called electric charges. Rubbing objects together can cause these electric charges to move from one object to another.

This girl is rubbing a balloon on her wool sweater. The balloon picks up electric charges from the sweater. These electric charges cause the balloon to stick to the wall.

Electricity can be stored in a battery. The electric charges move through the battery. They move in a path called a circuit. When the circuit is complete, the bulb lights up.

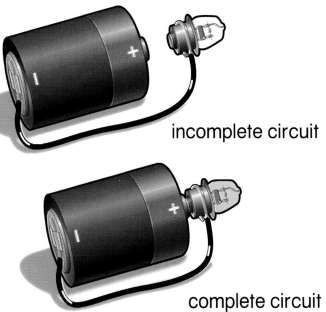

incomplete circuit

complete circuit

You use electricity in your home. When you plug in a lamp, electric charges move from the outlet through the lamp cord. Then the circuit is complete and the lamp lights up.

Mixtures and Solutions

When you mix two or more materials together, you make a mixture. This salad is a mixture. You can easily separate each piece.

Some liquids can mix together to make a solution.

This is another kind of mixture. It is a solution. The powdered drink mix dissolves in cold water to make lemonade. Other kinds of powders only dissolve easily in hot water.

Some materials do not mix with water. The oil floats on top of the water. The sand sinks to the bottom.

Water Cycle

Water moving from the clouds to the earth and back to clouds again is called the water cycle.

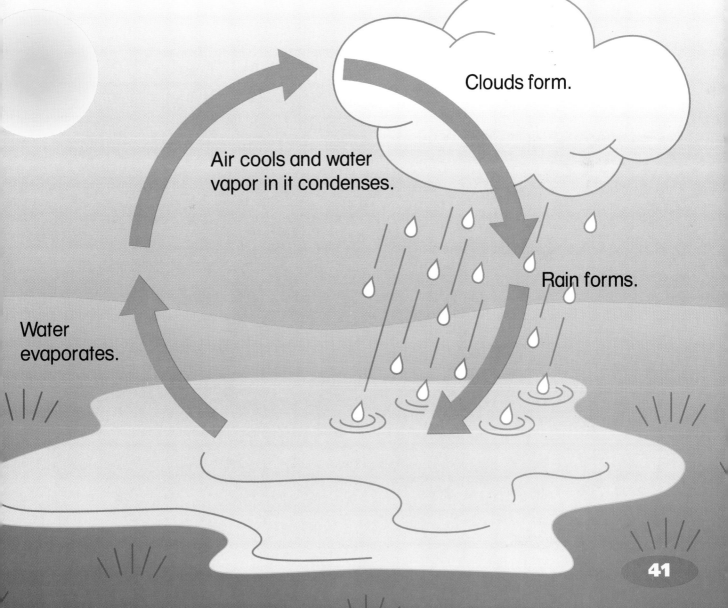

Clouds form.

Air cools and water vapor in it condenses.

Rain forms.

Water evaporates.

Solar System

The sun is the center of our solar system. The planets in our solar system move around the sun.

Name each planet. Count them. How many planets are in our solar system? Which planet is the largest? Which one is closest to the sun?

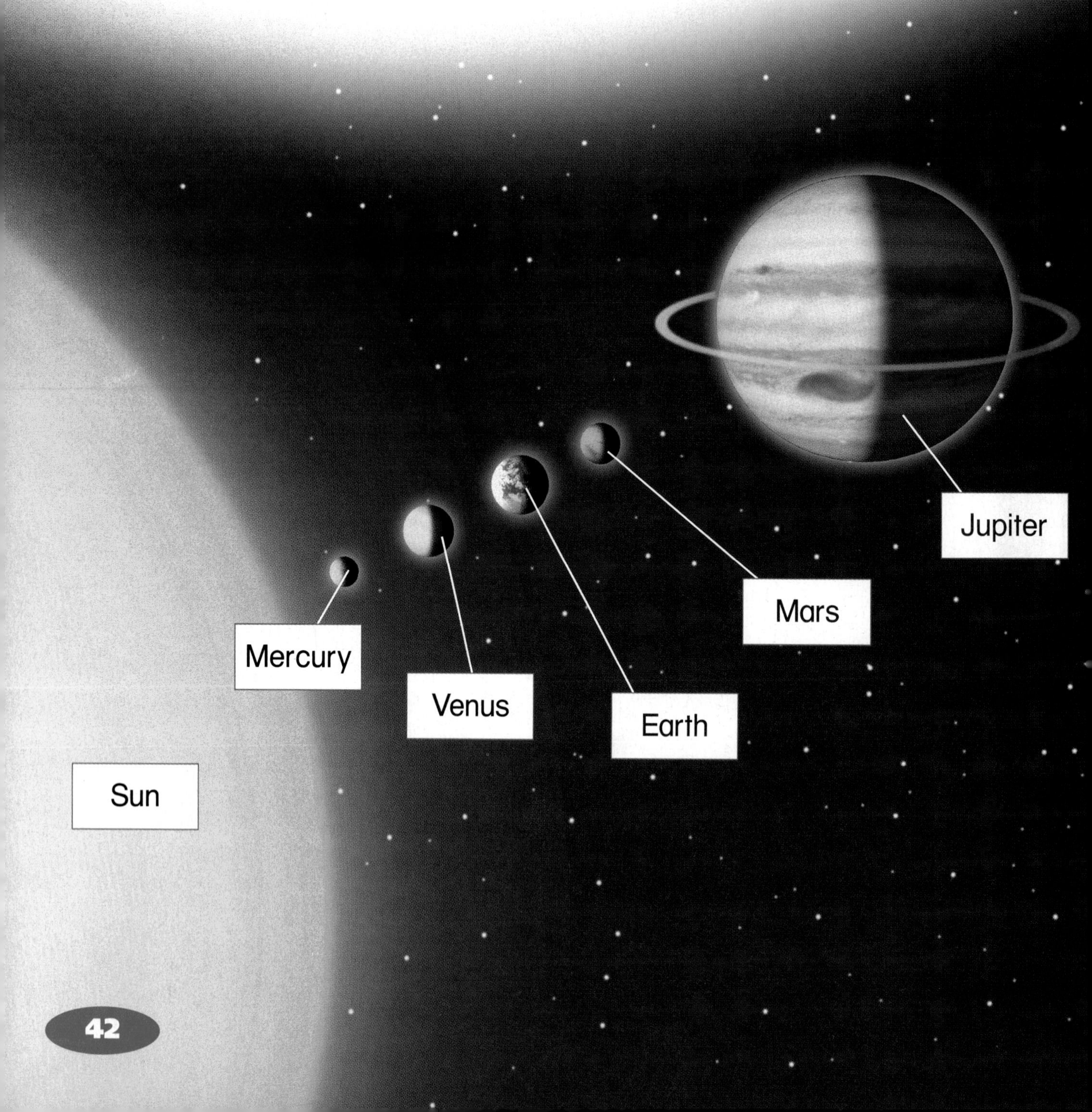

Jupiter

Mars

Mercury

Venus

Earth

Sun

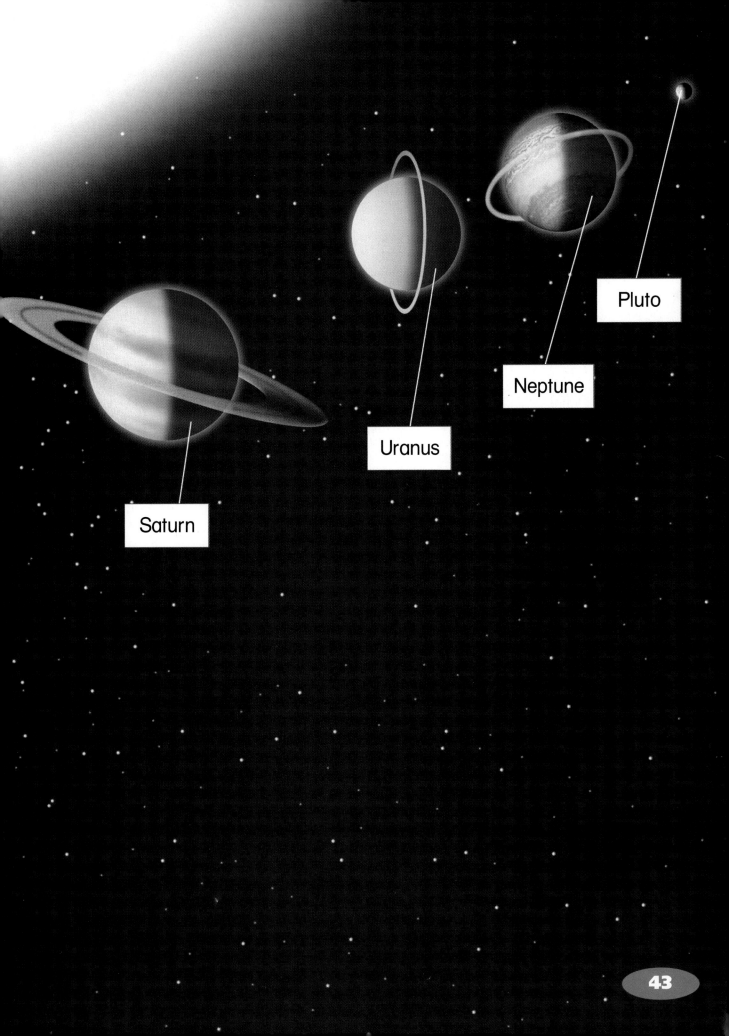

Saturn

Uranus

Neptune

Pluto

Space Exploration

Scientists use special equipment to learn about space. The Mars Pathfinder was sent to Mars. Astronauts do not travel on the Mars Pathfinder. Cameras, computers, and other equipment record information. The information is sent back to Earth.

Look at the picture of the Space Shuttle. Astronauts who travel on the Space Shuttle do experiments in space. They learn what it is like to live without gravity.

The Mars Pathfinder carried the Sojourner Rover to Mars. The Sojourner Rover collected important information. ▶

The Digestive System

When you eat, you chew and swallow food. The food goes down a tube called the esophagus. Then it goes into your stomach. Next it is digested in the small intestine. Most digestion happens in the small intestine. Food that is not digested goes into the large intestine. Then it passes out of the body.

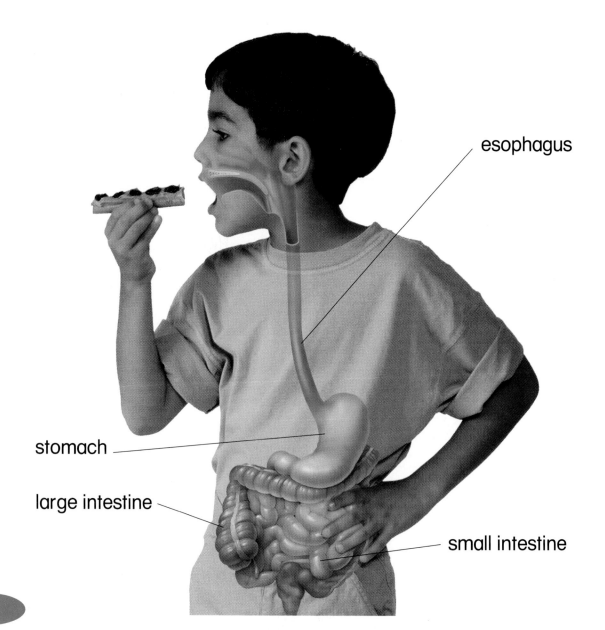

esophagus

stomach

large intestine

small intestine

The Heart and Lungs

When you breathe, your lungs take in air. Air contains oxygen, a gas that your whole body needs.

Your heart pumps blood to every part of your body. Blood is pumped away from your heart in tubes called arteries. It travels back to the heart in tubes called veins.

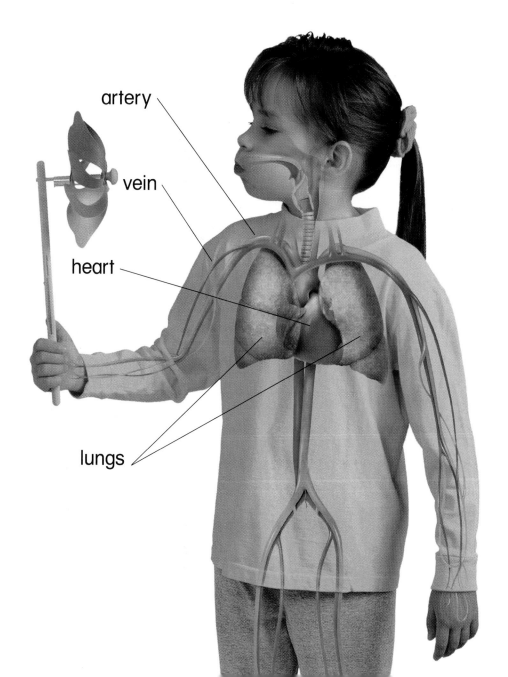

artery

vein

heart

lungs

The Brain and Nervous System

Your brain tells your body what to do. It helps you move, think, feel, and remember. Your brain sends messages through the nerves. Nerves are pathways that lead to and from your brain.

When you see a ball, your brain sends a message. Nerves carry the message to your arm and hand. Your arm and hand move to catch the ball.

brain

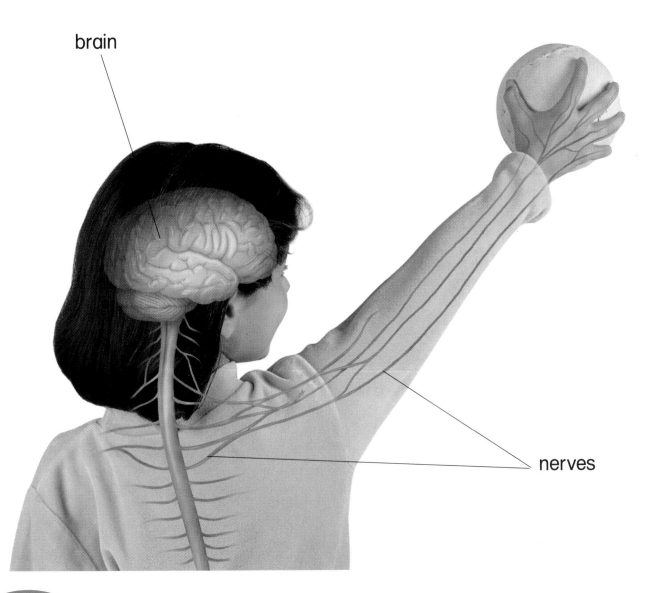

nerves

The Eye

You see things because light travels through your eyes.

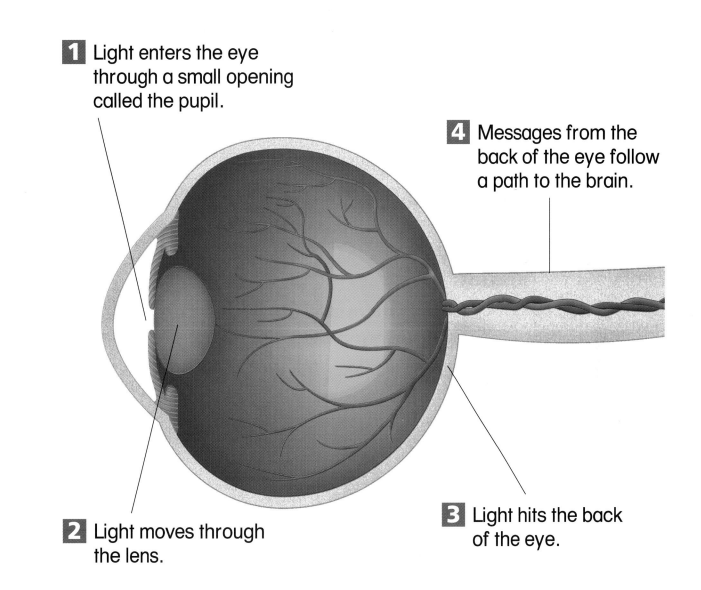

1 Light enters the eye through a small opening called the pupil.

4 Messages from the back of the eye follow a path to the brain.

2 Light moves through the lens.

3 Light hits the back of the eye.

Using Measuring Tools

You can use tools to measure how long something is. Most scientists measure length in centimeters or meters.

Measure length with a metric ruler.

1. Find a pencil. Line up the eraser of the pencil with the end of the ruler.

2. Look at the tip of the pencil. Find the centimeter mark that is closest to the tip of the pencil.

3. About how long is the pencil? Record.

Measure length with a meter stick.

What is the length of your classroom? Measure with a meter stick.

Measure length with a tape measure.

Find something round in your classroom. Use a tape measure to measure around it.

Using a Thermometer

A thermometer measures the temperature. When the temperature gets warmer, the red line moves up. When it gets cooler, the red line moves down.

Some thermometers have a Celsius and Fahrenheit scale. Most scientists use the Celsius scale.

Measure temperature with a thermometer.

1. Put a thermometer in a cup of cold water.

2. Observe the red line in the thermometer.

3. Put the thermometer in a cup of warm water.

4. Observe the red line again.

5. How did the red line in the thermometer change?

Using a Pan Balance

A pan balance is used to measure mass. Mass is how much matter an object has. Make sure the two sides of a pan balance are level before you use it.

Measure mass with a pan balance.

1. Choose two objects. Which one do you think has more mass?

2. Put an object on each side of the pan balance.

3. Which side of the pan balance is lower? The object on the low side has more mass than the object on the high side.

Using a Hand Lens

You can use a hand lens to make objects look larger than they really are. This helps you see parts of the object that you might not notice without the hand lens.

Observe a penny.

1. Look at a penny through a hand lens.

2. Move the hand lens closer to and farther from the penny. Notice that the penny seems to change size. Notice that the penny can look clear or blurry.

3. Hold the hand lens so that the penny looks clear. Tell what you observe that you did not see without the hand lens.

Using a Calculator

A calculator can help you do things, such as add and subtract. This chart shows how much paper a school recycled each month. Use a calculator to figure out how much paper they recycled in all.

1. To add a number, press the number. Then press the ➕ sign.

2. Do this for each number in the chart.

3. When you have added all the numbers, press the ＝ sign.

4. The answer should be 98.

Month	Paper Recycled in kilograms
September	7
October	12
November	13
December	9
January	11
February	14
March	9
April	15
May	8

Using a Computer

You can learn about science at a special Internet website. Go to www.sfscience.com .

1. Use the mouse to click on your grade.

2. Find a topic you would like to learn about. Click on that topic.

3. You can click on an arrow to go to another page. You can also click on words with lines under them.

4. Tell about 3 things that you learned at the website.

1,000 B.C.	725 B.C.	450 B.C.	175 B.C.	100 A.D.

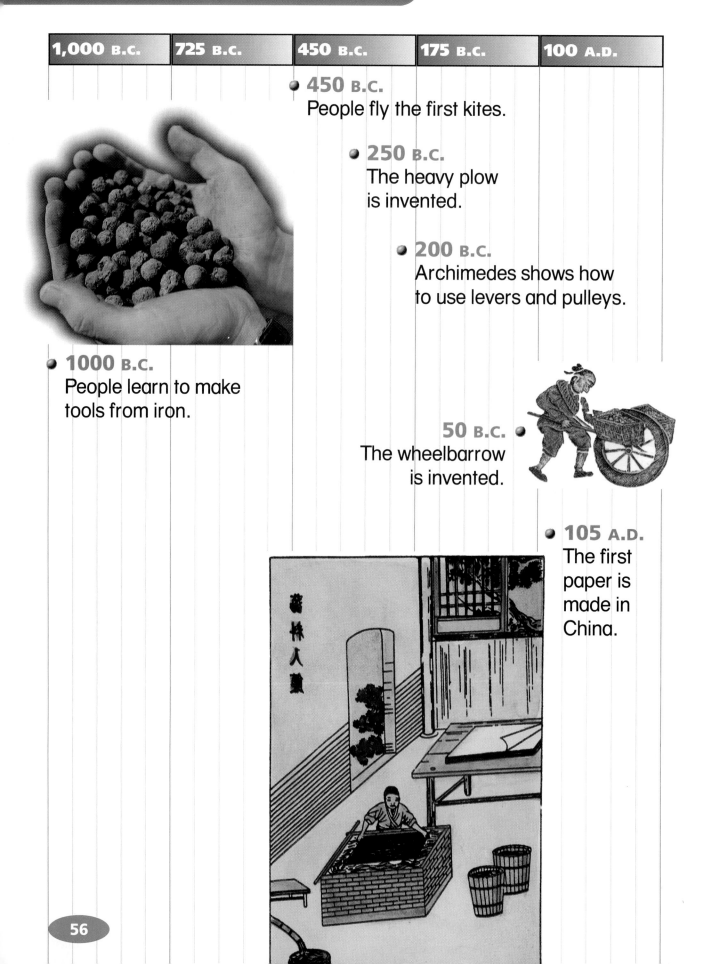

450 B.C.
People fly the first kites.

250 B.C.
The heavy plow is invented.

200 B.C.
Archimedes shows how to use levers and pulleys.

1000 B.C.
People learn to make tools from iron.

50 B.C.
The wheelbarrow is invented.

105 A.D.
The first paper is made in China.

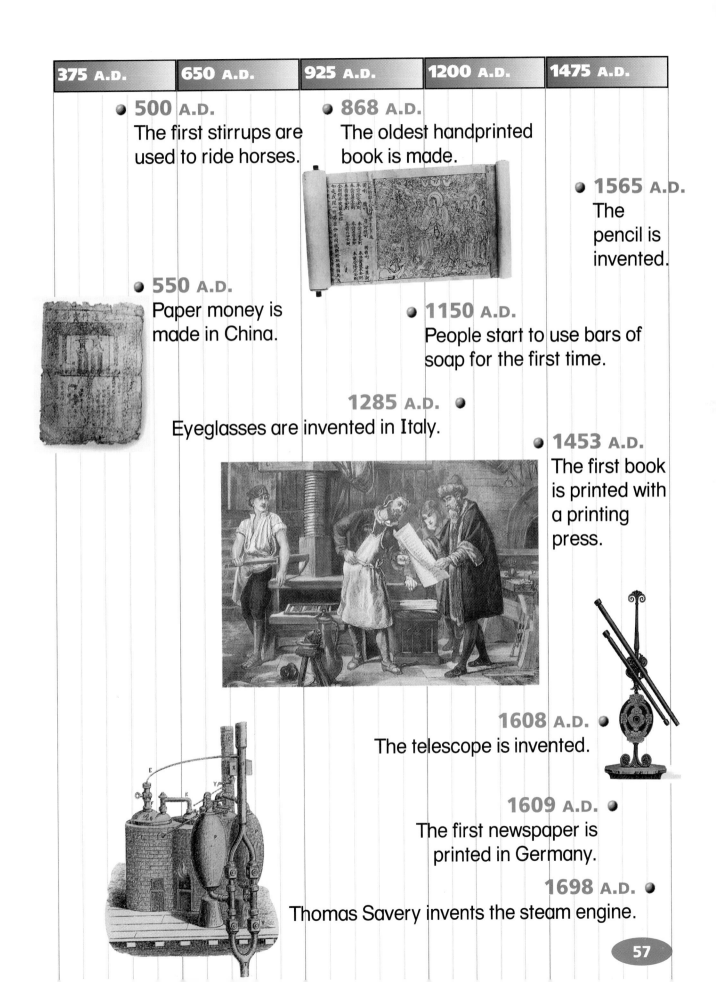

375 A.D.	650 A.D.	925 A.D.	1200 A.D.	1475 A.D.

500 A.D.
The first stirrups are used to ride horses.

868 A.D.
The oldest handprinted book is made.

1565 A.D.
The pencil is invented.

550 A.D.
Paper money is made in China.

1150 A.D.
People start to use bars of soap for the first time.

1285 A.D.
Eyeglasses are invented in Italy.

1453 A.D.
The first book is printed with a printing press.

1608 A.D.
The telescope is invented.

1609 A.D.
The first newspaper is printed in Germany.

1698 A.D.
Thomas Savery invents the steam engine.

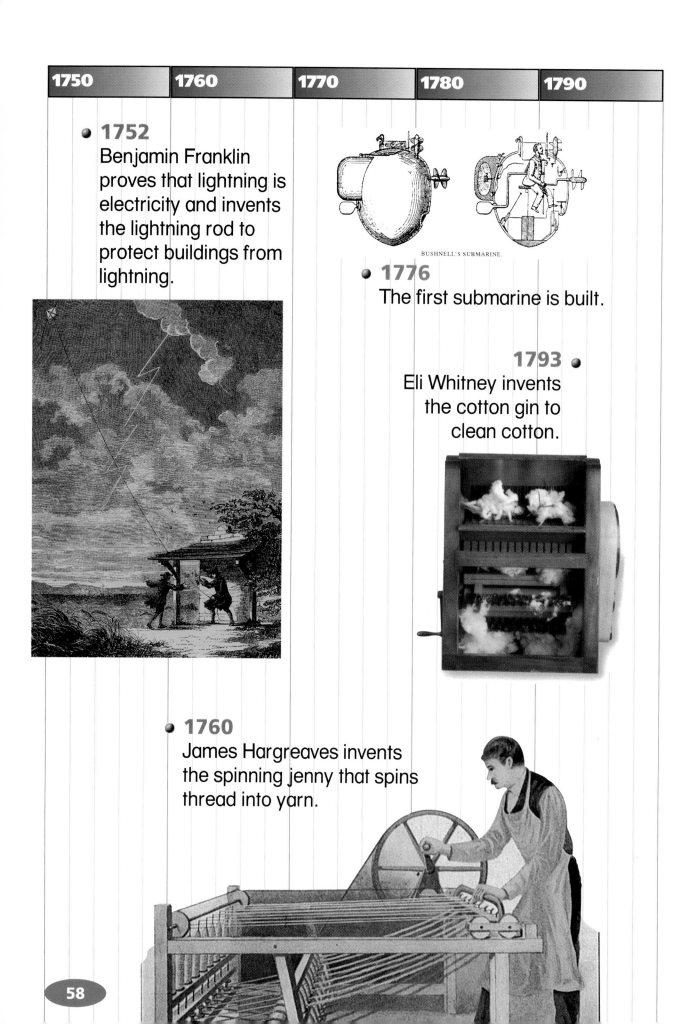

| 1750 | 1760 | 1770 | 1780 | 1790 |

1752
Benjamin Franklin proves that lightning is electricity and invents the lightning rod to protect buildings from lightning.

BUSHNELL'S SUBMARINE.

1776
The first submarine is built.

1793
Eli Whitney invents the cotton gin to clean cotton.

1760
James Hargreaves invents the spinning jenny that spins thread into yarn.

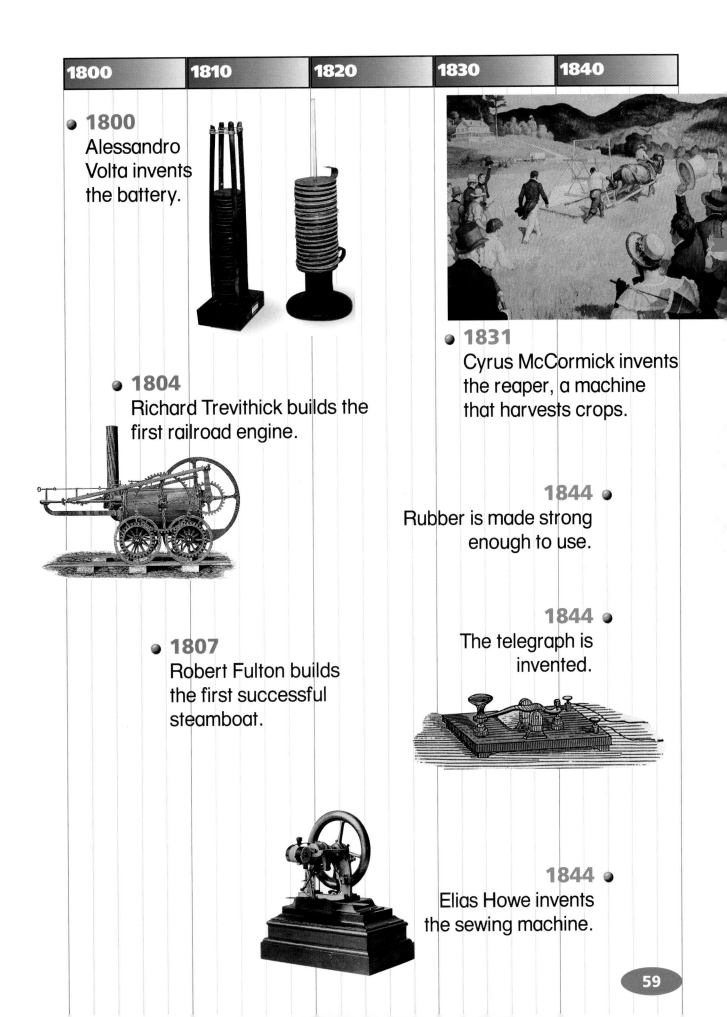

1800
Alessandro Volta invents the battery.

1804
Richard Trevithick builds the first railroad engine.

1807
Robert Fulton builds the first successful steamboat.

1831
Cyrus McCormick invents the reaper, a machine that harvests crops.

1844
Rubber is made strong enough to use.

1844
The telegraph is invented.

1844
Elias Howe invents the sewing machine.

| 1850 | 1855 | 1860 | 1865 | 1870 |

1856

Henry Bessemer shows
how to make strong steel.

1861

Coast to coast communication in
the U.S.A. is made possible with
the telegraph.

1858

The first rubber eraser is put on the end
of a pencil.

1857

The passenger elevator is invented.

1861

Nicolaus August Otto makes
the first engine powered by gasoline.

1863

James Plimpton makes the
first set of roller skates.

1865

The first fax machines
are used.

1873

The typewriter
is invented.

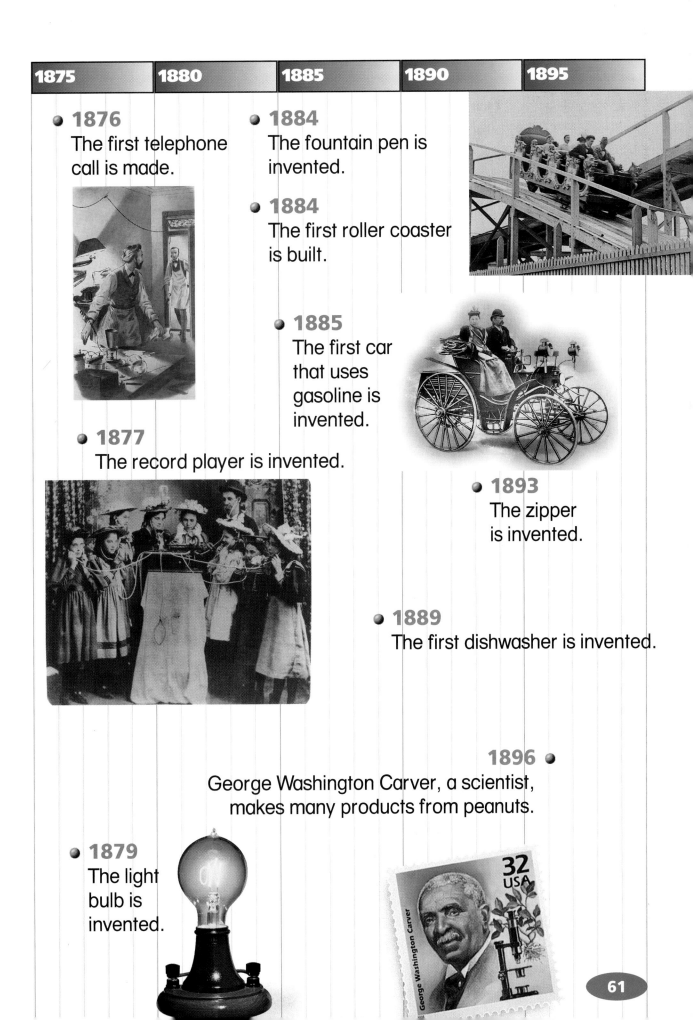

| 1875 | 1880 | 1885 | 1890 | 1895 |

1876
The first telephone call is made.

1884
The fountain pen is invented.

1884
The first roller coaster is built.

1885
The first car that uses gasoline is invented.

1877
The record player is invented.

1893
The zipper is invented.

1889
The first dishwasher is invented.

1896
George Washington Carver, a scientist, makes many products from peanuts.

1879
The light bulb is invented.

32
USA

George Washington Carver

1900	1905	1910	1915	1920

1902
William Carrier makes
the first air conditioner.

1903
The first crayons are made.

1903
The Wright brothers fly the first airplane.

32 USA
Kitty Hawk 1903

1920
Radio
entertains
millions of
people in
America.

32 USA
Radio Entertains America

1906
The first radio broadcast
is heard.

1906
The first cartoon is made.

1907
Leo Baekeland
invents plastic.

1913
The refrigerator is invented.

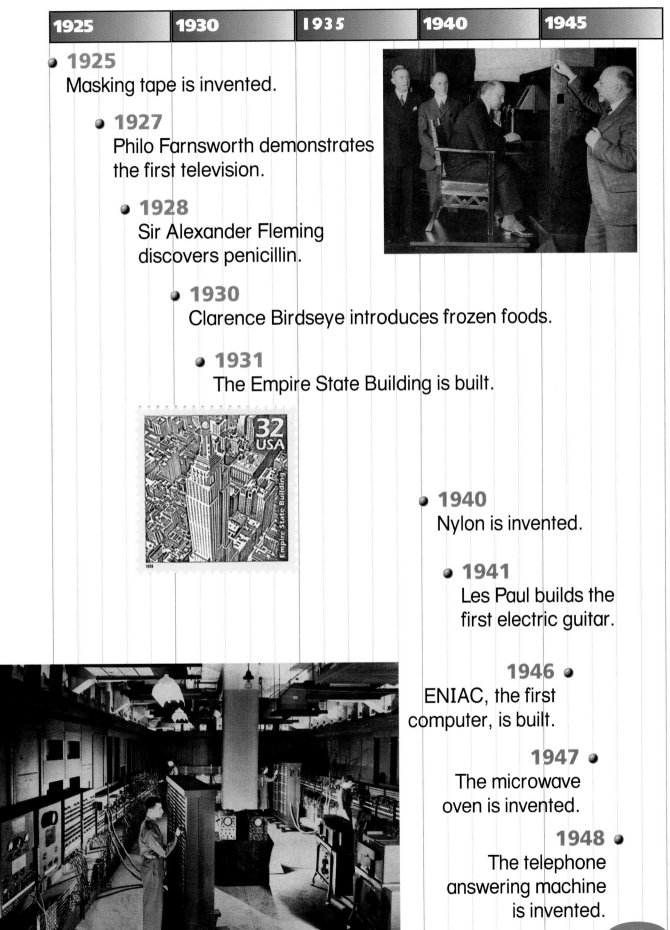

| 1925 | 1930 | 1935 | 1940 | 1945 |

1925
Masking tape is invented.

1927
Philo Farnsworth demonstrates the first television.

1928
Sir Alexander Fleming discovers penicillin.

1930
Clarence Birdseye introduces frozen foods.

1931
The Empire State Building is built.

1940
Nylon is invented.

1941
Les Paul builds the first electric guitar.

1946
ENIAC, the first computer, is built.

1947
The microwave oven is invented.

1948
The telephone answering machine is invented.

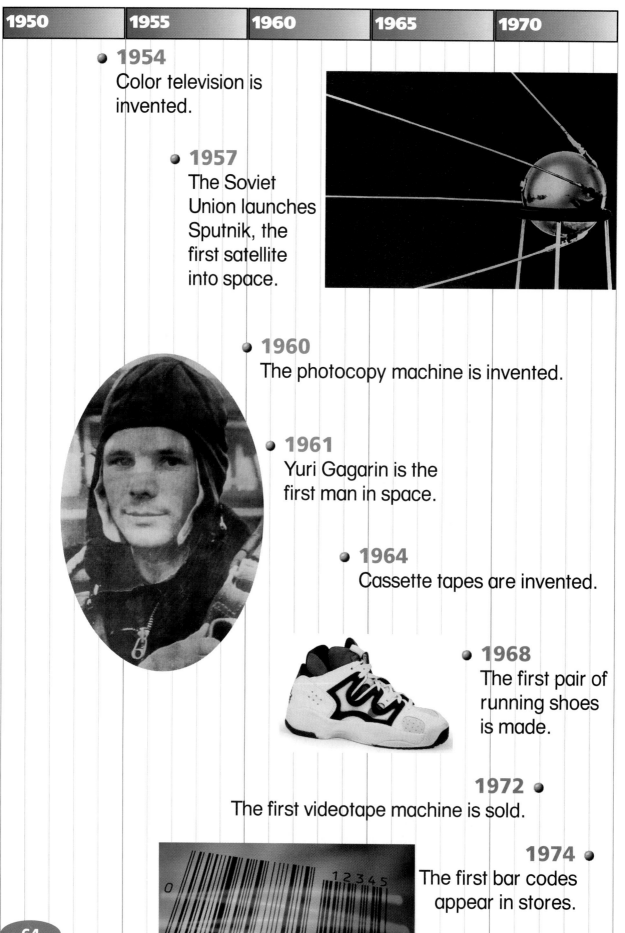

| 1950 | 1955 | 1960 | 1965 | 1970 |

1954
Color television is invented.

1957
The Soviet Union launches Sputnik, the first satellite into space.

1960
The photocopy machine is invented.

1961
Yuri Gagarin is the first man in space.

1964
Cassette tapes are invented.

1968
The first pair of running shoes is made.

1972
The first videotape machine is sold.

1974
The first bar codes appear in stores.

0 1 2 3 4 5

0 1234 56789

1981
The first space
shuttle is launched.

1975
The first personal
computer goes on sale.

1983
Cellular phone networking starts in the U.S.A.

1985
The first compact discs are sold.

1990
The Hubble Space
Telescope is launched.

1994
The Internet
becomes popular.

1998
John Glenn, age 77,
is the oldest person
to fly in space.

Glossary/Index

A

abdomen, A36, A44. The abdomen is a body part of an insect.

air, B10. Air is made of gases. People breathe air.

animal, A30. An animal is a living thing. Most animals can move around on their own. Animals eat plants or other animals.

aquarium, 33. An aquarium is a tank or glass bowl in which living fish, other water animals, and water plants are kept.

artery, 47. An artery is a tube in the body that carries blood away from the heart.

attract, B52, B60. Attract means to pull toward.

B

balance, D38. Balance means to stand without falling.

Big Dipper, C56. The Big Dipper is a group of stars that looks like a cup with a long handle.

blizzard, C39. A blizzard is a very strong snow storm.

blowhole, A55. A blowhole is a hole on top of a dolphin's head. Dolphins use a blowhole to breathe air.

bones, D29, D30. Bones are the hard part of the body. Bones hold the body up. Bones move when muscles pull them.

brain, 48. The brain is a part of the body that is inside the head. The brain controls the body. It helps people move, think, feel, and remember.

breathe, A55. To breathe is to take air into the lungs and then let it out.

C

cactus, A57. A cactus is a plant that usually has spines but no leaves. Most cactuses grow in very hot, dry places.

centimeter, B58. A centimeter is a unit for measuring length.

crosswalk, D42, D44. The white lines on the street that show the safest place to walk make up a crosswalk.

D

desert, A57. A desert is a dry place on the surface of the earth.

digestion, 46. The process of breaking down food is called digestion.

dinosaur, 37. A dinosaur is an extinct animal that lived millions of years ago. There were many different kinds of dinosaurs.

dissolve, 40. When something dissolves, it spreads evenly throughout a liquid.

dolphin, A55. A dolphin is a mammal that lives in the ocean. Dolphins use a blowhole on top of their heads to breathe air.

E

Earth, C48. Earth is the planet we live on. Earth is the third planet from the sun.

electric charge, 38, 39. Electric charges are the tiny bits of electricity in all matter.

electric circuit, 39. Electricity moves in a path called an electric circuit.

endangered, 30, 31. When a plant or animal is endangered, it means that very few are living.

esophagus, 46. The esophagus is the part of the body that squeezes food down to the stomach.

evaporates, B17. When water evaporates it changes into a gas called water vapor.

exercise, D36, D44. Playing and moving are ways to exercise.

F

feathers, A34. Feathers cover a bird's body.

flippers, A54. Flippers are wide, flat body parts that help some animals swim.

flood, C38. A flood is a large amount of water on land that is usually dry.

floss, D27. To floss is to clean between the teeth using a special kind of thread.

foam, B39. Foam is a lightweight material used to make cups and other things.

fog, C34. Fog is a cloud that is near the ground.

Food Guide Pyramid, D34, D44. The Food Guide Pyramid shows the food groups. It shows what foods to eat in order to stay healthy.

forest, A56. A forest is a large area covered with trees.

fossil, 36. A fossil is a part or print of a plant or animal that lived long ago.

freeze, B16. To freeze is to harden from cold. When water freezes, it turns into a solid.

fruit, A17, A20, A24. A fruit is the part of a plant where seeds are. An apple is a fruit.

fur, A34. Fur is the hair that covers some animals.

G

gas, B10, B20. Gas takes up space. It can change shape and size. Air is made of gases.

germs, D37. Germs are tiny living things. Some germs can make you sick.

gills, A55. Gills are the openings in the body that let fish breathe in the water.

globe, C17. A globe is a sphere with a map of Earth on it.

H

habitat, A52, A60. A habitat is a place where plants and animals live.

hail, C34. Hail is ice that falls from clouds.

hand lens, 53. A hand lens is a tool that makes objects look larger.

head, A36, A44. The head is a body part. It is one of the three main body parts of an insect.

heart, 47. The heart is the part of the body that pumps blood to other parts of the body.

hibernate, C43, C44. Hibernate means to spend the winter in a deep sleep.

I

insect, A36, A44. An insect is an animal that has three main body parts and six legs.

L

large intestine, 46. The large intestine is a part of the body. Food that is not digested goes into the large intestine. Then it passes out of the body as solid waste.

leaves, A12, A20, A24. Leaves are part of a plant. Leaves use light, air, and water to make food for the plant.

liquid, B8, B20. A liquid takes the shape of its container. Water is a liquid.

living things, A50, A60. Plants and animals are living things.

lungs, 47. Lungs are the part of the body that take in air.

M

machine, B56. A machine is a tool that makes work easier.

magnet, B52, B60. A magnet is an object that attracts some kinds of metal.

map, B48. A map is a drawing of a place. You can use a map to get from one place to another.

maze, B51. A maze is an area with many paths.

migrate, C42, C44. Migrate means to move from one place another when the seasons change. Some animals migrate to warm places in the winter.

mixture, 40. When two or more materials are mixed together, they form a mixture. The materials can easily be separated.

moon, C52. The moon is an object in the sky that moves around Earth.

mountain, C16. A mountain is a very large hill.

muscles, D28, D30. Muscles are a part of the body that help it move.

N

nerves, 48. Nerves are pathways in the body that carry messages to and from the brain.

nonliving things, A50, A60. Nonliving things cannot grow or move on their own.

O

object, B6, B20. An object is a thing you can see or touch.

observe, D6, D16. When you observe, you notice many things.

ocean, A54. The ocean is the large body of saltwater that covers much of the earth's surface.

Orion, C57. Orion is a group of stars that looks like a hunter wearing a belt.

oxygen, 47. Oxygen is a gas we need to breathe.

P

pan balance, 52. A pan balance is a tool used to measure mass. Mass is the amount of matter in an object.

parent, A42, A44. A parent is a mother or father.

phases, C53, C60. The shapes of the lighted part of the moon are called phases.

planet, 42, 43. A planet is a body of matter that moves around the sun.

plant, A8. A plant is any living thing that can make its own food from light, air, and water.

pull, B46, B60. A pull makes things move. When you put clothes away, you pull to open the drawer.

push, B46, B60. A push makes things move. To close the drawer, you push it shut.

R

recycle, C20, C22. Recycle means to take something that has been used and make something new from it.

repel, B52, B60. Repel means to push away.

reuse, C20, C22. Reuse means to use something again.

roots, A8, A20, A24. Roots are a part of a plant. Roots take in water and hold plants in the soil.

S

scales, A34. Scales are the hard plates that cover the bodies of some animals. Some fish, snakes, and lizards have scales.

sea turtle, A54. A sea turtle is a turtle that lives in the ocean.

sea urchin, A54. A sea urchin is a small animal that lives in the ocean. Sea urchins are covered with sharp spines.

season, C40, C44. A season is a time of the year. The seasons are spring, summer, fall, and winter.

seed, A14, A20, A24. A seed is a part of a plant that can grow into a new plant.

seed coat, A14. A seed coat is the outside layer that protects a seed.

senses, D10, D16. You use your senses to observe. The senses are seeing, hearing, smelling, touching, and tasting.

shadow, B30, B42. A shadow is made when something blocks the light.

shell, A34. A shell is a hard covering that protects some animals. Turtles have shells.

simple machine, B56, B60. A simple machine is a tool with few or no moving parts that makes work easier. A wheel and axle, inclined plane or ramp, lever, and pulley are four kinds of simple machines.

small intestine, 46. The small intestine is a part of the body that helps digest food. Most of the digestion happens in the small intestine.

soil, C12, C22. Soil is the top layer of the earth. Plants grow in soil.

solar system, 42, 43. The sun, the planets and their moons, and other objects that move around the sun form the solar system.

solid, B8, B20. A solid is an object that takes up space and has its own shape.

solution, 40. A solution is a mixture in which one material dissolves in another.

star, C56. A star is an object in the sky that gives off its own light.

stem, A8, A20, A24. The stem is the part of a plant that takes water and sugars to other parts of the plant and holds it upright.

stomach, 46. The stomach is a part of the body. Food is mixed in the stomach until it becomes liquid.

sun, C50. The sun is the star in the center of our solar system. All of the planets in our solar system move around the sun.

T

tadpole, A42. A tadpole is a very young frog or toad. Tadpoles have tails and live only in water.

teeth, D26. Teeth are used to bite and chew. Children usually get their first teeth before they are one year old. Permanent teeth replace first teeth later.

telescope, C52, C60. A telescope makes objects that are far away look closer.

temperature, C28, C44, 51. Temperature is how hot or cold something is.

terrarium, 32. A terrarium is a glass container in which plants or small land animals are kept.

thermometer, C32, C44, 51. A thermometer measures the temperature.

thorax, A36, A44. The thorax is a body part of an insect.

tornado, C39. A tornado is a very strong wind that comes down from the clouds in the shape of a funnel.

V

vein, 47. A vein is a tube in the body that carries blood to the heart.

vibrate, B26, B42. Vibrate means to move back and forth very fast.

W

water cycle, 41. The way water moves from the clouds to the earth and back to the clouds is called the water cycle.

water vapor, C34, C44. Water vapor is a form of water in the air. When liquid water evaporates, it changes to a gas called water vapor.

weathering, C8, C22. Wind, water, and ice can change rocks. This is called weathering.

wind, C30. Wind is moving air.

Acknowledgments

Illustration
Borders Patti Green
Icons Precison Graphics
Materials Icons Diane Teske Harris

Front Matter
iv T PhotoDisc, Inc.
iv B Walter Stuart
v B Artville
v B INS Tom McHugh/Photo Researchers
viii TL Dr. E.R. Degginer/Color-Pic, Inc.
viii TR Arthur Hill/Visuals Unlimited
ix T Adam Jones/Photo Researchers
ix B NASA
x T Marsha Winborn
x BL Telegraph Colour Library/FPG International
x BC Peter Correz/Tony Stone Images
x BR Phillip Engelhorn/Tony Stone Images

Unit A
4 Pauline Phung
8, 32b, 54 Walter Stuart
14 Rebecca Merrilees
16c Michael Carroll
26 Judy Moffatt
40 Tom Leonard
46 Marsha Winborn
48 Eileen Hine
52 Kristin Kest

Unit B
3 Hyewon Shin
4 Annie Lunsford
12, 13 Ginna Magee
17 Dara Goldman
20 Diane Teske Harris
22 Stacey Schuett
24, 36, 56, 60 Tom Leonard
33 Don Tate
38a Carol Stutz
44 Marshall Woksa
48, 49 Eileen Hine
55a Elizabeth Wolf

Unit C
4 Trudy L. Calvert
17c John Edwards
18b Diane Paterson
21a Precision Graphics
24a-c David Wenzel
26 Donna Nelson
32a Roger Roth
46 Walter Stuart
54, 55 Elizabeth Wolf
56 John Edwards

Unit D
4 Georgia C. Shola
16a Carol Stutz
18 Cristina Ventoso
27c Diane Teske Harris
28b, 29b John Edwards
32 Marsha Winborn
40, 41 Diane Paterson
42 Pauline Phung
36, 37 Robert Lawson

Photography
Unless otherwise credited, all photographs are the
property of Scott Foresman, a division of Pearson
Education. Page abbreviations are as follows:
(T) top, (C) center, (B) bottom, (L) left, (R) right,
(INS) inset.

Cover: Rick Iwasaki/Tony Stone Images

iv PhotoDisc, Inc.
v L Artville

v R Tom McHugh/Photo Researchers
viii T Dr. E. R. Degginger/Color-Pic, Inc.
viii B Arthur Hill/Visuals Unlimited
ix T Adam Jones/Photo Researchers
ix B NASA
x L Telegraph Colour Library/FPG International
Corp.
x C Peter Correz/Tony Stone Images
x R Philipp Engelhorn/Tony Stone Images

Unit A
1 Jeff Hunter/Image Bank
2 C D. Demello/Wildlife Conservation Society
headquartered at the Bronx Zoo
2 BL Greg Marshall/National Geographic
2 B-Background Pete Saloutos/Stock Market
2 T Vincent O'Bryne/Panoramic Images
16 L William J. Weber/Visuals Unlimited
16 R Joseph L. Fontenot/Visuals Unlimited
17 L William J. Weber/Visuals Unlimited
17 R Joyce Photographics/Photo Researchers
22 B David R. Frazier/Tony Stone Images
30 T Francois Gohier/Photo Researchers
30 BC PhotoDisc, Inc.
30 CC PhotoDisc, Inc.
30 BL PhotoDisc, Inc.
30 BR PhotoDisc, Inc.
32 Stephen Dalton/Photo Researchers
34 Tiger-Tom McHugh/Photo Researchers
34 Bluejay-Elvan Habicht/Animals Animals/Earth
Scenes
34 Goldfish-George Bernard/Animals
Animals/Earth Scenes
34 Turtle-Bill Beatty/Visuals Unlimited
34 Turtle shell-Maslowski/Visuals Unlimited
34 Tiger stripes-Tim Davis/Photo Researchers
34 Goldfish scales-G. I. Bernard/Animals
Animals/Earth Scenes
34 Bluejay feathers-Thomas Martin/Photo
Researchers
36 TR Artville
36 CL Artville
36 CR Artville
36 BR Leroy Simon/Visuals Unlimited
37 TL Artville
37 TR Leroy Simon/Visuals Unlimited
37 BCL Artville
37 BR Artville
37 BCR Artville
37 BL Artville
38 Artville
42 Anup & Manuj Shah//Animals Animals/Earth
Scenes
43 TL E. R. Degginger/Color-Pic, Inc.
43 TC Stephen Dalton/Photo Researchers
43 TR Tom McHugh/Photo Researchers
50 T PhotoDisc, Inc.
50 C Rod Planck/Photo Researchers
50 BL Brock May/Photo Researchers
56 Background Doug Sokell/Visuals Unlimited
56 TR Joe McDonald/Visuals Unlimited
56 CL Leonard Lee Rue IV, NAS/Photo
Researchers
56 BR Fred Unverhau/Animals Animals/Earth
Scenes
57 Background Doug Sokell/Visuals Unlimited
57 TR C.K. Lorenz/Photo Researchers
57 CL Richard Kolar/Animals Animals/Earth
Scenes
57 BR C.K. Lorenz/Photo Researchers

Unit B
1 A. Gin/Picture Perfect
2 B Sunny Cor Inc.
2 C Grantpix/Photo Researchers
2 T Vincent O'Bryne/Panoramic Images

Unit C
1 Chuck Szymanski/International Stock
2 B ESA/SPL/Photo Researchers
2 Inset-c Joseph Sohm/ChromoSohm/Corbis
Media
2 C Royal Mat Inc.
2 T Vincent O'Bryne/Panoramic Images
3 CR NASA
3 CL NASA
8 L Dr. E.R. Degginger/Color-Pic, Inc.
8 C Dr. E. R. Degginger/Color-Pic, Inc.
8 R Arthur Hill/Visuals Unlimited
16 L Paul Chesley/Tony Stone Images
16 R Larry Ulrich/Tony Stone Images
17 L Tony Stone Images
17 R Dr. Ed Degginger/Bruce Coleman Inc.
28 B D. Young-Wolff/PhotoEdit
34 L Adam Jones/Photo Researchers
34 R Wendy Shattil/Bob Rozinski/TOM STACK &
ASSOCIATES
35 L Doug Miller/Photo Researchers
35 R Joyce Photographics/Photo Researchers
38 ©Tom Stack & Associates/Wm. L. Wantland
39 L ©Tom Stack & Associates/Merrilee Thomas
39 R Aaron Strong
/Liaison Agency
40 TL Bill Beatty/Visuals Unlimited
40 TR Bill Beatty/Visuals Unlimited
40 BL Bill Beatty/Visuals Unlimited
40 BR Bill Beatty/Visuals Unlimited
42 John Gerlach/Visuals Unlimited
42 Inset Maslowski/Visuals Unlimited
43 L Lindholm/Visuals Unlimited
43 R Tom J. Ulrich/Visuals Unlimited
48 NASA
50 Eric R. Berndt/Unicorn Stock Photos
52 T John Bova/Photo Researchers
53 L John Bova/Photo Researchers
53 R John Bova/Photo Researchers
55 Photo Researchers
56 Royal Observatory Edinburgh/SPL/Photo
Researchers

Unit D
1 William Sallaz/Duomo Photography Inc.
2 C Michael Newman/PhotoEdit
2 B Larry Mulvehill/Photo Researchers
2 T Vincent O'Bryne/Panoramic Images
3 B Myrleen Ferguson/Photo Edit/Picture
Network International
8 Myrleen Ferguson/PhotoEdit
9 L Maresa Pryor/Animals Animals/Earth Scenes
9 R Lon Lauber/Alaska Stock
26 L Telegraph Colour Library/FPG International
Corp.
26 C Peter Correz/Tony Stone Images
26 R Philipp Engelhorn/Tony Stone Images
27 Nancy Sheehan/PhotoEdit
34 Elizabeth Simpson/FPG International Corp.
36 R Michael Newman/PhotoEdit

End Matter

4 Bob Kalmbach, University of Michigan Photo Services

30 T Dan Suzio/Photo Researchers

30 BL Marianne Austin-McDermon

30 BR Paul M. Montgomery

31 TL Art Wolfe/Tony Stone Images

31 TR Gary Carter/Visuals Unlimited

31 B Dr. & TL Schrichte/Tony Stone Images

36 T A. J. Copley/Visuals Unlimited

36 BL Denver Museum of Natural History/Photo Researchers

36 BR E. R. Degginger/Color-Pic, Inc.

44 B NASA

45 NASA

56 T Cliff Hollenbeck/Tony Stone Images

56 B The Granger Collection, New York

57 T British Library

57 CL Ancient Art & Architecture Collection/Ronald Sheridan Photo-Library

57 CC Corbis Media

57 CR Culver Pictures Inc.

57 BL The Granger Collection, New York

58 T Drawing by F. M. Barber in 1885/Bushnell

58 CL Deutsches Museum

58 CR Smithsonian Institution

58 B Culver Pictures Inc.

59 TL Museo Nazionale Della Scienza & Della Tecnica Leonardo da Vinci Milan

59 TR Newell Convers Wyeth/International Harvester Company

59 CL Stock Montage

59 CR Stock Montage, Inc.

59 B Smithsonian Institution of Physical Sciences

60 C Otis Elevator Company

60 B Hagley Museum and Library

60 T Culver Pictures Inc.

61 TL Corbis Media

61 TR Culver Pictures Inc.

61 CR Corbis Media

61 BL General Electric

62 BL Karen M. Koblik

62 BR Corbis Media

63 T Corbis Media

63 C Public Domain

63 B University of Pennsylvania Libraries

64 T UPI/Corbis Media

64 CL UPI/Corbis Media

64 CR Corel

64 B William Whitehurst/Stock Market

65 TR NASA

65 TL Computer Museum, Boston

65 C PhotoDisc, Inc.

65 B NASA

Science in Texas

T1

Unit A

A Beautiful Tree in Texas

The state of Texas has many different kinds of trees that grow in parks, fields, and towns. One of the most beautiful is the pecan tree.

What is the state tree of Texas?

Think about the kinds of trees where you live. What do they look like?

Reading • Read the sentences in the box. Look at the pictures. Answer the questions.

> The people of Texas named the pecan tree to be a **symbol** for the state. A symbol is an object that stands for something.
>
> Pecan trees grow in many parts of Texas. They grow to about 30 meters or 100 feet tall. Their trunks can be more than a meter, or about three feet, around.

A   B

1. Which picture shows a tree that is a symbol of the state of Texas?

2. Which picture shows another symbol of Texas?

Reading • Read the sentences in the box. Look at the pictures. Answer the questions.

> The pecan tree grows tall and wide with many branches and leaves. They make the pecan a good shade tree for Texas.
>
> The pecan has nuts that we eat. The pecan nuts grow in hard, brown shells that are 3 to 5 centimeters long.

A   B   C

1. Which picture shows a good place to cool off on a hot Texas day?

2. Which picture shows the pecan nut's hard brown shell?

3. Which picture shows the fruit inside the pecan nut?

Writing • Draw a picture of a strong, tall, wide pecan tree. Describe the things the Texas state tree can give and do for you.

What do pecan trees need to grow?

Which things in the picture can help pecan trees grow? Most plants need air, soil, water, and sunlight.

Writing • Find three things in the picture that can help pecan trees grow. Draw and label each one.

Reading • Read the sentences in the box. Look at the pictures. Answer the questions.

Pecan trees give the people of Texas many things. The thick tree trunk is used to make wooden things. The trees make nuts that are used for food. The trees' leafy branches make cool shade.

1. Which picture shows only the trunk of the pecan tree?

2. Which picture shows the part of the pecan tree used for food?

3. Which picture shows the part of the pecan tree that makes cool shade?

A

B

C

Reading • Read the sentences in the box. Look at the pictures. Answer the questions.

Pecan trees are home to many animals. Birds can build nests in the branches. Small insects and worms can find new homes in the trunks. Small animals can eat the pecan nuts that drop to the ground.

1. Which picture shows the part of the pecan tree where birds can build their nests?

2. Which picture shows the part of the pecan tree where insects and worms can find a new home?

3. Which picture shows the part of the pecan tree that small animals can eat?

C

A

B

How is a pecan tree like a pecan nut?

Have you noticed that sometimes the adult plant does not look very much like the seed or baby plant? When will they look more alike?

Reading • Read the sentences in the box. Look at the pictures. Answer the questions.

A pecan tree grows into a big tree from the tiny pecan seed. With water, sunlight, and clean air, the seed grows into a green stem with small leaves. As the small tree grows, it gets taller with more branches, leaves, and seeds of its own.

1. Which picture shows a pecan tree seed?

2. Which picture shows a small pecan tree?

3. Which picture shows a tall pecan tree?

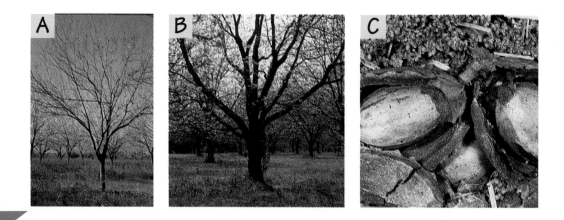

A Log Cabin in Texas

Some of the first people in Texas built log cabins for their homes. Using simple machines, they lifted large logs to make cabins. These people started new lives in Texas.

Dallas

El Paso

Austin

Houston

San Antonio

Why did early settlers build log cabins?

Think about how the land looked. What could the settlers use to build homes? What did they use to build the log cabins?

A

B

Reading • Read the sentences in the box. Look at the pictures. Answer the questions.

> Settlers came to Texas to live in a new part of the country. They built homes by cutting trees to make logs. The logs were set in a square and stacked on top of each other to make the walls of a log cabin.

1. Which picture shows what the settlers used to build their new homes?

2. Which picture shows a settler's log cabin?

T10

Reading • Read the sentences in the box. Look at the pictures. Answer the questions.

> The settlers used cut trees as wheels to roll the heavy logs. The builder could push or pull the logs into place with the help of these wheels. The settlers used wagon wheels to move heavy objects from the forest to the log cabin.

1. Which picture shows a tree used to roll heavy objects?

2. Which picture shows a wagon wheel?

3. Which picture shows a log cabin?

Writing • Draw a picture of a wagon with wheels. Describe the wheel shape and how many wheels the wagon has.

What simple machines did the settlers use?

Which things in the picture can help people build homes?

Writing • Find three simple machines in the picture that helped people build a log cabin. Draw and label each one.

Reading • Read the sentences in the box. Look at the pictures. Answer the questions.

The pulley is a simple machine that makes lifting heavy objects easier. The pulley uses a wheel and a rope to lift heavy objects up to high places, such as a log cabin roof. A builder pulls on the rope of the pulley to lift heavy objects.

1. Which part of the pulley is the wheel?

2. Which part of the pulley is the rope?

3. Which part is the heavy object that needs to be lifted?

Reading • Read the sentences in the box. Look at the pictures. Answer the questions.

Settlers used simple machines to help them lift heavy objects. They could lift logs by putting a flat board over another log to form a lever. Then by pushing down on one end of the board, a log could be lifted onto the log cabin wall.

1. Which is the log that needs to be lifted?

2. Which log helps the lever work to lift heavy objects?

3. Which piece of wood is used as a lever?

Do Texans still use simple machines?

Have you ever used a lever, wheel, ramp, or pulley? How did you use them?

Reading • Read the sentences in the box. Look at the pictures. Answer the questions.

> Simple machines help people work and play. Wheels and ramps help you move, push, or pull heavy things. A lever will open a lid. A pulley will move big objects to high places.

1. Which simple machine will help you push or pull heavy things?

2. Which simple machine will help you open a lid?

3. Which simple machine will help you move big objects to high places?

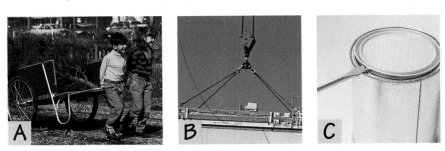

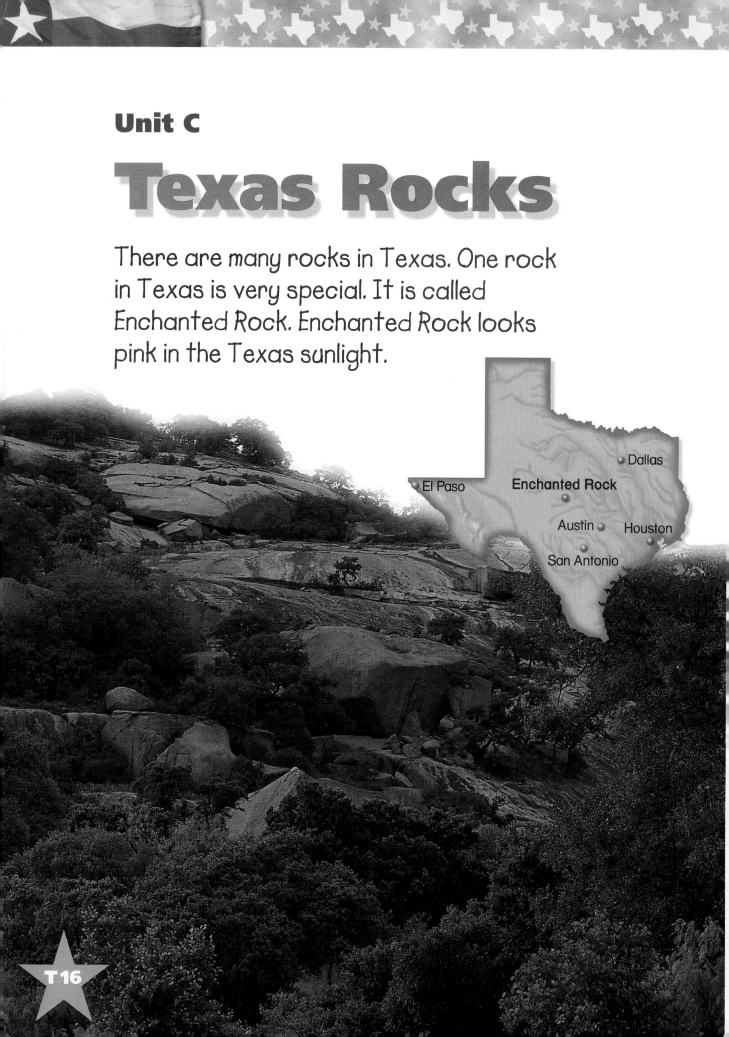

Unit C

Texas Rocks

There are many rocks in Texas. One rock in Texas is very special. It is called Enchanted Rock. Enchanted Rock looks pink in the Texas sunlight.

Dallas

El Paso   Enchanted Rock

Austin   Houston

San Antonio

What is the Enchanted Rock?

Think about the kinds of rocks where you live. What do they look like?

B

A

C

Reading • Read the sentences in the box. Look at the pictures. Answer the questions.

Enchanted Rock is made of pink **granite**. Granite is a very hard rock. Enchanted Rock is 129 meters tall. It is the second largest rock in the United States.

Granite looks dull and feels rough. It can be used to make buildings and statues.

1. Which picture shows the giant Enchanted Rock?

2. Which picture shows a piece of granite?

3. Which picture shows a statue made of granite?

Reading • Read the sentences in the box. Look at the pictures. Answer the questions.

Enchanted Rock has many legends. **Legends** are stories told many times. Native Americans told legends about crying voices on the giant rock. They also told legends about ghost fires. Enchanted Rock got its name from the legends.

A

B

C

1. Which picture shows a Native American telling a legend?

2. Which picture shows a ghost fire on the giant rock?

3. Which picture shows the color of Enchanted Rock?

Writing • Think of a story about Enchanted Rock. Draw a picture of your story. Describe your story. Is your story a legend?

What can you do at Enchanted Rock?

Which things in the picture would be fun to do?

Writing • Find three activities in the picture. Write a sentence to tell about each one.

Reading • Read the sentences in the box. Look at the pictures. Answer the questions.

> Do voices really cry at Enchanted Rock? The crying is creaking made by the rock. Creaking sounds are squeaky noises. The sun heats the rock in the day. At night when the rock cools, it creaks.

A

B

1. Which picture shows the moon over Enchanted Rock?

2. Which picture shows the granite rock during the day?

Reading • Read the sentences in the box. Look at the pictures. Answer the questions.

> Pink granite is found in many parts of Texas. Workers cut the rock into large, flat pieces. They make the pieces smooth and shiny with machines.
>
> The smooth, shiny granite can be used to build buildings. The Texas State Capitol building is made of granite.

1. Which picture shows the rough and dull granite?

2. Which picture shows the smooth and shiny granite?

3. Which picture shows the granite walls of the Texas State Capitol building?

A

C

B

Why was granite used to make the capitol building?

Granite is used to make buildings. How might granite make buildings strong?

Reading • Read the sentences in the box. Look at the pictures. Answer the questions.

At first, the builders of the capitol were going to use a rock called limestone. The pink Texas granite is much harder and stronger. The capitol needed to stand for a long time, so they built it with the beautiful pink granite of Texas.

1. Which picture shows the Texas State Capitol building?

2. Which picture shows a piece of pink granite.

Unit D

The Hot Sun in Texas

It can get very hot in Texas during the spring and summer months. You can take care of yourself by knowing how your body works when it is hot outside.

How does your body work in Texas heat?

Think about playing outside on a hot, sunny day. How does your body feel?

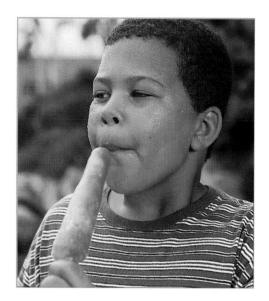

Reading • Read the sentences in the box. Look at the pictures. Answer the questions.

> When your body gets hot, it tries to cool down. To help keep cool, your body sweats. The sweat comes out of tiny pores in your skin. Then the sweat cools your body.

1. Which picture shows what happens when you feel hot?

2. Which picture shows something that does not happen when it is hot?

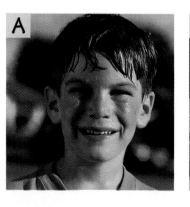

Reading • Read the sentences in the box. Look at the pictures. Answer the questions.

Do you get thirsty when it is hot? Your body loses water when it sweats. Your body needs to put back the water that you sweat out.

Drink water! You need eight glasses of water a day. In hot weather, you need even more. This will keep your body working at its best.

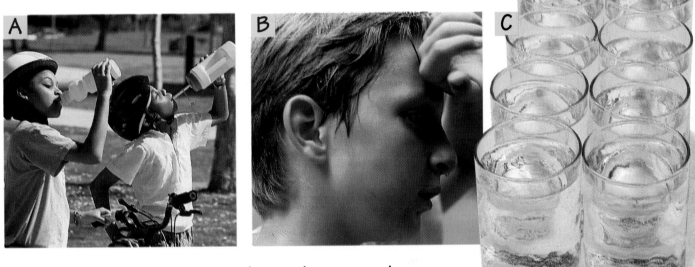

A
B
C

1. Which picture shows how much water you should drink every day?

2. Which picture shows what you should do when it is hot?

3. Which picture shows the body losing water?

Writing • Draw a picture of a hot, Texas day. Write to tell how your body cools itself.

How can you protect your skin from the hot Texas sun?

Which things in the picture can help keep your skin safe in the sun?

Writing • Find three things in the picture that can help keep your skin safe from the sun. Draw and name each one.

Reading • Read the sentences in the box. Look at the pictures. Answer the questions.

> Keep your skin safe!
> Wear a hat and keep your shirt on. Clothes help protect your skin from the sun.
> Wear sunglasses. They help keep out the sun's rays, too. They protect your eyes and face.
> Stay in the shade. Play under an umbrella or a tree. The sun is not as strong in the shade.

1. Which picture shows a good place to be outside?

2. Which picture shows clothes that keep your skin safe from the sun?

B

A

Reading • Read the sentences in the box.
Look at the pictures. Answer the questions.

> **Sunscreen** helps block out the sun's rays. Put sunscreen on your skin before you go outside.
>
> Put it all over your skin. Your ears, neck, and feet need sunscreen, too.
>
> If you swim, put more sunscreen on after you swim.

1. Which picture shows sunscreen?

2. Which picture shows a good time to put sunscreen on?

When are the best times to be outside?

Have you noticed that some times of the day are hotter than others? When are the best times to play outside?

Reading • Read the sentences in the box. Look at the pictures. Answer the questions.

> In Texas, the sun is hottest from late morning to late afternoon. It is best to stay out of the sun then. If you are out in the sun, only stay out for a short time, rest, and drink plenty of water.

1. Which picture shows a cool time in the morning?

2. Which picture shows a hot time in the afternoon?

3. Which picture shows what to do when you are outside in the hot sun?

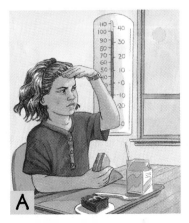

A

B

C

Writing • Look at each picture. Draw the clothes you would wear if you were in each picture. Write a sentence about your pictures. Tell how you would dress for a hot or cold day.

Share your pictures with the class. Tell what you would do to stay warm or stay cool.

Glossary

granite a very hard rock found in Texas, that comes in many colors, one of which is pink

legend ancient stories

lever a tool that looks like a bar and is used to pry or lift

log cabin homes built from logs; the first people to come to this country built this type of home

pecan tree tree found in Texas that is used as a state symbol

pulley a tool made of a wheel and a rope and used to lift heavy objects to high places

ramp a sloped surface used to raise or roll objects up a hill or to a higher level

simple machine a tool that is used to do work; wheels, levers, pulleys, and ramps are examples of simple machines

sunscreen lotion that protects the skin from the sun

symbol an object that stands for something else

Index

W9-ANU-810

DEPRESSION MODERN

MARTIN GREIF

DEPRESSION
MODERN

THE THIRTIES STYLE
IN AMERICA

UNIVERSE · BOOKS · NEW · YORK

Published in the United States of America in 1975
by Universe Books
381 Park Avenue South
New York, N.Y. 10016

© 1975 by Martin Greif

Library of Congress Catalog Card Number: 75-11140
ISBN 0-87663-257-6

Printed in the United States of America

Designed by Robert Reed

CONTENTS

ACKNOWLEDGMENTS

The idea for this book is Larry Grow's. Having heard me talk about the 1930s on and off for the past ten years, he suggested that I stop talking and start writing. For his impatience, good counsel, and friendship, I am grateful.

For reasons that go far beyond the compilation of this book, I am indebted to Donald Deskey, Wallace K. Harrison, George Fred Keck, Raymond Loewy, Edward Durell Stone, and Russel Wright, young men all during the Great Depression who have taught me, among other things, that Browning knew what he was talking about when he wrote the opening lines of *Rabbi Ben Ezra*. After coming to know Donald Deskey and Russel Wright in particular, I doubt that I will ever again fear old age.

The photographer Robert Damora, the designer John D. Gerald, and the architects W. E. Bentzinger, John A. Holabird, Jr., Samuel E. Homsey, Wesley V. Pipher, and T. Trip Russell have all responded generously to requests for information about design during the Great Depression.

Kay Sakier has graciously shared with me her memories of the 1930s as has Lillian Kiesler, artist and friend, whose dedication to the genius of her late husband, Frederick Kiesler, is the stuff of fine poetry and even greater love.

Of the many people who have supplied me with rare archival material for this book, several have been unstinting and tireless in their energies and detective work. Of these, H. E. B. Anderson, Director of Information of The Austin Company, Cleveland, Ohio, emerged from dank storage basements, dust-covered and disheveled, more than once in my behalf, and Diane Thaler, secretary to Raymond Loewy, mixed efficiency with wondrously earthly humor in assisting me through ten years of Mr. Loewy's files. William B. May, Jr., arranged a guided tour through one of his properties so that I could have a first-hand architectural understanding of a 1930s apartment house, from boiler room to penthouse. Peggy S. Huffman of the Hedrich-Blessing Studio, Chicago, Illinois, has come up with solutions to every problem sent her, even though the clues were often as slender as a thread. I acknowledge, too, the extraordinary cooperation of Robert P. Scott, Manager, Advertising and Public Relations, Burroughs Corporation, Business Forms and Supplies Group, Rochester, New York; Alan K. Lathrop, Curator, Northwest Architectural Archives, Minneapolis, Minnesota; Isobel C. Lee, Vice President, Steuben Glass, New York City; and Nicholas Polites, Walter Dorwin Teague Associates, Inc., New York City.

I am grateful, also, for the assistance of Douglas Hahn, B. Altman & Co., New York City; Byron S. Campbell, Aluminum Company of America, Pittsburgh, Pennsylvania; Clara H. Noack, County Clerk, Alpena County, Michigan; Alvin F. Gunther, Gibbons—Hollyday & Ives, Inc., New York City; Eileen Wosick, Ogden & Company, Milwaukee, Wisconsin; Richard B. Sinclair, Armstrong Cork Company, Lancaster, Pennsylvania; Robbie Y. Kestner, The Wm. H. Block Co., Indianapolis, Indiana; Robert C. Reese, Campana Corporation, Batavia, Illinois; Annchen T. Swanson, The Chase Manhattan Bank, N.A., New York City; Wilbur George Kurtz, Jr., The Coca-Cola Company, Atlanta, Georgia; Peggy James, Colorado Springs Fine Arts Center, Colorado Springs, Colorado.

Also Bob Fuller, CBS Radio, New York City; Dixie Lee Stringer, Columbia Public Schools, Columbia, Mississippi; L. Henry Liese, Cranbrook Educational Community, Bloomfield Hills, Michigan; Janice C. Greer, Dictaphone Corporation, Rye, New York; Lucille Wolz, County Clerk, Ector County, Texas; Edward Markey, Electrolux Corporation, Stamford, Connecticut; Ann Oliva, The Emporium, San Francisco, California; Helen E. Noah, First Federal Savings and Loan Association of New York, Bronxville, New York; Michael C. Contezac, U.S. Department of Agriculture Forest Service, Madison, Wisconsin; Elizabeth D. Marshall, The Great Atlantic & Pacific Tea Company, Inc., Montvale, New Jersey; Eleanor Adams, Halle's, Cleveland, Ohio.

Also David M. Nellis, The Hecht Co., Washington, D.C.; J. D. Atkins, Houston First Savings Association, Houston, Texas; A. L. McCormick, Principal, Edward L. Bailey Junior High School, Jackson, Mississippi; Eunice McMurtry, Johnson & Johnson, New Brunswick, New Jersey; Neal J. Seiser, S. C. Johnson & Son, Inc., Racine, Wisconsin; Warren R. Erickson, The Meyercord Co., Chicago, Illinois; E. H. Daws, U.S. Postal Service, Miami, Florida; Anne Read, Herman Miller, Inc., Zeeland, Michigan.

Also Charlotte La Rue, Museum of the City of New York; M. L. Melville, NCR Corporation, Dayton, Ohio; Frank P. Howard, Oregon State Highway Division, Salem, Oregon; Ann Whyte, Pan American World Airways, Inc., New York City; Jack Shuba, Pennzoil Company, Los Angeles, California; C. E. Weber, Precision Spring Corporation, Detroit, Michigan; Frida Schubert, RCA, New York City; H. T. S. Heckman, Republic Steel Corporation, Cleveland, Ohio; Chris Sanson, *The Shreveport Times,* Shreveport, Louisiana; John W. Hubbell, Simmons Company, New York City; Kathy Leonard, Southern California Gas Company, Los Angeles, California.

Also M. Forster, Star Electrical Supply Co., Newark, New Jersey; Lillian Owens, Time Inc. Archives, New York City; David J. Gizer, Trans-Lux, New York City; George Schoepfer, Triborough Bridge and Tunnel Authority, New York City; Jean C. Burnett, Wadsworth Atheneum, Hartford, Connecticut; R. H. Vogt, Wear-Ever Aluminum Inc., Chillicothe, Ohio; and J. R. van Leuwen, F. W. Woolworth Co., New York City.

Many people searched through musty files and corporate archives to supply me with information and photographs which, for lack of space, have not been included in this book. I am pleased, therefore, to record my debt to Edward A. Metzger, Borchard Management Corporation, New York City; Bev Eastman, Eastman's Gaslight Room, Detroit, Michigan; Leo DeFer, Boulder Valley Public Schools, Boulder, Colorado; Lee L. Burtis, California Historical Society, San Francisco, California; Ann Tellman, Cannon Mills, Inc., New York City; Peg Dann, The Cincinnati Historical Society; Joan Levers, The Children's Hospital, Denver, Colorado; Otto W. Hilbert, Corning Glass Works, Corning, New York.

Also Robert F. English, Cutler Mail Chute Division, Cutler-Federal, Inc., Eaton Park, Florida; Albert C. Kelley, Medical Products Division, The De Vilbiss Company, Somerset, Pennsylvania; Lu Ann Porter, Dunbar Furniture Division, General Interiors Corporation, Berne, Indiana; David Hartley, *The Herald Statesman,* Yonkers, New York; Kenneth L. Bowers, Hershey Foods Corporation, Hershey, Pennsylvania; Nancy Burt, Hollywood High School, Hollywood, California; Augustin S. Hardart, Jr., The Horn & Hardart Company, New York City; E. P. Hogan, International Silver Company, Meriden, Connecticut; H. Ray Goldwire, Kimble Division, Owens-Illinois, Inc., Vineland, New Jersey; Arthur Riback, National Restaurants, Inc., New York City.

Also Grace Teed Kent, Longchamps Restaurants, New York City; Robert A. Mann, The B. Manischewitz Company, Newark, New Jersey; K. D. Magill, The Mennen Company, Morristown, New Jersey; Martin H. Feinman, Modernage Furniture, Miami, Florida; A. J. Swartz, Modine Manufacturing Co., Racine, Wisconsin; John F. Majeski, *The Music Trades,* Englewood, New Jersey; Frank Lloyd, The Philadelphia Art Alliance; Robert E. Buckley, Pittsburgh Corning Corporation; Ross R. Fernow, Glass Advertising & Promotion, PPG Industries, Pittsburgh, Pennsylvania; William J. Bassett, *The Daily Item,* Port Chester, New York; Lloyd B. Plummer, San Diego Federal Savings and Loan Association; Marsha Lane, Schenley Affiliated Brands Corp., New York City; Mayor Betty Davis, City of South Haven, Michigan; Dan P. Thornton, Spreckels Sugar Division, Amstar Corporation, San Francisco, California; Phyllis McCullough, Thonet Industries, Inc., York, Pennsylvania; Willis Ranney, United Airlines, Chicago, Illinois; Robert L. Mason, U.S. National Bank of Oregon, Klamath Falls, Oregon; Donn Dutcher, Western Union Telegraph Co., Mahwah, New Jersey; and Dorothy B. Strayer, The White Plains Hospital, White Plains, New York.

The furniture of Frederick Kiesler pictured in this book is, with two exceptions, from the collection of Martha Bartos and was originally designed for Mr. and Mrs. Charles Mergentime. Of the remaining two pieces, the aluminum kidney-shaped tables are from the collection of Mr. and Mrs. Donald Grossman, and the aluminum coffee table is shown in an original photograph taken in 1936. I am grateful to the owners of these important Kiesler pieces for permission to reproduce them in these pages.

In the compilation and writing of this book I have been encouraged by my friends Clive Driver, David Lindstrom, and, especially, Helen Iranyi, all of whom have had to put up with a great deal of talk about the 1930s. Finally, I have been fortunate in my editor, Lou Barron, without whose thoughtful advice and gentlemanly kindness *Depression Modern* would have been an entirely different book.

PREFACE

Photos in an album, yellowed, faded, worn. Moments frozen in memory worlds ago, but recorded only forty years ago in time. Fragments distant, but startlingly familiar.

My mother at twenty, handsome and slender, her evening dress shaped to her figure, bias-cut and backless, clinging and revealing, soft and flattering. My father at twenty-six, proudly showing off his first-born on a spring morning in 1933, an uncle (his eye to the camera) reflected carelessly in the curved, steel-rimmed window of the local bakery. My elder brother at four, at play in the courtyard of a new apartment house with round-cornered casements, his tricycle and the scooter of a small friend streamlined to resemble the latest Chrysler "Airflow" motor car. A neighbor, looking older than her twenty-one years, her small felt hat worn rakishly to one side and revealing waved hair set close to the head, a sleek figure in black crêpe de Chine jacket and white jabot, posed before the gleaming glass block and Vitrolite façade of Ann's Beauty Salon. A birthday party in the late 1930s for a five-year-old, the neighborhood children (four of whom, round-faced and banana-curled, are named Shirley) crowded expectantly around the oblong blonde-wood dining table, its matching, gift-laden sideboard, gracefully rounded, smooth, and mass-produced without ornament, set beneath a frameless, circular, peach-tinted mirror. A snapshot of an infant in the summer of 1939, the author at fourteen months, asleep in a polished-enamel perambulator, maroon in color, a horizontal band of three slender steel stripes across its side, a baby carriage with lines like the family's Pontiac, a line that starts with a parabolic curve and ends in a long backward sweep, the same line recurring in photograph after photograph, in clothing and furniture, in automobile and storefront—the fundamental line of an age. And then—seen against the Trylon and Perisphere, the vast white curves of the New York World's Fair—my parents, young and American, their backs turned to events in Europe, their eyes widened and corrupted by the modern wonders of "The World of Tomorrow," a glass and steel and streamlined phoenix emerging triumphant from the devastation of the Great Depression.

Each succeeding generation is false to its predecessor in reconstructing and interpreting the events of the past, in selecting and stressing the details that conform to its notion of an age recently become history, in sentimentalizing or libeling the days and years of its elders. And—in punishing its parents by distorting their era, their time in the sun—my generation is no different from any other.

Perhaps no American period in memory has been so falsified and fictionalized as that of the 1930s. TV shows are set in the period for no apparent reason. Articles on this or that aspect of it appear daily in newspapers and in popular magazines. Its entertainers and celebrities—many second-rate and justly anonymous to two generations—are rediscovered and packaged as momentary, but passing, fancies. Its styles and fashions are ransacked and adapted and briefly revived by the chic and by the middle-class young. Inevitably, Hollywood—most responsible for our "first-hand" vision of the '30s as we view old films on television—distorts it still further by creating it anew as plastic fodder for today's motion pictures. This time, however, the shadow is twice removed from the substance (the Dream Factory's original vision of itself forty years ago being once removed from reality), and reflects, of economic necessity, the present obsession with raw sex and violence, eternal concerns treated quite differently during the Great Depression. The sycophantic imitations of Bogdanovich, the very face and voice of Streisand, the make-up of Dunaway, the pin-striped suits of Redford and Newman are totally false to the 1930s—hard-edged vulgarizations of its soft-edged sophistication and calculating condescensions to its naïve innocence.

The Hollywood of the '70s, aware of the superficial parallels between the two decades, grinds out "period" fantasies, set gratuitously in a mythologized Depression, whether the time is integral to the plot or not. But the characters are all either Steinbeck-poor or Brenda Frazier-rich. And the clothes are wrong, the hairdos oddly contemporary, the music ludicrously anachronistic—either Scott Joplin (then passé and at least twenty years ignored and forgotten) or the clipped rhythms of a Cole Porter or a Harry Warren, muted, modernized, and Muzak'd. Whether the date portrayed is 1931 or 1938, the settings are alive, conspicuously, with Art Deco—all zigzags and neo-Cubist designs, ersatz Lalique, and procelain statuettes of flappers in cloche hats—the Jazz Age mysteriously set down, as if by some strange time machine, in the midst of the Great Depression. But for those in the audience who might be watching, only the Pierce-Arrows, the Hupmobiles and Packards are right, a concession not so much to accuracy as to the only shared history left us: the history of America's veneration of the automobile.

The current vogue for things bizarre and, particularly, for the extravagant, the exotic, and the erotic, has crescendoed through the 1960s into the present decade. It explains, perhaps, the enormous popularity of Art Deco today and why, of all things associated with the '20s and '30s, Art Deco has most captured the imaginations of the gay set, the decorators, the admen, and other trend-setters —and, ultimately, the fancies of the young, the kitsch collectors, the falsely sophisticated, and most other trend-followers.

At its best (and it was frequently superb), Art Deco was a style consummately Parisian, "smart" rather than pretty, embraced not by the French avant-garde, not by the conservative old-rich, but by those who liked to think of themselves as tastemakers: couturières, decorators, theatrical designers, and others catering to the *haut monde.* As such, Deco was of passing importance, a snobbish badge of exclusivity adopted by the few and known to still fewer, a style characterized by its use of luxurious materials: Macassar ebony in furniture, shagreen and ivory as trim, the finest leather, lacquer, and enamel that money could buy.

In its self-indulgent pursuit of exclusivity and luxury, it appealed to those whose lives were devoted to modishness, a thing to be ridiculed in the pages of Evelyn Waugh once it traveled across the Channel, and a fashion totally Americanized (and bastardized) after it crossed the Atlantic to the land of mass production. And, as we shall see, it was obsessively romantic and backward-looking, finding inspiration in the ornate past, the very antithesis of the modern and its radical emphasis on functional simplicity. As the plaything of the fashionable, the palliative of the vain, Art Deco's orchidaceous flowering in the '20s was to be withered, ultimately, by the cold winds of the Depressed '30s. And once it sacrificed its urbane exclusivity on the mechanized altar of the American assembly line, it lost its very *raison d'être.*

Deco in America enjoyed a short-lived vogue as superficially applied decoration on lipstick holders, cigarette cases, compacts, and the like. But there is no Art Deco to be found in my family album. Nor is there any in the albums of anyone else I know. I can find no ebony furniture, no stylized African sculpture or cubistic decoration in these photographs, even though my parents and their contemporaries did visit the dazzling interiors of Radio City Music Hall more than once in the decade, realizing, of course, that movie palaces and hotel lobbies were to be looked at and not lived in. There is, in fact, little of Deco, authentic or vulgarized, to be found in contemporary American magazines, either. *The Smart Set,* apparently, was not smart enough for it. *Fortune* was too conservative. *The New Yorker* (ridiculing most things "modern") restricted it to occasional appearances in jewelry advertisements. *Time* (frozen in its original 1923 format) ignored it, and *Life* was born too late for it. Although there are in the pages of these magazines glimpses of spoutless teapots with lids dizzily askew, of square Depression-glass dinnerware, or of zigzagging, geometric dress clips, asymmetric perfume bottles, and Jazz Age display type, these are far outnumbered by objects, layouts, and type faces that are simply curved, eloquently understated, elegantly unornamented. What impresses one most, in fact, in thumbing through magazines of the '30s, is clarity of line, simplicity, and directness—graphic precision largely free of hokey "trendiness," a much more recent journalistic invention.

And yet the belief persists today that Art Deco and the decade of the '30s are somehow synonymous, a popular misconception spread almost universally by contemporary pop-culturists and the advertising media, aped slavishly by fashionable magazines and the feature pages of our daily newspapers, and embraced enthusiastically, but ignorantly, by the young, the lazy, the unthinking, and those whose only view of the period is through the prismatic lens of Hollywood. When an Art Deco "festival" can be held annually at Radio City Music Hall, its once-elegant foyer and lounges polluted by dealers hawking to the multitudes everything from World War I song sheets to World War II platform shoes, all masquerading as gen-u-ine "Art Deco"; when *The New York Times* can report this phenomenon *uncritically* as a page-one event; when a slick magazine can include in its photographic gallery of Art Deco buildings masterpieces of the International Style; when an otherwise intelligent film critic can praise the brilliant modern design and almost-Bauhaus trappings of *Things to Come* (1936) as "vintage Art Deco"; when a popular TV talk-show emcee can babble knowingly about "Art Deco of the *1940s*," meaning snoods and veils and padded shoulder-pads—something has gone wrong with our critical vocabulary, if not our critical acumen. These people are all like the goose in the barnyard, honking at the rising sun, lacking memories and foresight. It is as if yesterday never happened and tomorrow will never come, as if everything from the recent past were one and the same, as if Bette Midler had invented the Wurlitzer jukebox.

It is time, I think, to have another look.

This book does not pretend to be a scholarly *dissertation d'un auteur*. It is, rather, an informal and informed appreciation of a period I happen to like. Although it is carefully and, I hope, accurately researched, it is essentially a personal document, an attempt, largely visual, to rescue the '30s—or one particular aspect of it—from those who, in their uncritical enthusiasm and perverse love for the decade, have distorted, suffocated, and nearly killed it.

As such, the book has two purposes. Its minor aim is to correct a misconception, that Art Deco was the predominant style of the 1930s—a misconception which obscures the essentially modern spirit of the time. On the contrary, the major American designers of the Great Depression hated Deco (which they considered "the modern deprived of its manhood") and despised its effete luxuriousness, adjudging its romantic backsliding a betrayal and perversion of modernism. What they created, largely in reaction against Deco, was a new machine art: honest, simple, and functionally expressive—values basic alike to the house, the school, the streamlined train, the cigarette lighter, the toaster, the saucepan, or the grand piano as these emerged from the designer's studio. What they created they called the "Modern," a term (to my eye, at any rate) still visually acceptable, but chronologically imperfect. I have chosen instead to call it "Depression Modern," suggesting both its time and its place: America in the 1930s.

The second aim of this book, its fundamental purpose, is to define and illustrate Depression Modern as the primary style of the decade, a design revolution which, in my opinion, was the turning point of modernism in America. By focusing on the period between two great expositions—Chicago's Century of Progress (1933–34) and the New York World's Fair (1939–40)—it shows that a relatively small group of young, brilliant, energetic designers of the 1930s attempted to create, perhaps for the first time, a national style that was uniquely American, despite its European borrowings—a style basically the same in New York, Mississippi, Arizona, Montana, Minnesota, or California. So revolutionary was this style, in fact, so all-pervasive, that in a period of only half a decade it changed the shape of virtually everything in the American home, including, finally, the home itself. So total was its success, so complete its acceptance (we live surrounded by its offspring today), that its origins in the 1930s and its innovative creators, if not completely forgotten, are now simply taken for granted. Thus does popular history reward the victors.

Depression Modern: The Thirties Style in America, by defining a neglected but important contribution to design, and especially through the pictorial recreation of that style in its album of contemporary photographs, intends to set the record straight.

As the decade began: the way things looked *before* Depression Modern.

DEPRESSION MODERN
AN APPRECIATION

*"Beauty, like truth, is never so glorious
as when it goes the plainest."*
—Laurence Sterne

"We should be more efficient, Sir, if less decorated."
—a Persian general to his emperor, fifth century B.C.

On a wintry Friday night in 1938, a throng of theatergoers, several primping in their evening clothes as they emerge from the blasts of a February wind, jostle their way through a fashionable crowd in the lobby of a New York playhouse. From the close perfumed warmth of the foyer, those nearest the chrome and glass doors can witness the frenetic bustle of the theater district in the hectic minutes before an 8:30 curtain. Outside, through frosty panes, moves a procession of the modern, a kaleidoscope of the mechanical, the metallic din of klaxons muted only by the icy wind.

Packard limousines, sleek and black, the iridescent neon of Broadway reflected in their slanted rear windows, disgorge the rich and privileged, their liveried drivers banished until the play's final act to coffee over red Micarta tables at the 42nd Street Cafeteria. In herds of twos and threes, fat arch-backed Yellow Cabs issue passengers picked up a quarter-hour earlier under the canopies and curved marquees of the Century, the Majestic, the Eldorado, and other smart apartment buildings on Central Park West. Suburban matrons, supping in town, their brightly lipsticked mouths freshened with after-dinner mints, dart between the cabs from the gleaming Thermolux vestibule of a wine-colored Long-champs across the street. Their unmarried daughters, playing at being career girls in the months before fashionable June weddings, leave unwashed china in apartment kitchenettes, silk stockings thrown hastily over the iron railings of dropped living rooms. Others, with their beaus, pass through leather-quilted doors pierced with chrome-ringed portholes, abandoning cups of steaming chocolate at the glass-brick fountain of the Taft Hotel. Young couples, their chesterfields and Persian lambs braced to the wind, hurry crosstown from streamlined Fifth Avenue buses, passing on their way the revolving doors and circular change booths of Automats and the ghostly blue mirrors of cheap chop suey joints, as the Sixth Avenue El rumbles overhead.

Suffusing all are the flashing lights of New York's Broadway in the late 1930s—urban America encircled, as it were, by a mechanical nimbus: the hissing and puffing A&P coffeepot sign. Adjacent, above a gaudy movie-vaudeville house, illuminated by a thousand bulbs, an enormous billboard, advertising MGM's *Test Pilot,* exploits the box-office popularity of Clark Gable and Myrna Loy— and the public's love affair with swift and shiny airplanes. Across the wide avenue at the Paramount, another blinking sign entices the radio fan to *The Big Broadcast of 1938,* with Fields and Hope and Flagstad and a dozen top stars of the airwaves aboard a dazzlingly white luxury liner. At Roseland, a few blocks uptown, a band breaking into swing announces the Lambeth Walk and the Big Apple, while a monocled Mr. Peanut, squinting grotesquely in red neon, is reflected in a passing Times Square trolley. Dominant over the east wall of the urban ravine, an enormous eleven-fished aquarium, advertising chewing gum, starts to flicker and sparkle, its colossal guppies blowing green and yellow neon bubbles. A photo-electric animated cartoon tells how to be a success at love, offering the example of a square-headed hero who smokes Old Golds. Beyond, a resplendent orange spurts radiance like a sun, an equally garish lemon looming higher than the orange. Both shimmer high above a theater showing the latest chapter of *The March of Time:* "Inside Nazi Germany."

Broadway on the night of February 4, 1938. The premiere performance of Thornton Wilder's *Our Town*—a play, ironically, that celebrates the timeless excitement of the ordinary.

In setting forth his story of the loves, deaths, and the patterns of everyday life in a small New England village, Thornton Wilder placed *Our Town* in the recent past: Grover's Corners, New Hampshire, in the year 1901, a time within living memory of many, if not most, of his audience. Presented on a stage bare of scenery, and reflecting both the sophisticated stripped-down art of the late 1930s and the innocent period of its setting, *Our Town* evoked the simple pleasures of a day just moments in time before the clamor of automobile traffic and the roar of whirling airplane propellers: a day, only thirty-seven years before, in which Editor Webb's wife baked pies in the oven of a wood-burning castiron range and Grover's Corners' only doctor made his rounds in a horse-drawn phaeton; a time in which George and Emily's young love blossomed over strawberry phosphates at the marble counter of the local drugstore.

The audience of *Our Town,* heirs of the 19th century, had lived with wide-eyed amazement through more than three decades of almost miraculous industrial growth, through a period of inventive progress intensified by a great war abroad. It had enjoyed (and was beginning to take for granted) the widespread mechanical wonders of the telephone and the radio, of talking pictures and the automobile, of speeding stainless-steel Burlington Zephyrs and transcontinental Flying Clippers. To this audience, the dimly familiar but alien world of Grover's Corners at the start of the century might never have existed. To this Depression audience, the world of 1901—with its buggies and wooden washtubs, its hot-water bottles and mustard plasters, its horsehair cushions and velvet hair ribbons —might just as well have occurred a thousand years ago on an uncharted island or on a distant planet. So far had America progressed in only thirty-seven years.

Thornton Wilder's *Our Town* stands midway between the opening years of the century's first and final quarters: midway between our generation of the 1970s and George and Emily's at the beginning of the 20th century. Exactly thirty-seven years separate its first performance in 1938 from the events in 1901 within the play itself. Exactly the same number of years separate its premiere from the present day. But if its first-night audience, repressing memories almost four decades distant, gazed as foreigners on the landscape of its youth, scarcely recognizing an earlier world portrayed so starkly that February night thirty-seven years ago, then we today look back with relative ease to a period equidistantly removed from us in time, but far less strange. We look back with an altogether different feeling of surprise at the physical world of 1938.

Look. The cabs, the cars, the planes, the buses, the restaurants, the lights, the bustle, the din are with us still. Nothing much has changed.

In 1934 Raymond Loewy executed a famous series of "evolution charts," illustrating the tendency toward simplification and sheerness in everything from automobiles, airplanes, and railroad trains to glassware and women's fashions. Many of the following charts also illustrate the origins of streamlining and of the new horizontality.

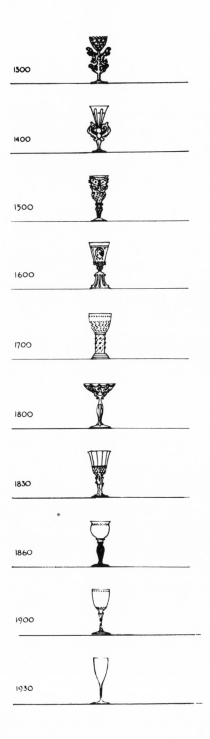

1300
1400
1500
1600
1700
1800
1830
1860
1900
1930

1630

1790

1850

1880

1890

1900

1910

1925

1934

3

In 1938, the average American wife, home-bound and dependent, listened to Kate Smith or Bing Crosby or Whispering Jack Smith while doing her daily housework. Her kitchen companion, if she were lucky or if her husband were working regularly, was a new table-model radio, placed securely atop the mechanical refrigerator, beneath the chrome and enamel electric wall clock and away from the exploring hands of little children. More frequently, however, in homes with only one radio, the living room console was turned up so that the housewife could enjoy *Aunt Jenny* while doing the wash in the family Toperator or Maytag or Bendix, or could listen to *Joyce Jordan, Girl Intern* while vacuuming the carpet with upright Kwik-Kleen or streamlined Electrolux. On the kitchen table, then as now, a two-slice automatic toaster. On the white square stove, its corners gently rounded, aluminum or stainless cookware with Bakelite handles. In the pantry or cabinet, in direct proportion to the family income, an assortment of electric appliances from waffle irons and coffee-pots to clothes irons and broilers, from oscillating fans and mixers to heating pads and sun lamps. And in the kitchens of the affluent: garbage disposals and automatic dishwashers, their ubiquity halted only by the oncoming clouds of a world at war.

One could catalogue endlessly the points of correspondence between the physical worlds of 1938 and today, between its mundane possessions and ours, between its mechanical triumphs and ours: glass walled, air-conditioned office towers and apartment buildings, television (both black-and-white and color), frozen foods, solar-heated homes, and on and on and on. All were demonstrably practical and commercially viable thirty-seven years ago, even if their widespread development was interrupted for almost a decade by the economies of war and by the necessary reconstruction of Europe.

But if we can so readily find in 1938 a mechanical world undreamed of in the America of *Our Town*, if we can easily recognize the functional similarities between the objects of 1938 and of today, how even more astonishing are the characteristic shapes of these objects, so familiar to us, so similar to those of our day, and so dramatically different from those of the previous decade of the '20s.

What is it, exactly, about the "shape of the '30s," and about the last half of the decade in particular, that so suggests modernity? What is it that makes an Eleanor Powell, tapping however ridiculously atop a sleek white battleship in 1936, so much more modern-looking than a Ruby Keeler, tapping just as ridiculously three years earlier aboard a dumpy sleeper shuffling off to Buffalo?

We needn't look to the rich or glamorous to discover just how modern the '30s were. Commonplaces will do, or even objects from Sears, Roebuck catalogues: bathroom scales or clocks or table lamps or basement burners. We need look no further, actually, than within the kitchen of Andy Hardy's mother, within the scrubbed and gingham pantry of Louis B. Mayer's idealized Middle America, to understand what it is that makes the decade seem so peculiarly contemporary. Mickey Rooney's 1938 screen-mother baked cookies in a kitchen very much like the kitchens of today, but vastly different from those of his Mickey McGuire days of the late '20s, a day in which a kitchen was a dreary affair furnished with a long-legged stove, a rickety china cupboard, and an enamel worktable set halfway across the room from a sink and washtub, standing stark and bare-limbed with plumbing rusting and exposed.

Although Judge Hardy, if he ever existed, exists no more, the 1938 kitchen of his wife still does. And it reflects in the material world, in the world of objects and of things, a revolution that occurred in the 1930s—a revolution in design and in the shape of things as dynamic as any that occurred in contemporary social thought: a movement from the vertical to the horizontal, from the straight line to the curve—both preferred, in their purest employment, for functional ends, and in their basest use, for the value of a marketable appearance.

Mrs. Hardy's stove, a gracefully rounded white square, set flush between glistening cabinet-counters and adjacent to a Monel metal sink, is as a building block in a functional and expressive unit of blocks arranged contiguously around the room. It is essentially an American design: the work of Norman Bel Geddes as filtered down through the popularized advertisements of Westinghouse and General Electric and Armstrong Floors and other corporations appealing to the American consumer. Mrs. Hardy's kitchen, its horizontal units of white blocks all exactly the same height and repeated in the long row of wall cabinets above, is identical to the one in which Penny Singleton, masquerading as Chic Young's Blondie, prepares dinner for Dagwood and Baby Dumpling, or in which Spring Byington as Mrs. Jones, the all-American Depression housewife, solves the pressing problems of her dim-witted husband. With its man-sized refrigerator and Formica cabinet tops, its Venetian blinds and inlaid linoleum floor, this modular kitchen is undoubtedly the most modern room in the 1938 house. It is, fundamentally, and with no substantial changes, the room in which we still prepare our meals today.

If the kitchen of 1938, glistening and utilitarian, bears little resemblance to that of just a few years earlier—say, to the kitchen of 1929—then the same dissimilarity is equally true of the objects found within both rooms. An electric fan, no longer standing at attention—as did its '20s predecessor— arches gracefully, its form resembling, consciously, that of an airplane, ovoid and gliding. A toaster, all polished chrome and curved, is longer and lower than the '20s model. It bears the same relation- ship to its earlier, taller, more vertical forebear as does the long, curved profile of the Broadway Limited to the straight up-and-down lines of a steam locomotive, or a streamlined Cord motorcar to the hulking boxlike frame of a tin lizzie. And the same observation might be made of the bread box or the coffee grinder or the tea kettle—each noticeably more horizontal and curved than its counterparts of 1929 or 1932.

Washing machine (*left*) de- signed by Henry Dreyfuss for Associated Merchandising Corporation, 1934. Streamlined Cadillac-Fleetwood coupe (*op- posite*), 1937.

* "We are rounding the corner," the noted furniture designer Kem Weber wrote in 1936, punning consciously on both the basic shape of the decade and on its salutary effect upon an embattled econ- omy. Everything from radios and mirrors to washing machines and ladies' hats was by that time sport- ing the new rounded look—a look which affected even Hollywood's ideal of feminine beauty. As hopelessly out of vogue as a dialless, vertical telephone was the angular face of a Katharine Hepburn, who, in 1938, was labeled "box-office poison," in part because she in no way resembled such stylish moon-faced lovelies as Rochelle Hudson and Arline Judge. And, if the rounded face was not the new ideal, how else explain the contemporary popularity of those chinless singing zeroes, Harriet Hilliard and Frances Langford? Or of that skating cipher, Sonja Henie? But we are racing ahead in time to the end of a decade before examining its start.

What rational explanation, we ask, can be found for this singular phenomenon, a change in the preference for shapes that informed an age? And what has it to do with the Great Depression?

America, in spite of the Depression, and perhaps because of it, had looked around and found itself shabby and wanting, its tastes and forms determined, largely, by influences from abroad, its production geared to meet the needs of a passing social order. Its tastemakers, the millionaires who were willing to go back 3,000 miles or 300 years for their choicest possessions, no longer existed in any great number, and those who did, those who still controlled American corporations and industry, were now understandably prejudiced against sending their capital to foreign shores. They looked

instead to economic recovery through the development of a new set of wants, through an American appetite for things both fresh and new. The result, nurtured in the depths of the Depression, was a new materialism, fostered by a new breed of creative designer to whom an America of industriousness, material progress, and opportunity was no mere myth. Out of their talents and creative efforts, and through the peculiarly American marriage of art and industry, came an impulse toward forms that were fresh and intelligent. Forms that grew out of current needs, instead of archaic needs. Forms that assimilated new materials and functioned to meet contemporary wants. This new materialism, turning its back on the luxuriousness of the 1920s,

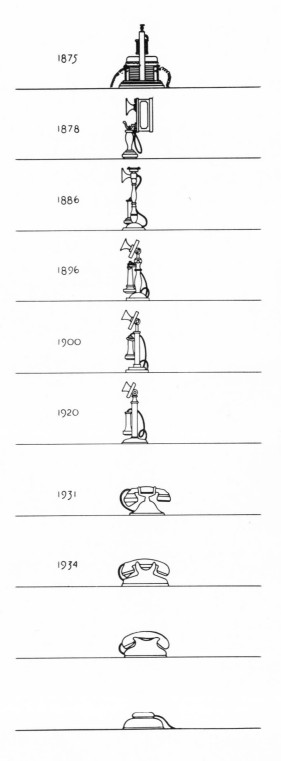

1875

1878

1886

1896

1900

1920

1931

1934

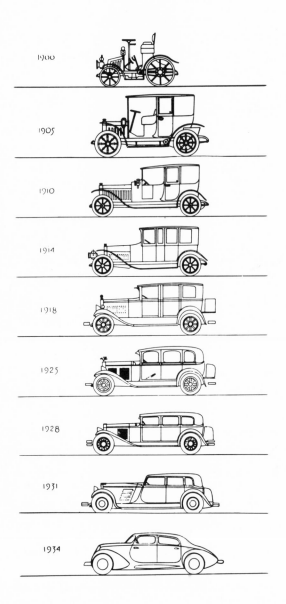

1900

1905

1910

1914

1918

1925

1928

1931

1934

and concentrating on simpler, more useful objects, reflected an authentic social mood, an attitude of interest in things created expressly for its peculiar age. And out of it—in automobile and railroad train, in home and in office, in department store and corner shop—developed the identifying features of a style as different from the Art Deco of the 1920s as it is similar to its offspring in the 1970s.

Because of these physical correspondences, because of the many similarities between the landscape of material objects then and now, the era of the Great Depression is ultimately far closer to us in experiential time than the year 1901 was in measured time to Thornton Wilder's audience. Even if Hollywood escapists did occasionally exploit as sexual metaphor the ta-ra-ra-boom-de-ay of the gilded '90s, it is hard to imagine during the Depression a widespread nostalgia for the year 1901. There was none, in fact. America in the 1930s, down on its luck, but believing nonetheless in the material benefits of mechanized progress, sought its way out of the Depression not through a nostalgic return to its preindustrial past, but through the creation of new objects, of needed and necessary things, well designed and inexpensively mass-produced. While some sang cynically of paper moons on cardboard seas, others dreamed, optimistically, of an American Era in which everyone, rich and poor alike, would share in the material riches of the nation—of a time in which all Americans would own a multitude of simple, useful, beautiful objects bought in stores created consciously as a golden mean between the five-and-dime and Tiffany's.

We are materialists, most of us. In recognizing how much closer we are to 1938 in our mundane likes and wants than 1938 was to 1901, we can begin to understand our present fascination with the years of the Great Depression. The parallels are all too obvious, even if superficial. Business is down. Unemployment is up. Social concerns are high. "Movements" are rife. Most of us want more, not less; sooner, not later. Everyman his own Henry Fonda. Everywoman her own Sylvia Sidney. In the face of corruption and ineptitude in high places, of public scandal and private disaster, the new Forgotten Man awaits a new leader, a new savior, an apocalyptic symbol fluttering blue and aery wings in a Busby Berkeley sky—an NRA eagle for the 1970s.

In these correspondences—both emotional and mundane—we are all, in a sense, children of the '30s, our eyes still earthbound despite the recent conquest of the moon. After all, to a generation raised on matinees at the Pix or the Luxor or the Bijou, didn't Buster Crabbe accomplish even greater interplanetary feats every Saturday afternoon?

Let us now move backward in time. And to Paris.

"*J'suis Français, j'suis Chauvin.*" Chauvinism—irrevocably French by dint of its very derivation—is a highly justifiable national trait when it comes to assessing Art Deco. For the French, and the French only, have a right to claim Deco as their own.

To have entered the fashionable salons of Paris in the decade before 1925, to have walked within the houses in the Faubourg St. Honoré or within the shops in the Boulevard des Capucines, was to marvel at the opulence of a Tamerlane, his riches plucked and plundered from the corners of the globe, or to comprehend in all their lush and lavish sensuousness the promises of Herod to his Salome. Here—amid Egyptian, Chinese, African, and Islamic *objets d'art*, scattered like rose petals at the feet of the epicene Heliogabalus—were furnishings wrought luxuriously in amboyna and in ivory, in Macassar ebony and silk brocade, in marbrite and Caucasian walnut, in repoussé leather or in silvered bronze. In their fine and detailed craftsmanship, each uniquely wrought for a single wealthy patron, the elegant pale sycamore and chrome furniture of Pierre Legrain, the inlaid ivory sofas of Marcel Coard, the moulded opalescent glass of René Lalique, the lacquered wood and ivory furniture of André Groult, or the sensuous sculptures of Gustav Miklos suggest nothing less than the royal court of *Le Roi Soleil*—Versailles resurgent, as it were, in 20th-century France.

Art Deco, then, is unmistakably French. And yet the term itself is English, a fact so obvious that it should give us pause.

We know, of course, that Art Deco derives its name from the great 1925 Paris exhibition, *L'Exposition Internationale des Arts Décoratifs et Industriels Modernes*, in which the style, in full flower, reached its culmination. We know, too, that the exhibition popularized this most conservative of styles and that the public embrace, antithetic to its exclusive nature, ultimately killed it. We know, finally, that today the term has somehow come to be applied to the complete range of artistic production of the 1920s and 1930s and that it is now applied equally, but indiscriminately, to the priceless furniture of

Clément Rousseau and to Bronx apartment houses, to junk jewelry and the covers of *Vogue,* to the Chrysler Building and the films of Rogers and Astaire.

What we forget, however, is that the French, precise as always, referred originally to the style as *l'art décoratif moderne,* carefully distinguishing the real thing from *le modernisme:* the style it became once it lost its sybaritic exclusivity and once it was reduced to a handful of surface motifs reproduced inexpensively for the masses. Curiously—but not so curiously once one thinks about it—both the English and the Americans have from the first referred to the style as "the modernistic." Until recently, that is. For the past fifteen years or so, we've been calling it Art Deco, a term that never existed in its own peculiar day.

Deco, like any rare plant, transplanted badly. It was brought back by Americans such as Donald Deskey and Joseph Urban, who discovered it in Paris, and by Europeans such as Frederick Kiesler and Josef Hoffmann and Paul Frankl, who foresaw America as a rich and logical ground for cultivation. Their works, commissioned in the late '20s by the Rockefellers and others similarly rich, remained true Deco—private, exclusive, luxurious. And, like anything else exclusive, there was precious little of it.

But others returned from Paris, too, ready to give the great American public its share of European smartness. Department store buyers, merchandisers, and fashion designers came back filled with enthusiasm, exotic color, and a few easily applied surface motifs. And what they created was called "the modernistic." Characterized, generally, by zigzags and asymmetrical patterning, it reduced the wealth and endless variety of Art Deco to a handful of decorative motifs: a squiggle here, a stylized sunburst there. True Deco had been soft, preferring lavish curves and curlicues in hand-wrought ballustrades and flower-patterned metal grillwork. But the modernistic was hard and largely angular, its zigzags and fluted columns far easier to stamp on machine-pressed objects from picture frames to refrigerator doors. Deco, characteristically understated, was dependent on a cumulative vision of luxury, each element in a room seen in relation to the whole effect. Deceptively subtle, it could be likened to a time bomb with a built-in detonator that required, merely, the sensory heat of sight and touch to activate it. The modernistic, however, all glittering surface and hollow substance, was more simply a bomb.

By 1930, the modernistic filled the lobbies of New York hotels and skyscrapers. It got into glassware and lipstick holders, compacts and cigarette cases. It altered advertising and the packaging of soap powders. It caused old-fashioned marble cake to change its name, for a day or two, to Cubist cake. It riddled the drug business—atomizers, perfume bottles, and other trifles were particularly hard hit. Even venerable commercial institutions tried it: Bon Ami Cleanser, abandoning in early 1929 its soft and fluffy baby chick ("It never scratches"), a trademark for almost half a century, replaced it with a black and yellow ziggurat, the ultimate in fashionable chic. Six months later the baby chick was back. And with it came the Great Depression.

Hard times bring with them the need, and the impulse, for stocktaking. America looked at itself and found itself fat. It felt the need for simplification. Gradually, therefore, the tide of the modernistic—the first wave of pseudo-modernism in America—began to ebb on every shore. On every shore, that is, but one. Hollywood had its own peculiar reason for holding on.

Early in its history, Hollywood had developed a visual vocabulary all its own, a pattern of symbols and conventions that spoke meaningfully, directly, and clearly to its audience, many of whom, because they could not read the subtitles of the silent cinema, would not have been able to follow the simple story line without these recognizable signposts. Long after the advent of sound had rendered them useless, Hollywood retained many of these conventions. And one of these visual symbols had to do with the modernistic vogue. It identified a particular moral evil. Until well into the '30s, every demimonde and every kept woman on the silver screen was always accommodated with a modernistic interior.

The modernistic Southtown Theater, Chicago, Illinois, 1931.

The equation was simple—"modern" equals sex —a formula all the more important in American films after William Randolph Hearst and all the other Forces of Good, attempting to put Mae West out of business, brought an end in Hollywood to sexual "explicitness," '30s-style. The very symbol of female license, therefore, whether in gangster's moll, banker's mistress, or high-priced whore, became the "smart" modernistic boudoir. Yards of white satin, a bed without posts, a chair without feet, and a mirror without frame—for the woman

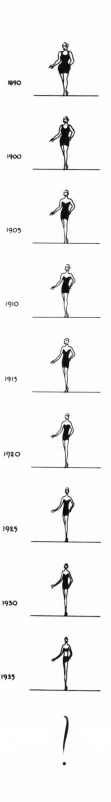

1650

1700

1730

1780

1810

1830

1880

1900

1920

1934

without morals. And, as an added mark of wantonness, the demimondes, when not in step-ins, seemed always to wear modernistic diamond clips on the straps of diaphanous nightgowns. It must have been painful to turn over in bed.

All the virtuous girls, of course—loyal wives, jilted sweethearts, innocent shopgirls, and all the other virgins—came out of sensible colonial bungalows, where they wrung their worried hands in chintz-covered sitting rooms or peered anxiously through lace-curtained windows, awaiting the return of fallen or transfigured heroes. And they never slept in beds. They only occasionally died in them.

Helped along by Hollywood, although gradually becoming moribund, the modernistic craze lasted into the early '30s. And well it should, since a 1932 automobile would have been designed in 1929, a 1932 skyscraper in 1928. But very early on, with the Depression deepening and the future looking bleak, with America tightening its belt and starting to think thin, the modernistic became a term of derision. After all, when William Van Alen, architect of the Chrysler Building, was called the "Ziegfeld of his profession," it wasn't meant to be a compliment.

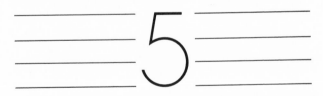

5

The style which in its day was called Modern, but which I have chosen to call Depression Modern, developed out of several sources: economic, social, and artistic. But, essentially, it was a direct response to the vogue for the modernistic. It was, in fact, its very antithesis. The modernistic was a collection of motifs applied superficially to objects for the sole effect of novelty. In its quest for sophistication, for mere smartness, it masqueraded as something "modern." It was, however, merely eclectic, a watered-down borrowing of elements from the past which its predecessor, Art Deco, had earlier ransacked for its own magnificent needs. Depression Modern, on the other hand, was an art stripped bare of all ornamentation, an art in which the American home and office and factory—and everything in them—were built for just one purpose: to work, and to look as though they worked.

Ideally, the Depression Modern style was spare. Although the earliest examples did exhibit a certain amount of decorative detail, the style became purer and purer, until, finally, a Depression Modern house, or airplane, or chair, or chemical plant could be said to be without a single detail that could be called extraneous, without any embellishment, without a line that did not seem inevitable. There was nothing in Depression Modern to distract the eye or the mind. It was clean and uncluttered, direct and innocent.

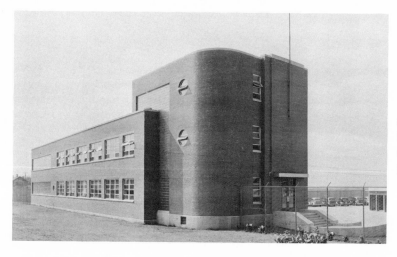

Administration building of Federated Metals Company, Hammond, Indiana, designed and built by The Austin Company, 1937.

The objectives of Depression Modern were efficiency, economy, and right appearance. Frequently these objectives were met; frequently they were not. Because the style was so directly related to the world of commerce, its chief designers and innovators were often required to compromise their ideals —sometimes against their will, more frequently with their consent. Many of these men and women became millionaires. Others did not. All of them shaped not only the world of the '30s, but our present day as well. In creating Depression Modern, a style which survived unchallenged until the late 1940s, they contributed, ultimately, to many contemporary wonders of technology. But, at their worst, they also planted some of the seeds that blossomed into the present *age de merde*. Consequently, both sides of Depression Modern—its achievements and its failures—are reflected in the photographs in this book.

Few generations have better understood themselves and their times than did the designers of the '30s. They knew what they were creating, they knew why they were creating it, and they even had a premonition of what their place in history would be because they had created it. They knew that they

31

hated the modernistic. They knew that they were on to something different. And they knew that it was modern. Given the clarity and consistency of their vision and the number of primary sources in which their thoughts appeared, one wonders why popular history has included and continues to include them under the collective umbrella of the term Art Deco. Especially when they thought completely otherwise.

In support of this thought, one could quote from the published writings, or speeches, or notebooks of Raymond Loewy, Donald Deskey, Russel Wright, Walter Dorwin Teague, Vahan Hagopian, Dorothy Liebes, Marianne Willisch, Gilbert Rohde, or other designers of the Depression. But we can discover a great deal about the '30s just as well by taking a look at what was being taught in American schools of the period.

Astonishingly, a most wonderful description of the Depression Modern style has been preserved in the pages of a mere schoolgirl's notebook. It is correct in almost every point, even though it was taken down in childish Palmer penmanship by a teenage student in 1937. This is how the world of modern design looked to a homemaking class in a St. Paul, Minnesota, high school almost forty years ago:

> Different times and different countries have their own art. Modern is only a relative term. Things may be old-fashioned today and in the future be modern.
>
> What is modern and what is not modern is mainly governed by our ideals of beauty at that particular time.
>
> Art of today must be created today. It must express the life about us. Ours is a complex age. It is much more complex than any previous age. Invention, machinery, industry, science and commerce are characteristic of today. Individuals must have a way of relaxing from this complexity. Thus, we seek to surround ourselves with those things which have the effect of simplicity and which allow us to relax and forget our restlessness.
>
> The modern trend in design is an expression of a desire for honesty of materials, an escape from some of the imitative and over-decorated periods of the past.
>
> What is more natural and sensible, than to make the home simple, restful and easy to care for, to counteract the many demands of our social and business activities?
>
> *Design*—style is the expression of the times. Modernism is the style of reason, of square, of circle and horizontal line. Good forms and decoration together with good construction will always appeal.
>
> The smart modern today is as lightly and delicately scaled as are the Sheraton, Hepplewhite, and Adam designs in Georgian furniture, while still adhering to its original principle, that of functionalism.
>
> *Materials*—these new ideas demand new materials. One of the most conspicuous of these is glass which is used of itself, for itself, but not always by itself.
>
> It may be used as transparent glass, mirrors, and Vitrolite, which is black glass. Other new materials are Celanese and rayon, Monel metal—copper and nickel alloy—Bakelite—paper and rosin—lacquer fabrics, cork plates, linoleums, rubber flooring, aluminum, wall paper—Japanese veneer—French straw paper.
>
> Modernism is recognized by:
> > Simplicity
> > Unbroken lines
> > Use of pure colors
> > Contrasts in light and shadow
> > Honesty in materials: steel is steel, copper is copper and paint is recognized as paint and not made to resemble marble.

"Ours is a complex age." There is something poignant about these words, offered as they are as an explanation for the simplicity characteristic of the style of the 1930s. One wonders whether our St. Paul schoolgirl actually believed them or whether she was simply taking down, verbatim, her teacher's words. So removed in time from energy shortages, space exploration, and the threat of nuclear devastation, her thought suggests that simplicity in design was an escape, a refuge from the material world of the Depression, rather than a celebration of it, as was more likely the case.

On the contrary, most contemporary designers of the 1930s believed that in their time, nearly two hundred years after the start of the Industrial Revolution, America had for the first time shown a substantial accomplishment in relating machine-inspired design to a machine-inspired way of life. They believed that an earlier world, having come to an end in October 1929, placed them at the threshold of a new American era, one in which they, finally, were able to come to grips with the world of the machine. They believed that in creating new shapes and forms, simple and unornamented, they would succeed in adjusting humanely to a machine-driven world as their predecessors, in aping the eclectic styles and fashions of earlier periods, had failed.

The result of this belief, I think, was a succession of unusually shaped, but aesthetically pleasing, structures and objects that appeared during the Great Depression from coast to coast, in large city and small town, from Maine to California. Considering how the pioneering efforts of Sullivan and Wright had been largely ignored in their own country, the wide acceptance of the Depression Modern style marked probably the first—and, I lament, the last—time in America in which the purely functional was made to appear beautiful. It was surely the last successful attempt to realize the decorative inherent in the functional. And this was especially true of American industry, contemporary design having had its purest expression in the machine itself and then, logically, in its architectural counterpart, the factory.

The Church and Dwight factory, pictured in these pages, is a case in point. The owners of this company, makers of Arm & Hammer Baking Soda,

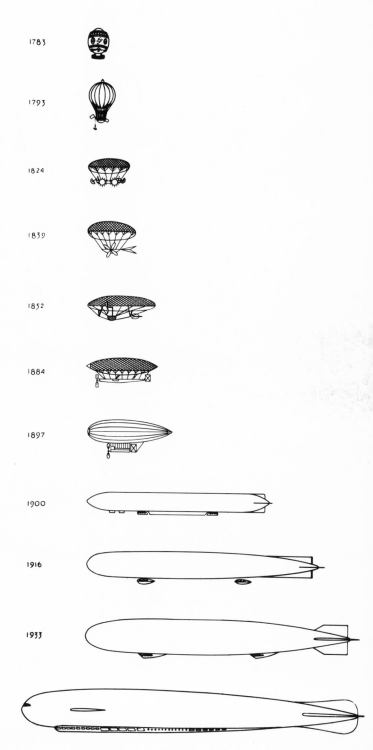

1783

1793

1824

1839

1852

1884

1897

1900

1916

1933

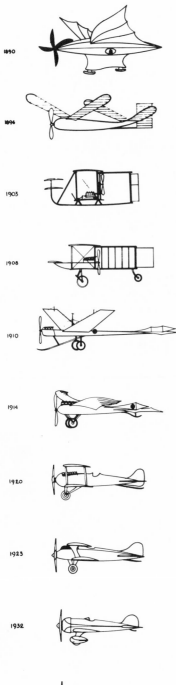

wanted a structure reflecting the purity of their product, and The Austin Company, consequently, designed a white brick, air-conditioned building in which the only ornament was its pattern of fenestration, a pattern dictated largely by function. The basic curve of the factory, that which gives it its singular shape, is purely functional: it is built around a seven-story industrial tank, necessary for the production of the company's product. To our eyes, the building appears as stark, as simple, and as primitively beautiful as it did in 1938. It could have been built only in a day that boasted of the essentially simple lines of its complex macadam

Church and Dwight factory, 1938.

parkways and cloverleafs, its bridges, and the massive, concrete dams of TVA.

"We achieve a high degree of simplicity because we are a primitive people," the designer Walter Dorwin Teague wrote in 1939. "We have reverted again to a primitive state of human development. We are primitives in this new machine age. We have no developed history behind us to use in our artistic creations. We have no theories, no vocabulary of ornament, behind us to use in our work. That is why so much of our modern work today has a certain stark and simple quality that relates it very closely to the primitive work of Greece and the primitive work of Egypt and the primitive work of most people who were discovering their techniques and their tools.''

''We should be very careful to deny ourselves the luxury of decoration in the things that we do,'' Teague cautioned, ''because we have no decoration today that is significant to us, that has a meaning. The Greeks, in their great day, in the design of the Parthenon, had at their command a vocabulary of ornament that they had inherited through years of work, that had become significant to them and was very useful in the creation of their internal rhythm. *But we have no ornament.''*

He was correct, of course. But the absence of an ornament for the modern day did not mean that lesser minds could not find one. And find one they did. Washing machines and apartment house façades, typewriters and gas pumps, space heaters and vacuum cleaners yielded their new unbroken surfaces to the strange cult of the ''three little lines,'' three parallel lines intended to suggest ''modernity'' to the consumer, three parallel lines marring surfaces everywhere in America. Few objects of the '30s escaped the plague of this unholy trinity, suggesting one reason why the Depression Modern

Interior of bar-lounge car, designed by Raymond Loewy for the Pennsylvania Railroad, 1936.

style is so frequently, and incorrectly, mistaken for the modernistic dilution of Art Deco. But these lines were far more than the modernistic zigzag gone straight. They were intended as a catch-all ornament for a day which rightly had no ornament.

Teague and his colleagues Norman Bel Geddes, Raymond Loewy, George Sakier, Russel Wright, Lurelle Guild, Eleanor LeMaire, and many others called themselves industrial designers, the very term ''decorator'' having become associated, pejoratively, with the effete luxuriousness of the antediluvian past. Most of them believed in ''the rhythm of design,'' in the idea that the design of a period reflected, unconsciously, the spirit of an age. And in this belief they were undoubtedly correct. For it is a characteristic of any period that all of its creations have a certain family resemblance, an underlying unity of form which does not spring uniquely from the imagination of the artist, but rather reflects the surrounding world and especially the prevailing modes of production. The world of the 1930s was especially fond of a particular line, a curved line, recurring again and again, a line with a sharp parabolic curve at the end, which it called the ''streamline.'' And it was the streamline which contemporary designers considered the characteristic ''rhythm'' of the age.

Streamlining, of course, had begun with the modern world's love of high speed. It was an attempt to increase the speed of moving mechanical objects by removing as many wind-deflecting obstacles as possible, designers having studied and observed the sleek, ovoid body of the porpoise and the unbroken surface of the teardrop. The first airplanes, trains, and automobiles had been vertical box-like affairs. By 1933, however, the modern streamlined ideal was the ovoid, gliding form and the smooth, continuous, unbroken surface of gleaming steel bodies. The speed of these new, sleek, streamlined vehicles caught the imagination of the public from the first display of the Burlington Zephyr at the Chicago World's Fair. And the subsequent appearance, throughout the decade, of other streamlined trains and ships and planes and motorcars made for lively page-one tabloid copy and for exciting footage in Paramount and Movie-tone newsreels. Americans, then even more than now, lived vicariously.

Streamlining, ultimately, became the vogue—and a way of marketing items which were never designed with speed in mind. Furniture and clothing, clocks and typewriters, electric irons and toasters, even false teeth and coffins, were hawked to Depression consumers as "streamlined," even though, with the possible exception of coffins, none was designed to transport its owner anywhere, at any speed. Although we may easily ridicule the commercial perversion of the streamline theory as typical of an age that was considerably less than golden, the streamline vogue was nevertheless an inherent reflection of the spirit of the decade. "Now, one reason why we are streamlining so many things today," Teague wrote in 1939, "things which will never move and have no excuse for being streamlined in the sense that they need to be adapted to the flow of air currents, is simply because of the dynamic quality of the line which occurs in streamline forms, and it is characteristic of our age. We are a primitive age, a dynamic people, and we respond only to the expressions of tensions, of vigor, of energy. And this line occurs constantly throughout our bodies—a muscular male body or a beautifully formed female body."

Teague's words, so simple and direct, suggest the WPA murals then being painted in post offices, courthouses, and other public buildings throughout America: graphic panoplies, symbolic mosaics of ocean liners and airplanes, of bridges and highways, of iron foundries and assembly lines, and, everywhere, the muscular figures of bare-chested men and Amazonian women, workers all for material prosperity and the national good.

No. Depression America adopted simple forms not as an escape from its complex age, but, rather, as a celebration of it.

"New ideas," our St. Paul schoolgirl had written, "demand new materials." And if Art Deco had plundered the riches of the world in its pursuit of luxury, if it had doted on amboyna and ivory and shagreen, on rare fabrics and even rarer woods, then Depression Modern, in its pursuit of the elegantly simple, of the direct and the useful, created its own materials. And most of them were machine-made. For the 1930s was, above all, a decade of alloys and of steel, of plastics and of glass. No wonder documentary films of the time favored montages to symbolize the mechanical progress of America: molten metals and blazing furnaces, whirring presses and hair-netted assembly-line women, gushing oil wells, and Brobdingnagian reapers decimating amber fields of grain—God, as it were, crowning the nation's good with Prosperity and ball bearings.

If the Depression had produced a Walt Whitman to catalogue its sights and sounds, its movement and its spirit, the poet would have heard a new America singing. And singing a new song—its vocabulary a scramble of Latin and Greek suffixes and chemical terms, its words as synthetic as the substances they describe, a litany to the scientific wonders of the age. Celluloid, Pyralin, Fiberloid, and Nixonoid for combs and buckles, buttons and dresser sets. Tenite, Plastacele, and Lumarith for lamp shades, watch crystals, bathroom accessories, fountain pens, and eyeglass frames. Ameroid for cigarette holders, chessmen, buttons, ashtrays, and piano keys. Vinylite for floor tile, toothbrushes, synthetic glass, and steering wheels. Coltrock and Bakelite, Durez and Durite, Insurok and Indur, Makalot and Resinox, Textolite and Arcolite for clocks and automobile parts, telephone instruments and typewriter parts, door knobs, kettle handles, radio cases, and electrical parts. Catalin, Marblette, Ivaleur, and Fiberloid for costume jewelry, cutlery handles, buttons, buckles, knobs, and rods of synthetic glass. Micarta, Formica, Textolite, Lamicoid, Panelyte, Insurok, Synthane, Dilecto, Phenolite, and Spauldite for store fronts, table tops, radiator covers, paneled walls, doors, sink tops, and automobile parts.

And in the world of glass there were Aklo and Tuf-flex, Vitrolux and Thermolux, Thermopane and Vitrolite, Glastone and Extrudalite. Heat-absorbing glass and sculptured glass. Tempered and laminated glass. Fiber glass and ultra-violet glass. Invisible glass and one-way glass. Colored mirror glass in peach and blue, in gunmetal and gold. And, above all, there was glass block. Everywhere.

Used abroad for many years, particularly in Holland, glass block (sometimes called brick) won a rather belated acceptance in the United States by 1935, becoming, finally, the most firmly established material of modern building, in part because

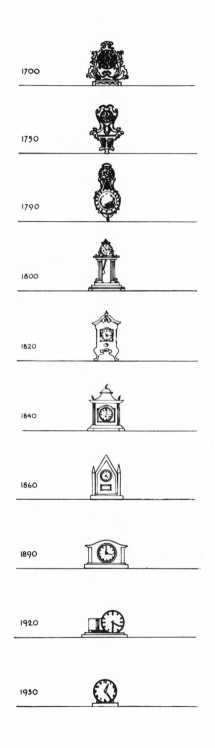

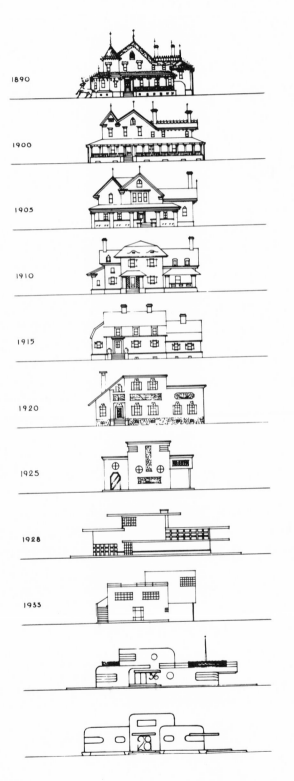

1890
1900
1905
1910
1915
1920
1925
1928
1933

it lent itself less readily to stylistic adaptations than any building material that had yet appeared. Its very existence demanded a "modern" setting. Used as wall or window, as inner partition or simple decoration, for bar or soda fountain, and even (for the fanciful) in furniture, glass block gave translucence without visibility, light with little heat transmission (making it perfect for America's first air-conditioned buildings), effective sound insulation, and low maintenance costs since it required no finish.

In the late 1930s, America's leading manufacturer of glass block publicized its product in trade magazines by building a glass Depression Modern playhouse, a veritable fantasy of Insulux, for Shirley Temple. In magazine advertisements that must have startled conservative architects, the dimpled moppet was shown, trowel in pudgy hand, building a towering glass-block structure, her smile of easy childish confidence antedating the Castro Convertible girl by at least a decade. Glass block, enormously popular in its day, vanished from the scene at about the same time that Shirley Temple did. But both, like them or not, were hallmarks of their age.

In metals and plastics, in cork and glass—new materials for new ideas. And even old materials were re-explored to serve the new: wood and nickel, aluminum and leather providing texture, grain, vibration, glint, and glow—all necessary for an art that preferred no ornamentation if it were to be considered new. Let us not for a minute underestimate the American public's fascination with things new and inventive. Let us not forget Barnum's fable of the Egress. Cellophane, a sensation when exhibited at Chicago's Century of Progress Exposition in 1933, was no less exciting six years later when used in a publicity stunt that could have taken place in no other decade. To celebrate the opening of the first community of

Levitt houses on Long Island, and, of course, to promote sales, the entire chorus line of Broadway's *Babes in Arms* appeared in force, each with a pair of enormous scissors, to inaugurate a shiny, new model home. It had been wrapped, from top to bottom, in cellophane. An enormous, glittering gift-wrapped package, topped with a huge plastic bow. And this while Christo was still in rompers. In 1939 they called it a publicity stunt. Today we call it art.

Mass education in America, especially on the college level, has produced a cultural game for our times, a game, for lack of a better name, called "Associations." And this has come about because postgraduate cultural life is little more than a random, but never-ending, short-answer quiz, a continuation of art and literature and music served up raw in textbooks and in lecture halls, the mass regurgitated and ill-digested. The mark of an educated man today is measured by his ability to come up with the right set of "associations" or responses to a given list of artists' names, identifying in turn the artist's field and, for extra points, the titles of his works. According to the rules of the game, if one can name an author and match him with the titles of his books, one is, ipso facto, educated—whether one has read the author's work or not.

Most of us have more than once overheard the game in progress, or even innocently participated in it, over drinks at the country club, or at a cocktail party, or while queuing up to see the latest trendy Mel Brooks film. We've heard it over restaurant tables, or at the office coffee machine, or amid the babble and chatter of TV talk shows. "Picasso," one bored man says to another. "Modern artist—*Guernica*," the other responds, equally bored. Ten points and another sip of scotch. "Debussy." "French composer—*La Mer*." Fifteen points and back to the golf game. "Ingmar Bergman." "Swedish director. Very interesting." Five points: incomplete, but cogent; accurate and masterfully concise. And so it goes, the names changing every season to remain in touch with the ins and outs of popular culture. "Art Deco." "The 1930s."

Ask any hundred educated Americans the names of two important designers of modern furniture (or even one) and chances are that thirty will be able to do so. And, of those thirty, twenty-nine will almost certainly mention Le Corbusier, Marcel Breuer, or Mies van der Rohe, Europeans all. The chance is probably zero that anyone will bring up the names of the American designers Donald Deskey, Gilbert Rohde, Kem Weber, or Russel Wright. And this is only natural in a culture which sees itself, still, as stepchild to its Continental masters.

The formidable accomplishments of Mies, Breuer, and Corbu notwithstanding, this native inferiority complex is indeed a pity. For at the very time in which the superb creations of the three Europeans were being meticulously handcrafted for a small, but discriminating clientele, Deskey's metal-tubing chairs were already being turned out by the thousands at a Grand Rapids factory, and the other three

Americans were in the process of designing mass-produced furniture of sound proportion, simple finish, and structural integrity—furniture that would radically change the appearance of the American home, and in numbers that would have astonished the European designers. In the conception of their furniture, neither Deskey, nor Weber, nor Rohde, nor Wright had been directly influenced by European models, and all four were attempting nothing less than the creation of a modern American style.

Of the four, the most versatile was Donald Deskey, his life a continuous round of inventive genius, interrupted only by retirement at the age of 80. Those who glibly play "Associations," if they know his name at all, will respond invariably with the fact that Deskey had designed the interiors of Radio City Music Hall. An achievement, to be sure. But only one, and hardly the most important, in a career spanning more than five decades.

Some day a book will be written about Deskey, his life and his accomplishments, and it will have as its title, one hopes, *Contemporary American,* an apt description of the man himself and also the punch line of a frequently told, but true, story about him—a story which tells us worlds about the goals of modern American design in its early days. Already famous at the age of thirty, Deskey, in the late 1920s, had created for a conservative manufacturer a modern room in which revolutionary use had been made of cork, asbestos, glass, and metal, the total effect of which was extremely simple. A visitor, shown Deskey's room, his eyes open wide with astonishment, commented with surprise on the manufacturer's sudden interest in "the new modern style." "That's not modern style," the manufacturer replied, "that's good contemporary American."

Good contemporary American. This was the ideal not only of Donald Deskey, but of the entire movement of Depression Modern, an ideal seeking expression in architecture and in machinery, in transportation and in furnishings—an ideal implying honesty, and simplicity, and functional expressiveness. And it had its most demonstrable impact, perhaps, in home furnishings—in accessories and, especially, in the design of modern American furniture.

In periods of transition, such as that of the Great Depression, it takes considerable time for the changes wrought in social and economic life to find a general expression in the arts. It is, in fact, a basic law that the creative expression of an era must conform to the general development of that period. The creative artist, after all, senses new directions long before the public becomes aware of them, and he realizes that the new and contemporary expression in art only reflects the change in modes of living in which each individual himself takes active part. For this reason, at the threshold of a new era, Americans, in the first years of the Great Depression, found themselves with an already well-developed modern outlook toward life, one born of economic necessity, but with a correspondingly conservative inclination toward modern art.

As a consequence, then, Depression Modern did not take hold over night. It was through small things, through accessories—through glassware, pottery, metalware, table linens, and woodenware—that modern design found its first wide-scale success in America. The repeal of Prohibition in 1933, perhaps more than any other single event, led multitudes of Americans to the back door of contemporary design. It introduced Americans—and particularly the American woman—to the new social institution of the cocktail hour, an event for which designers created the cocktail shaker, the ice bucket, the snack tray, and an assortment of inventions deemed necessary for enjoying the new pastime. Drinking, for America, became superbly modern, and most of its new forms reflected good contemporary design. Once invaded, the American home was vulnerable. And as it became increasingly populated with ultra-modern ice tongs and cheese boards, pitchers and ashtrays, all created of shimmering new materials, all as modern as Amelia Earhart, the next logical place in which Depression Modern could succeed was in the world of American furniture itself.

The average American couple, beginning married life in the early '30s, bought a suite of machine-made bedroom furniture, decorated most frequently in mock Tudor or Stuart or Italian Renaissance style. Characterized by indifferent design, poor construction, and even poorer materials, such suites were known in the trade, with more than just a little contempt, as "borax"—a wonderful American term that has all but vanished from the language. Because hawkers of the then-famous cleanser, Twenty Mule Team Borax, had offered as free premiums cheap and garish kitsch, the word "borax" came to be associated with the "extra" values offered by commercial furniture manufacturers: "extra" carving, "extra" large-size frames, "extra" glossy finish.

For more than three generations in America, from furniture showroom to the pages of Montgomery Ward, one bought a "suite" of furniture, more frequently pronounced "suit." For more than three generations, a bedroom suite consisted of a dresser, a vanity, a chest, and a bed. A dining room suite consisted of a buffet, a china closet, a server, a table, and six chairs. Regardless of the change in the life or tastes of the people, borax or refined, the form remained essentially the same, year in and year out. Manufacturers put Chippendale ornament on a dresser and called it Chippendale, despite the fact that Chippendale had never designed anything even vaguely resembling a

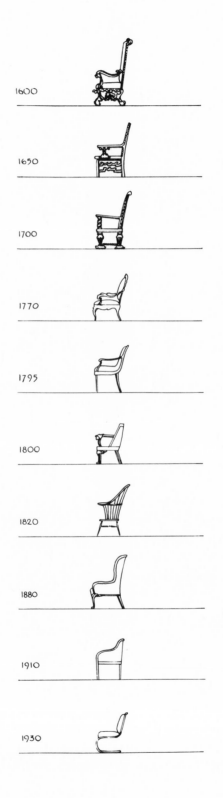

1600

1650

1700

1770

1795

1800

1820

1880

1910

1930

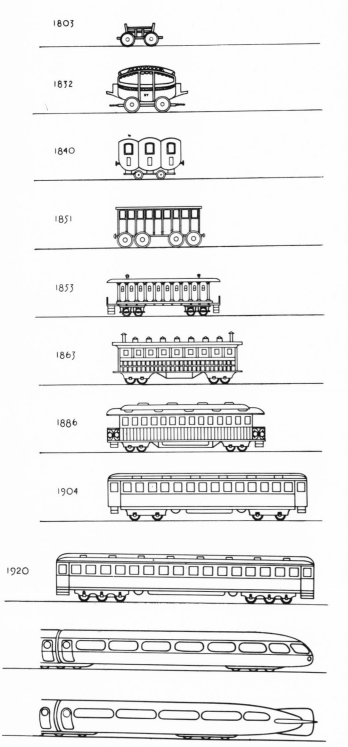

1803

1832

1840

1851

1853

1863

1886

1904

1920

dresser. On the same basic form they put Spanish, or Adam, or Queen Anne decoration, and changed the name of the style accordingly. By changing the faces on the same chassis, they had borax, or highly ornate, or any period style the public wanted. But then came the Great Depression, and, with it, its all-embracing revolution in design.

With every major change in economics or political life has come a new period in furniture. And the Depression brought no exception to the rule. America was in a new economic and political era, and styles were changing all about it. By 1933, the same pattern we have already witnessed was forcefully in progress: designs, once created exclusively for the wealthy in the late '20s, were being mass-produced inexpensively for the common man of the '30s. What visitors to the Century of Progress Exposition witnessed in the year in which FDR replaced Hoover was a dynamic demonstration of a new artistic principle: a New Deal, as it were, for the world of American design—a belief, almost religious in its fervor, that modern design could be a means of improving the quality of contemporary life. What fairgoers saw was something as new in furniture as the Burlington Zephyr had been in transportation. Modern American furniture, although it never ceased completely to be sold in suites, was now being offered in individual pieces that could be grouped or fitted into the needs of the newer, smaller, servantless, more efficient American home. In the highly commercial world of mass-produced furniture, the interchangeable unit, the modular, the sectional—that which we so take for granted today—was finally born.

The appearance of sectional furniture offered flexibility to a depressed industry and economy to a consumer who could now only infrequently afford the purchase of an entire matching suite. Early in the decade, Gilbert Rohde created for the

Herman Miller Furniture Company a complete "plan for comfortable living," which featured small units that could be combined and rearranged into innumerable schemes of interior decoration, making a good deal of variety possible on a single investment, and including chests designed intelligently as ensembles so that the consumer could use one, two, or three to fit any wall space. At about the same time, in 1933, Russel Wright's many-sided furniture and three-piece sectional sofas for Heywood-Wakefield illustrated the identical principle of functional versatility.

If any one person in the '30s best represents Depression Modern as more than just a commercial development, but as a social force straining for a better home for a happier people, then it is Russel Wright. And no other designer of the period more clearly represents the contemporary quest for a modern native-American style. His address before the New York Fashion Group in 1938 reveals his vision in all the forcefulness of its youthful vigor. In it, he tells the wonderful story of how, in having visited the handsome Bauhaus exhibit at the Museum of Modern Art a few days before, he had bumped into a German acquaintance, who accused American designers of being artistically backward. They were backward, he declared, because their work consisted entirely of copies of designs that had been executed in Germany years ago. Wright, as he tells the story, quietly fumed, his blood reaching the boiling point:

> My thoughts raced backward over personal experiences. Years of learning that Europe was the source of all culture. And then of finally going to Europe, rejoicing and reveling in the treasures there. Years of learning to talk in parrot fashion about Old World charm and New World barbarism. And then at last my sudden discovery as I looked again at our skyscrapers—our buildings and streets, our fat farm buildings, our gleaming rivers of traffic that I had not seen for months. I realized that America does have a very definite character of its own—that in all that we make here is a distinct visual pattern decidedly different from anything Europe does. Although our work is usually crude and raw, we seem to have our own conception of scale and it is grander than the European conception; our use of form is bolder and more vital; our use of color is distinctly our own.
>
> Why, then, must our museums and our art schools and our press and our critics still look to Europe; why must Europe always be advanced to us as the criterion? Why must our designers and our artists suffer most of their lives under the handicap of America's inferiority complex? Why don't they look around them? . . .
>
> Why can't someone, a Museum of Modern Art or a New York World's Fair, put on an exhibit in which they would dramatize all design that is American? First, let them parade those unconscious developments free from any aesthetic inferiority complexes. Our bridges. Our roads. Our factory machinery. Our skyscrapers. Let them throw a spotlight on our shining bathrooms and our efficient kitchens. Roll out our trick cocktail gadgets—our streamlined iceboxes—our streamlined pencil sharpeners. Let them show our electric light bulbs on white velvet like jewels. The work of Frank Lloyd Wright. Our gasoline stations. Our movie theatres. Our cafeterias. No matter how vulgar they are. Our handsome business machines. Our sport clothes. Our particular brand of shooting galleries and barber shops. Our gleaming fat automobiles. Then let them arrange our home furnishings in this parade. Let them put a magnifying glass (if they feel they need it) over these things to find the American character. But I am sure that they will not need it for the continuity of character will then become apparent. Let them do this without recourse to European standards in their selection. It has never been done. But I know that they will find that there is a distinct American character of design in all that is American and that our home furnishings *tie in to this character.* Not until then, will we know of what elements this American character consists.
>
> Rid yourselves of the American inferiority complex, forget European standards, look at the American scene, and *have more respect for it.*

Russel Wright, then only thirty-four years old, was speaking from long, personal experience, as the creator of "American Modern," a unique line of furniture—the most popular produced during the Depression, and the one that made his name a commonplace in tens of thousands of American homes.

"American Modern" furniture, created first in 1935 for the Conant-Ball Company and popularized by R. H. Macy, was an almost immediate commercial success. It grew out of Wright's long-stated belief that America had to reject European tradition in order to relate the functional modern style, so prevalent abroad, to its own needs. In forcing himself to examine these American needs, he determined that Americans, faced with a raging economic Depression, were working out new ways of living and in so doing were eliminating the useless and the invalid values of an outmoded culture. In trying to simplify their lives, Americans were trying to become more efficient. And of their new surroundings they were now demanding honest value, simplicity, sturdiness, and new innovations pertaining to comfort. These, he believed, were the basic requisites of American taste. Because of its mechanical facility, because of its dominant spirit of enterprise and its basic lack of Old World tradition, America was ripe for the development of a national style. And Wright's contribution to this style was his famous line of "American Modern" furniture—a line followed in succession by fabrics, bedspreads, lamps, table linen, china, glass, and giftware, all bearing the same name or its later variant, as war broke out in Europe, the "American Way."

"American Modern" bedroom, 1935.

Attempting to discover modern design of inherently American character, Wright turned to maple—the wood of the pioneer forefathers, which, because of its availability, strength, and hard surface, had been used since colonial times for furniture making. But it was not until 1935, and the advent of "American Modern," that maple came into its own for contemporary furniture. Wright's use of solid lumber uncovered by veneer helped not only to bring down production costs for modern furniture, but tended also to provide for greater freedom of design, facilitating, for instance, the rounded or cushion edge which became, ultimately, one of the identifying features of 1930s furniture. His return to full, hardy craftsmanlike forms gave his maple designs great adaptability to a large number of American homes, enabling "American Modern" to fit compactly into a small apartment or to be used more expansively in larger homes.

Wright was largely responsible, too, for the enormous popularity of light-colored woods in the '30s, for, with his "American Modern," he was the first to use a bleached maple finish for commercial furniture, calling it (at his wife's suggestion) "blonde," a term which became almost synonymous with American furniture of the late '30s and which paved the way for the invasion of "Swedish Modern" that ended the decade.

The "American Modern" line, in units that could be purchased separately and inexpensively, included living room, sunroom, dinette, and bedroom furniture. With its curves and flowing lines, this innovative furniture broke away completely from the geometric, packing-box type of modern so common at the beginning of the decade, nonetheless fulfilling the basic precepts of modern design, its careful proportions following the basic requirements of use and comfort. Russel Wright's "American Modern" furniture, perhaps more successfully than any other design of the decade, attempted to break out of the confining straightjacket of imitated European modernism, creating in its place a modern furniture with a strong affinity for the American home. If Wright believed that he had succeeded in creating a basic "American Modern" design, then thousands of Americans agreed with him.

Inevitably, their children and grandchildren thought otherwise. For "American Modern," and its many imitators, can be found now, battered and worn, in thriftshops and Salvation Army stores all over the nation.

Main Street. Any small city, U.S.A. The present.

The street lies bare, littered, crumbling. Its buildings, boarded and deserted, await the wrecker's ball, the looter's sack. In days or weeks, the sun will shine for the first time in half a century on three-story buildings a block away. In two years, or maybe three, a ribbon of highway, cars and trucks breathing fumes of black carbon, will bisect the city, its traffic passing from here to there, from there to here, as if the city no longer existed. These are the streamlined cars of yesterday. And this is its Main Street.

The Superette, where food stamps lately marked the closing of the city's aerosol-spray plant, was once The Gem, where posters, advertising *Rosemarie* and "Wednesday Bank Night," were affixed to green Micarta walls. Beneath the grit-encrusted glass block of the padlocked Erin Bar & Grill lie the cracked shards of Vitrolite, black and shattered. A group of squatters, patient until the end, play dominoes on ancient wooden milk crates before the storefront *Iglesia de Jesus,* once Gus's Bake Shop and, in 1933, the first "modern" store in town, its remodeled façade of stainless steel and glass superimposed upon the dull red brick of a late-Victorian building. And then the Carlton-Pickwick Restaurant, its elegant Thermolux and Formica interiors and its flesh-tinted rounded mirrors long ago replaced by the simulated stone, brick, and wood of a later day—all three textures falsely plastic and all grotesquely mixed, beneath fake colonial chandeliers, in the anarchistic style of the 1960s.

The Carlton-Pickwick. Gus's Bake Shop. The Gem. This might have been the very street on which my parents strolled the night they decided to marry and to face the Depression together more than forty years ago.

My mother and father, like America's Main Street, like the Broadway of Thornton Wilder's *Our Town*, are dead. America, always careless of its past, has been particularly cruel to the authentic heritage of the Depression, never, after all, having really loved it, never having wanted to be reminded of it. It has been abandoned to the modern carrion—to the romantics, to the distorters, to the collectors of kitsch.

The odd mirror-covered building on Times Square, its blue-tinted glass once reflecting the excitement of the Crossroads of the World, is like the windows of Ecclesiastes—blind, unseeing—its glass long ago shattered into thousands of pieces. Curtain time on the new Broadway is no longer at 8:30. And the theater where *Our Town* opened on February 4, 1938, Henry Miller's Theater, is now a hardcore pornographic movie house, late shows Friday and Saturday at midnight.

My parents lie dead, buried beneath a stone which my mother had designed at my father's death, never herself having lived to see its completion. Surrounding them, so unlike the graveyard scene in *Our Town*, with its black umbrellas and its dead conversing from wooden folding chairs, are the tombstones of my family—cold marble, bearing names existing only in memory and faces recorded in the fading pictures of my family album. An aunt, whom I had never known, murdered at fourteen in 1932. A second-cousin, the victim of meningitis, dead at eight in 1933. The bearded old man, for whom I'm named, asleep since 1937. My father's father, one of thousands struck down in 1918 by the influenza epidemic, and the first to be buried in the crowded cemetery from a motor-driven hearse, the single greatest distinction of his thirty-seven years, and the only fact that I have ever learned of his history in my thirty-seven years. And, standing like mute soldiers in row on silent row, the graves of others, whose eerie oval photographs, mounted under glass upon their 1920s stones, continually walk the corridors of my childhood dreams.

So strange to notice that these gravestones, like everything else in the coldly material world, bear the signs and symbols of the times in which they were made. How odd and grimly humorous, that death, like life, should observe the vogues and fashions of the day. The stone of 1932, probably already old-fashioned when it was chosen by a Depression family grieving for its youngest child so cruelly slain, is clearly modernistic, a vertical ziggurat in black and gray, its angular lines celebrating the suddenness of earthly loss. My grandfather's stone is nondescript, a borrowing of the classical and traditional, as eclectic as anything created in that final year of World War I, sentimental but cold, a monument to the ubiquity of death. My namesake's gravestone, curved and white, a simple and direct marker for a simple man, is plainly Depression Modern, its graceful lines suggesting the infiniteness of eternal rest.

But, as I look upon this 1937 stone, so sleek (dare I say streamlined?), I smile in recognition of its single ornament, three slender parallel lines. The cult of the unholy trinity. It has left its mark upon my namesake's grave and, hence, on me.

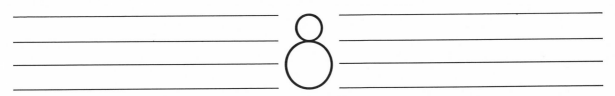

August 12, 1939. The pages of *The New Yorker*. The sophisticated column, "The Talk of the Town."

Looking at one of the newer buses, streamlined to cleave the trade winds that sweep Fifth Avenue, we wondered again what another generation will think of the bogus functionalism which seems to be the keynote of our own. We can remember our grandmother's house quite clearly. Outside, it was an atrocity of scrollwork and irrelevant turrets; inside, a dim museum in which animal and vegetable matter decayed quietly and respectably, under glass; altogether it was the typical house of its time. It was absurd, but it was saved from vulgarity by its innocence, and we still think of it with affection; and, because its furnishings were always rational though often hideous, we can easily imagine what it would have been like to live there. This nostalgia, we feel, is going to be a little harder for the grandchildren of many of our contemporaries. How to account, except by a sort of mass insanity, for a generation that designed everything, from automobiles to alarm clocks, to buffet a hypothetical tornado? How to picture one's ancestors, warm and alive, in all that steely symmetry? It is inevitable that the American home, in its current design, will presently come to be regarded as old-fashioned, but it is hard to believe that it will be remembered with love or pleasure. If your grandchildren think of you at all, surrounded by your bright, functional toys, it will be with terror or dislike, as a madman or stranger.

August 12, 1939. The very same page of *The New Yorker*. The very same sophisticated column ridicules with polite laughter an installment of Chester Gould's *Dick Tracy,* in which "the last picture shows the villains, a couple of fake European ambassadors, discovering a secret message concealed in the olive of a Martini cocktail." *O tempora! O mores!* How Watergate has stilled the laughter of such ridicule.

As H. L. Mencken once observed, "The prophesying business is like writing fugues; it is fatal to everyone save the man of absolute genius."

Let it suffice that no one on the distinguished *New Yorker* staff ever wrote a fugue.

Terror and dislike? Madmen and strangers? Hardly. Let the pages that follow speak of love and pleasure.

THE THIRTIES STYLE IN AMERICA

AN ALBUM

Design of the 1930s, from painting and sculpture to architecture and home furnishings, had its most important basis in the widely varied elements of American industry. The structures most closely related to industry, therefore, represent the peak of Depression architecture, factories in particular illustrating the contemporary trend toward simplicity and directness.

Among the most distinguished and extraordinary of American modern industrial buildings were those designed and constructed by The Austin Company of Cleveland, Ohio, whose advertisements in *Fortune* magazine throughout the Great Depression stood out above all others in their stunning—even startling—modernity. The Austin Company's structures of the 1930s remain to this day magnificent archetypes of the functional Depression Modern style. To see one is to experience in a moment the very "feel" of the period. The architectural models pictured here were constructed between 1936 and 1939.

Built in 1937, the Hecht Company warehouse, Washington, D.C. (above), and the Campana Sales Company factory, Batavia, Illinois (center), won mention in the prestigious Pittsburgh Glass Institute competition of that year. In the warehouse, glass block functions as wall and window, while, in the factory, it is effectively combined with terra-cotta facing. The warehouse was designed by Abbot, Merkt & Co.; the factory, by Childs & Smith and Frank D. Chase, associated architects.

Research laboratory of American Rolling Mill Co. (*above*), Middletown, Ohio, design and construction by The Austin Company, 1937.

Municipal Incinerator (*opposite page, right*), Shreveport, Louisiana, Jones, Roessle, Olschner, & Wiener, architects, 1935. The first building of its kind planned by architects. *Right* (*below*): Grain Elevators, W. K. Kellogg Co., Battle Creek, Michigan, Albert Kahn, architect, 1938.

Johnson & Johnson's Industrial Tape Building (*top*), New Brunswick, New Jersey, R. G. and W. M. Cory, architects, 1940. *Center:* Wyatt Clinic and Research Laboratories Building, Tucson, Arizona, Leland W. King, Jr., architect, 1935. *Right:* Forest Products Laboratory, Madison, Wisconsin, Holabird & Root, architects, 1933.

While most industries were foundering during the Great Depression, radio was burgeoning. In 1936, NBC constructed the "latest" in studios for its Hollywood station. It was outmoded before it was occupied. Its replacement, in 1938, was The Austin Company's "Radio City of the West" (*left*). Not to be outrivaled, CBS engaged the architect William Lescaze to design its Hollywood studios (*above, top*), completed in 1938, one year after its KNX transmitter (*above*) opened in the same city.

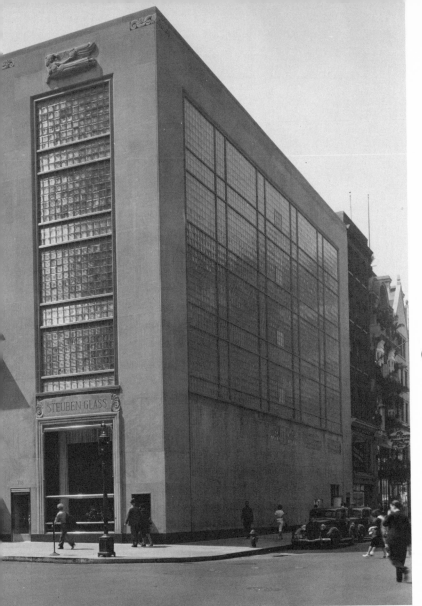

Corning-Steuben Building (*left*), New York City, 1937. In the structure and decoration of this building, designed by William & Geoffrey Platt and John M. Gates, the company's own products were utilized to the fullest extent: of the limestone walls which enclose the offices, 80% of the area is in glass block.

Right: In the same period in which glass was being used to great dramatic effect in the entrance lobbies of their buildings in New York's Rockefeller Center, Harrison & Fouilhoux designed General Electric's WGY Broadcasting Station in Schenectady, New York, completed in 1938. The façade (*below*), functional but warm, combined the use of red brick and glass block with chromium.

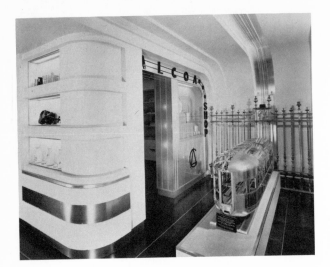

Expressive of the tension, vigor, and energy of a new age, the curve became the most dynamic characteristic of the 1930s style. Found everywhere—in shop and showroom, hotel and public building—the curve suggested the streamline, hence modernity, to the American consumer.

Completed in 1936, Lurelle Guild's Alcoa Showroom in New York City (*above*), advertised aluminum not merely in the products displayed, but in the structure itself: lighting fixtures, furniture, and display stands were all built of aluminum. *Below:* Raymond Loewy's design for New York City's Cushman's was the model for similar bake shops in cities and towns throughout America.

The Cataract Hotel (*above*), in Sioux Falls, South Dakota, designed by Harold Spitznagel in 1937, featured a lavish use of curves in its lobby, particularly in the entrance to its restaurant and cocktail lounge.

Below: Designed in 1937, Reinhard Hofmeister's two branch offices of the Chase National Bank in Rockefeller Center were circular banking rooms, with terrazzo counters and platform rails running in an unbroken line, and circular domes overhead providing troughs for reflector lights.

The Meyercord Company, a manufacturer of decalcomanias, opened its glass block office building in Chicago in 1938, decorating its interiors with its own products—notably in different patterns of Sans-Marb, an imitation marble so effective that only experts could tell that it was not real. Other applications of the company's products were suggested in decorative photomurals. All interiors and furnishings were designed by Abel Faidy; the building itself, by Julius Floto.

Three views of a combined living room—dining room—clients' reception room in Russel Wright's New York penthouse studio and apartment, 1934. The room was furnished entirely with special pieces, each experimental in character, and each serving multiple functions. Designed, in part, as a proving ground for furniture prior to commercial production, the studio illustrates Wright's principles of maximum flexibility of use.

Designed by Raymond Loewy and Lee Simonson for the 1934 Contemporary American Industrial Arts Exposition at New York's Metropolitan Museum of Art and planned to show that an office should be adapted to its function, this industrial designer's office and studio (*below*), intentionally resembles a clinic: a place where things are examined, studied, and diagnosed. It was constructed almost entirely of ivory formica and gunmetal.

Designed by Abel Faidy in 1936 for America's most innovative architectural photographers, the Hedrich-Blessing studio in Chicago featured a mirrored wall which doubled the apparent size of the reception room and reflected the photomural of the studio's work, then a radical decorative departure.

The private office (*opposite*), echoes the dramatic quality of the reception room. High and narrow, it emphasizes the proportions by a strip of photographs and by low, simple furniture. Because of its creative use of glass, the Hedrich-Blessing studio won the grand prize in the Pittsburgh Glass Institute competition of 1937.

A champion of good modern design, Henry Luce's Time Incorporated helped to popularize the idea of economic recovery through the creation of American functional objects, Luce's *Architectural Forum* remaining to this day the best pictorial record of excellent Depression Modern design. *Left:* Three views of Time Inc.'s conference room and reception areas, New York City, 1937.

In 1937, the architect William Lescaze designed rooms (*left and below*) for Time, featuring seating for interviews arranged in small sections and a receptionist's desk protected from cross-drafts by a glass screen tilted to avoid reflection.

Although only a small, local radio station, KSOO in Sioux Falls, South Dakota, required the same sound insulation needed by the large radio networks. In 1937, architect Harold Spitznagel, employing glass block and plate glass functionally and decoratively, produced the clean and efficient design pictured here.

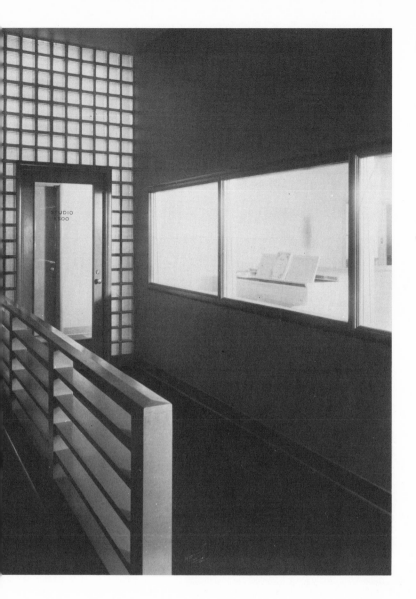

The Sioux Falls architectural office that Spitznagel designed for himself in 1937 (*right*), featured what was probably the only glass block desk in America—and certainly the only one that was illuminated from within. Stark Venetian blinds on curtainless windows were already a cliché of modernism in America.

The Johnson Wax Administration Building—designed for the Racine, Wisconsin, company by Frank Lloyd Wright in 1937—is admittedly a work of architectural genius, but it is as well reflective of the period in which it was planned. Its flowing curves and horizontality identify it clearly as a work of the late '30s. From the floor of its large room for typists rise slender white concrete columns that taper from nine inches at the base to eighteen-foot disks at the ceiling. Between these circles falls natural light through patterned glass-tube skylights. Wright designed all the original furniture for the building, including the three-legged chairs, which tip over if the typist does not sit with correct posture.

Office furniture designed for Herman Miller, Inc., by Gilbert Rohde, 1936.

This almost casual-looking furniture (*below*), was designed in 1939 by Edward Durell Stone for the penthouse offices of Simon & Schuster, New York publishers. Stone, having created an all-glass office pavilion down the center of a building rooftop in Rockefeller Center, designed light furniture especially conducive to its setting.

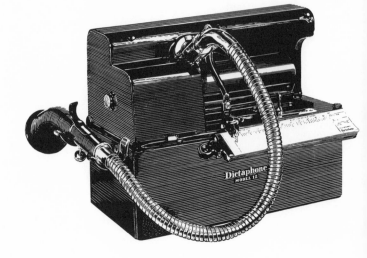

The general trend of greater simplicity and directness is reflected in the variety and improved appearance of business machines in the 1930s. As the decade progressed, such machinery grew sleeker and more horizontal. The 1933 Dictaphone (*above, left*), although featuring for the first time a cover over the moving parts, revealed nevertheless a vertical bias. Six years later, re-designed by Raymond Loewy, the "Cameo" model (*above, right*) was ten pounds lighter and decidedly more horizontal.

When, in 1933, Raymond Loewy re-designed the 1929 Gestetner duplicating machine (*below, left*), he created a functionally formed useful product (*below, right*), which was smoothly encased, its corners rounded off and its projections sheared away. The result was a new appearance of simplicity, efficiency, and attractiveness.

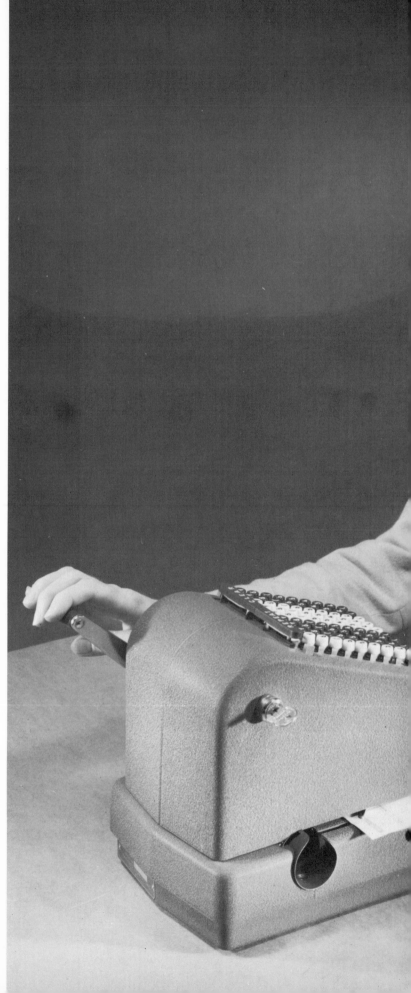

A late '30s model
of the Todd "Protectograph" check writer,
designed by Henry Dreyfuss.

Streamlined chromium pencil sharpener, designed by Raymond Loewy in 1934.

The 1935 model of the desk telephone set —designed by the engineering-design department of Bell Telephone Laboratories, with the assistance of an artist-consultant and an advisory committee of artists— was offered in a variety of finishes including ivory, gray, statuary bronze, oxidized silver, and in gold.

The Southern California Gas Co. commissioned E. C. and E. W. Taylor to design a display building that would emphasize the modernity of gas as a fuel as well as the appliances for sale. Gracefully curved, with well-organized lettering (silhouetted at night against lighted panels), the Hollywood structure opened in 1937.

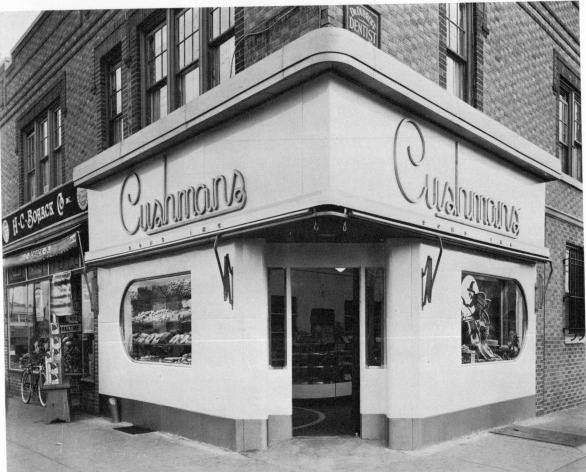

Raymond Loewy's store front for Cushman's Bake Shop in New York (1937), and its hundreds of imitations across the nation, introduced countless Americans to their first taste of "the modern."

An early example (1934) of glass and stainless steel used to remodel (and "modernize") a restaurant in Canton, Ohio. Two years later, the "Modernize Main Street" movement began as a nationwide effort to improve the depressed economy.

Opened in 1940 in Taunton, Massachusetts, and standing in sharp relief against older structures, this five-and-dime, typical of scores of Woolworth stores built during the Depression, graphically illustrates the "Modernize Main Street" movement.

The building as billboard, a '30s innovation. The Star Electric Building, Newark, New Jersey (*opposite*), designed in 1936 by Barney Sumner Gruzen.

The lobby entrance of the Rockefeller Center showroom of the National Cash Register Company, designed in 1939 by Reinhard & Hofmeister and handsomely arranged for display.

Model of rotary filling station, designed in 1934 by Raymond Loewy. As the motorist's car was driven onto the turntable, his car was serviced within two minutes with gasoline, oil, water, and air. Two of these red-white-and-blue porcelained-steel service stations were built in New York City.

The elevator bank and men's shoe department of the Wm. H. Block Co., Indianapolis, Indiana (*opposite, top*), modernized by Vonnegut, Bohn and Mueller, and Pereira and Pereira in 1934.

An unusual use of glass for the side walls of an escalator (*opposite, below*), designed in 1936 by Eleanor LeMaire for The Emporium, San Francisco, California.

John Vassos' Coca-Cola dispenser, 1933. Egmont Arens's A & P coffee packaging, 1934. Russel Wright's vending machine, 1934. Raymond Loewy's Elizabeth Arden cosmetics packaging, c. 1936.

Styled in 1937 for aviatrix-cosmetician Jacqueline Cochran and incorporating the motifs of sky-writing and revolving airplane propellers in the design, Raymond Loewy's "Wings to Beauty" cosmetics packaging (*opposite*), appealed to "contemporary-minded women" in a day before *Fear of Flying*.

Although the Depression world of streamlined transportation boasted the names of such prominent designers as Norman Bel Geddes, Henry Dreyfuss, and Otto Kuhler, Raymond Loewy's was the one best known to the American public. These visualizations of the future were executed by Loewy in 1938 as part of the exhibit on transportation at the New York World's Fair the following year. Included are a four-decker airplane, streamlined train, triple-unit truck, streamlined automobile, double-decker autobus, autotaxi, and single-masted ocean liner.

M̲ost famous of the streamlined trains of the early '30s, the Burlington Zephyr (*above*), built by the Budd Manufac-turing Company, captured the imagination of a speed-conscious America when it was first exhibited at Chicago's Century of Progress Exposition in 1934. An invitation to display it on the streets of Philadelphia, in front of the Art Alliance's Dynamic Design exhibit, was rejected the same year.

R̲aymond Loewy aboard his K4S streamlined locomotive (*opposite*), built for the Pennsylvania Railroad in 1936.

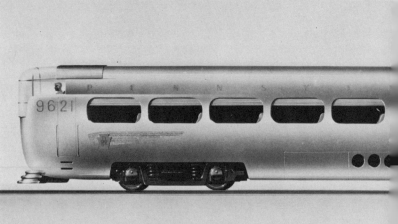

Raymond Loewy's "The Eagle" (*above, left*), a six-car, air-conditioned, streamlined train designed for the Missouri Pacific Railroad in 1938. The GG-1 electrical locomotive (*above, right*), the first butt-welded engine in the United States, designed with engineers of the Pennsylvania Railroad by Loewy in 1936.

Never built, this experimental single-unit fast-motorized commuter train (*opposite*), was designed by Loewy for the Pennsylvania Railroad in 1932. *Below:* The S-1 (*left*), designed by Loewy in collaboration with the Pennsylvania Railroad in 1937, was in its day the world's largest high-speed locomotive. Loewy's K4S (*right*), built in 1936.

The interiors of Raymond Loewy's trains reflected his belief that they should equal the standard of the modern home. *Above:* The curved interior of The Eagle's observation car, 1938. *Left:* Bar-lounge car, The Broadway Limited, 1936. Contemporary advertisements spoke of this car as "an intimate and smart club on wheels. Curved wall sections, murals, upholstered banquettes, rich carpeting, and 'sunbeam' mirrors lend distinction to travel and entertainment by rail."

Loewy's bar-lounge car, The General (*right*), 1936. Walls: gray harewood Flexwood. Ceiling: alcove, gold leaf; lower deck, rust. Floor covering: mauve taupe carpet. Chairs: rust, and natural-colored leather. Sofas: natural-colored leather. Tables: gray Micarta. Venetian blinds: gray paint. Bar counter: mahogany. Bar: redwood burl Flexwood, bronze opalescent trim. Mirror: flesh-tinted.

All concrete curves and buttresses, the World's Fair Station of the Long Island Railroad, 1939 (*opposite, top*), was pictured in the Fair's *Official Guide Book* in this manner: "The slogan of the Pennsylvania Railroad, 'From the World of Today to the World of Tomorrow in ten minutes for ten cents,' describes the service of the Long Island Railroad which brings you swiftly to the Fair from Pennsylvania Terminal in Manhattan. Twelve-car shuttle trains operate on a two-minute headway. The Long Island's World's Fair Station has a capacity of 20,000 persons an hour."

Ticket office, Burlington Railroad, Denver, Colorado, 1938 (*opposite, bottom*). The sweeping curves of the gleaming chromium-steel counter and the recessed fluorescent lighting were intended by architects Holabird & Root to suggest the lines of the Burlington's own famous streamliners.

The Douglas DC-3 (*right*), 1937. The most successful Depression civil airliner illustrates the ovoid gliding form and smooth, continuous surface of streamlining. Earning its nickname of "workhorse," the DC-3 eventually carried more than half a billion passengers over the years, not counting millions of servicemen during World War II.

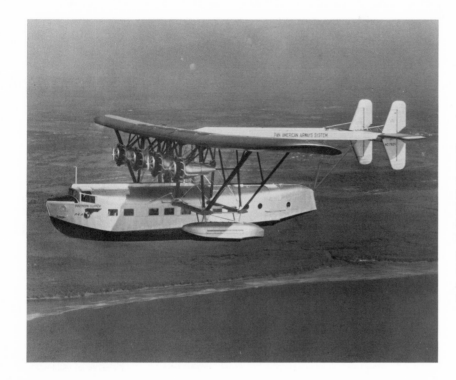

The first Flying Clipper (*left*), 1931. Flagship of the most famous airplanes of the decade, the Sikorsky S-40 captured the imagination of the nation when, in 1933, a brace of dancing chorus girls, led by Ginger Rogers, went *Flying Down to Rio* aboard its glistening wings. *Below:* The Dixie Clipper, last of Pan American Airways' Flying Clippers, 1939.

Brochure advertising TWA's Stratoliner, designed by Raymond Loewy, 1939.

Beauty and Convenience

CHARM
ROOM

This Charm Room for the ladies represents styling and design as advanced as the TWA Stratoliner itself. A masterpiece in convenient arrangement, the room has full view lighted mirrors, two smartly styled dressing tables, upholstered seats, wash basin with hot and cold water, built-in towel shelves, ash trays and handy waste containers. Mirrors are lighted by modern tube fixtures, while the entire room is softly illuminated by indirect lighting.

Interior, Dixie Clipper, 1939.

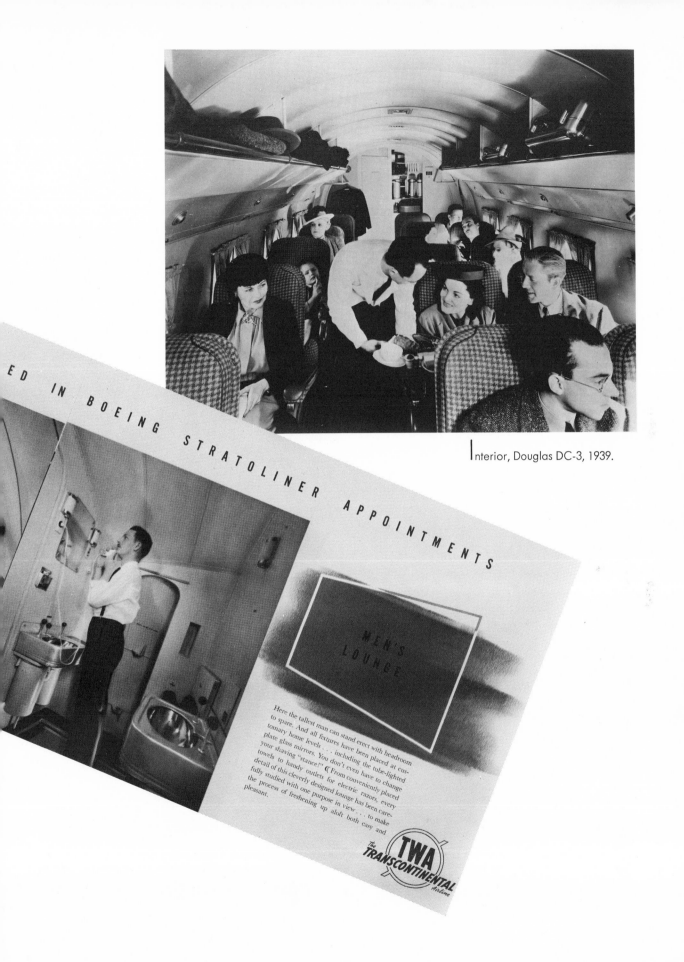

Interior, Douglas DC-3, 1939.

The *Princess Anne*, a Chesapeake Bay commuters' steamer, designed by Raymond Loewy in 1933 and launched in 1936, was the nearest approach to streamlining to appear on the Atlantic seaboard until Loewy's luxury liner, the *S. S. Panama*, made its maiden voyage in 1938. *Far left:* The Main Salon of the *S. S. Panama*, the first ocean liner decorated in the simple, restrained, contemporary American style. *Above and left:* the streamlined *Princess Anne*.

Although most people think of the Stude-baker as an innovative automobile of the late 1940s, it was already a trend-setter in the '30s. *Center:* The 1938 Studebaker President, selected by the American Federation of Arts as the "best looking car of the year," an unprecedented award. *Left:* 1939 Studebaker and S-1 locomotive with their designer, Raymond Loewy. *Right:* 1938 Studebaker Champion cruising sedan.

Because of the commercial success of Chrysler's Airflow in 1934, all Detroit turned to streamlining as automobiles became lower and more horizontal. *Counterclockwise, from left to right:* 1937 Lincoln Zephyr V-12, 1936 Cord, 1936 Plymouth sedan, 1937 Mercury, and 1938 Lincoln Zephyr. The justly famous, but short-lived Cord was America's most advanced front-engined automobile during the Depression.

The '30s was a decade of massive construction: public buildings, dams, highways—and, especially, bridges. Above, two of the finest: The Bronx-Whitestone Bridge, 1939 (*left*) and The Triborough, 1936 (*right*), both designed for New York's Triborough Bridge Authority by O. H. Ammann, Allston Dana, and Aymar Embury.

City offices, the police department, city jail, water department, rifle facilities, and assembly hall were included in Harold Spitznagel's design for the compact Municipal Building in Sioux Falls, South Dakota, completed in 1937. Executed in brick, with granite base and entrance, it expresses the Depression's rejection of superfluous decoration and waste space. The interiors, of flush wood panels or plaster, reflect the conservative, unpretentious exterior. The frescoes in the Commissions' room were painted by Edwin Boyd Johnson.

Although most American public buildings continued to imitate classical models, an increasing number turned to the contemporary Depression Modern style. *Opposite, from top to bottom:* Alpena County Courthouse, Alpena, Michigan, William H. Kuni, architect, 1935. Ector County Courthouse, Odessa, Texas, Elmer Withers, architect, 1938. State Capitol, Bismarck, North Dakota, Holabird & Root, architects, 1934. *Above:* State Capitol, Salem, Oregon, Trowbridge & Livingston and Francis Keally, associated architects, 1938.

During the Depression, the WPA constructed local post offices that were exceeded in ugliness only by those built today. One of the few exceptions, the U.S. Post Office at Miami Beach, Florida (*below*), opened in 1939. *Opposite* (*above*): The Houston (Texas) Building & Loan Association offices, John F. Staub and Kenneth Franzheim, architects, 1938. *Opposite* (*below*): Bronxville (New York) Federal Savings and Loan Association building, George F. Root III and Frederick J. Hartwig, architects, 1939.

Few public buildings of the '30s more dramatically demonstrated the trend of horizontality than did schools, several of which were worlds apart from the vertical blocks of the previous decade. *Left to right:* Edward L. Bailey Junior High School, Jackson, Mississippi, N. W. Overstreet and A. H. Town, architects, 1937. Cranbrook Institute of Sciences Building, Bloomfield Hills, Michigan, Eliel Saarinen, architect, 1938. Columbia High School, Columbia, Mississippi, N. W. Overstreet and A. H. Town, architects, 1937.

Museums, too, surrendered their traditional eclecticism and became increasingly modern, the decade culminating in Edward Durell Stone and Philip Goodwin's magnificent Museum of Modern Art, New York City, 1939 (*opposite*). *Right* (*above*): The nation's first modern museum structure, the Avery Memorial of the Wadsworth Atheneum, Hartford, Connecticut, Morris & O'Connor, architects, 1934. *Right* (*below*): Fine Arts Center, Colorado Springs, Colorado, John Gaw Meem, architect, 1936.

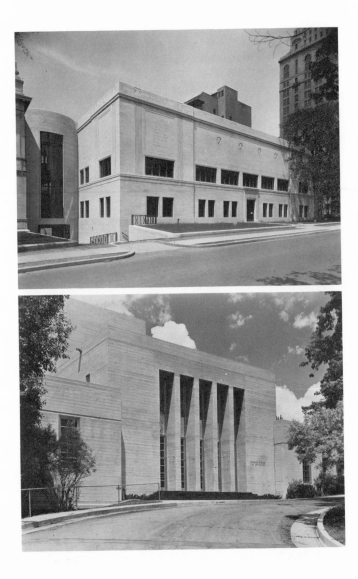

Trans-Lux Theater, New York City, Thomas W. Lamb, architect, 1938.

Hollywood Theater (*right*), Sioux Falls, South Dakota, Harold Spitznagel, architect, 1937.

Savar Theater, Camden, New Jersey, 1936.

In these streamlined, reclining movie theater seats (*opposite*), Depression youth emulated Ruby Keeler and Dick Powell "Pettin' in the Park." The smart aisle light reveals the cult of the unholy trinity. *Above:* Elegantly curved and unornamented, the '30s movie theater bore little resemblance to the rococo motion picture palaces of the previous decade. One of the most handsome Depression Modern theaters was Chicago's Esquire, designed by Pereira and Pereira and opened in 1937.

International Casino, New York City, 1937. Ingeniously designed by Donald Deskey to by-pass the local law limiting the number of bars in an establishment to one, this multi-leveled nightclub featured a spectacular "spiral" bar that served customers along the complete length of stairs. The casino boasted the first escalator in a place of public entertainment.

Ladies' Lounge, Hollywood Theater, Sioux Falls, South Dakota, Harold Spitznagel, designer, 1937.

Built in Mt. Kisco, New York, and completed in 1935, two years after it was designed, the house of Richard H. Mandel was a collaboration between architect Edward Durell Stone and designer Donald Deskey, functioning as "interior architect"—with the assistance of the owner, who was an associate of Deskey.

The exterior (*above*) illustrates the new horizontality, corners broken only by one flowing curve where a rounded glass block bay is introduced. Deskey's interiors (*opposite*), colorful and warm, but reinforcing the functionalism of the exterior, succeeded in bringing indoors the spaciousness of the new horizontality.

So intense was reaction to the Ulrich Kowalski house (*opposite and above*), designed in 1934 by Edward Durell Stone, that zoning ordinances in Mt. Kisco, New York, were modified to prevent "further desecration of the community."

Architectural model of the house of Mrs. Charles I. Liebman, Mt. Kisco, New York, designed in 1937 by Stone but never built.

Writing of his career, which has extended over fifty years, one of the great American architects, George Fred Keck, writes that architects "build at a given time, using all the devices, ideas, and materials and needs of *that* time, and what comes out is the result of such thinking." What came out of his assimilation of ideas current in the Depression was one of the best houses of the '30s: the Herbert Bruning residence in Wilmette, Illinois, designed in 1936.

The Herbert Bruning residence, 1936
(*above and following page*).

Living room, decorated by Gladys Freeman, in one of four guest houses, all designed by Edward Durell Stone, on Mepkin Plantation, Moncks Corners, South Carolina, winter home of Henry R. Luce, 1937.

Detail of living room, Albert C. Koch residence, Cambridge, Massachusetts, Edward Durell Stone, architect, 1936.

The most extraordinary house in Depression America was undoubtedly the residence (above) that Earl Butler built in Des Moines, Iowa, between 1935 and 1937. Working in close collaboration with his architects, Kraetsch and Kraetsch, Butler constructed a fire, tornado, earthquake, and termite-proof residence, permitting no conventional decoration since he believed that "simplicity and good design are much more restful and inherently beautiful in a home." Among the special features were an unusual central ramp, air conditioning, dishwasher and disposal, an electric eye to open and close garage doors, a small storage room for freezing game, an extra ice-cube freezer with a 675-cube capacity, and an intercommunicating telephone system.

Above: Central ramp. *Far left:* Basement recreation room. *Left:* Study.

The crescent-shaped residence in Lake Forest, Illinois, that George Fred Keck designed for B. J. Cahn in 1937. Having seen Keck's "House of Tomorrow" at the Century of Progress, Mrs. Cahn requested that he build "the house of the day after tomorrow." What Keck designed was one of the most beautiful houses in America, whether seen by day (*above*) or at night (*left*).

Right (*above*):
High-ceilinged living room,
rugless and curtainless for
ease in maintenance.
Right (*below*):
Bedroom with built-in beds.

Five views of the Frank Altschul Library, Stamford, Connecticut, designed in 1939 by Edward Durell Stone. A private retreat, planned for a publisher of limited editions and situated on a large estate, the structure featured sliding glass walls, then a novel architectural innovation. The interiors were designed by Virginia Connor.

Collier's House of Ideas (*opposite, above, and right*), an exhibit built in 1940 by Edward Durell Stone on a terrace in Rockefeller Center, introduced the use of redwood to the East. The furniture was designed by Jens Risom and Dan Cooper.

Harrison and Fouilhoux's *Ladies' Home Journal* House (*left*), built for the 1937 New York Home Show, featured a rounded glass wall which, at the push of a button, disappeared into the ground, admitting the garden indoors.

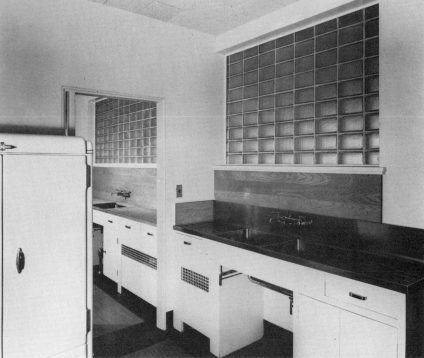

Completed in 1937, this dignified residence of steel, brick, and glass, built for Henry B. Robertson in Centerville, Delaware, was designed by Victorine and Samuel Homsey. Its interiors repeat the essentially simple forms of the exterior, the integration of design and decoration heightened by the almost complete absence of ornamentation.

The house of Alvin Greif (*above and opposite*), on Rivo Alta Island, Florida, designed by T. Trip Russell and Igor Polevitzky, and completed in 1938.

A striking transformation of a 19th-century brownstone in New York City by William Lescaze, designed for his own use and employing glass block several years before it was a popular building material, 1934.

A similar, and even more dramatic transformation of a 19th-century Chicago row house by James F. Eppenstein, 1939.

As modern today as the day it was built, this Chicago apartment house (*above*) was designed by George Fred Keck in 1937. (The photograph was taken in May 1975.)

Certainly the most beautiful apartment house constructed in New York during the 1930s, The Rockefeller Apartments (*opposite*), designed by J. André Fouilhoux and Wallace K. Harrison in 1936, clearly demonstrates the Depression Modern style: an unadorned façade and graceful curves.

The 1930s' love of the curve is everywhere evident in this Milwaukee apartment house, designed by Herbert W. Tullgren and completed in 1939—from the building's graceful bays and its circular driveway *(left)* to the entrance foyer of a typical apartment *(below)* and a hallway corridor leading to the lobby *(opposite)*.

Furniture designed by Russel Wright. *Opposite, above:* "American Modern" dining room, 1935. *Opposite, below:* "Blonde" maple "American Modern" living room with contemporary Morris chairs, each with adjustable back, 1936. *Above:* Upholstered sectional furniture designed for Heywood-Wakefield, 1933.

Furniture designed for Herman Miller, Inc., by Gilbert Rohde. *Opposite, above:* Laurel wood drop-front desk, c. 1936. *Below:* Corner of a living room, featuring radio end table, 1936. *Opposite, below:* Bentwood side chair and glass-top table with brush-chromium support, 1934.

Two views of a bedroom designed by Gilbert Rohde for Herman Miller, Inc., 1934.

B lack lacquer and chrome bedroom suite designed by Norman Bel Geddes for the Simmons Co., displayed in the window of Carson Pirie Scott during the second year of Chicago's Century of Progress Exposition, 1934.

Grand piano (*opposite, above*) designed by Walter Dorwin Teague for Steinway & Sons, 1939. Grand piano (*opposite, below*) designed by Russel Wright for Wurlitzer, c. 1932.

Detail of living room (*below*) decorated by John D. Gerald for B. Altman's "Modern House," New York City, 1937.

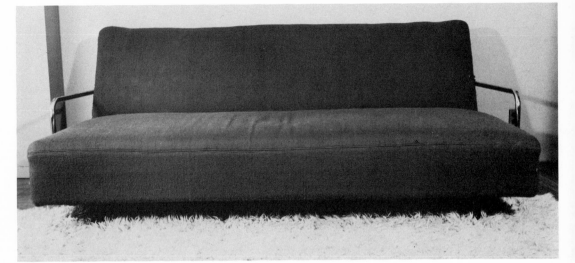

Sculptor, architect, designer, poet, visionary, Frederick Kiesler was a genius the majority of whose works are out of place in a volume dedicated to the mundane. But even Kiesler's furniture of the '30s was touched by the spirit of the times: the urge to simplify, to strip bare is everywhere apparent.

Far left, above: One of a nest of cast aluminum coffee tables, 1936. *Far left, below:* Aluminum kidney-shaped tables, 1938. *Center:* Bookcase with adjustable sycamore shelves and chrome supports, 1935. *Above, top:* Chrome couch/sofa/bed, originally covered with white leather and an excellent example of Kiesler's concept of multiple use of furniture, 1935. *Above:* Chrome ash tray, 1935.

"Modern Blue Kitchen," a model room designed to display the latest pattern of linoleum by the Armstrong Cork Company, 1936.

"The Kitchen of Tomorrow," as envisioned by the Briggs Manufacturing Company, 1935. The cylindrical structure in the foreground is an electric range.

Bathrooms designed in 1940 (*opposite*) and in 1938 (*above*) by Edward Durell Stone. The Leda and the Swan chair and mural reflect either the influence of the famous Surrealism exhibition of 1936 or a droll sense of humor; perhaps both.

Plumbing hardware (*below*), designed in 1932 by George Sakier.

Designs by Russel Wright. Smoking set *(opposite, above)*, chrome, cork, wood, and glass, 1933. Aquarium *(below)*, chromium and glass, 1933. Bookend *(above)*, c. 1930.

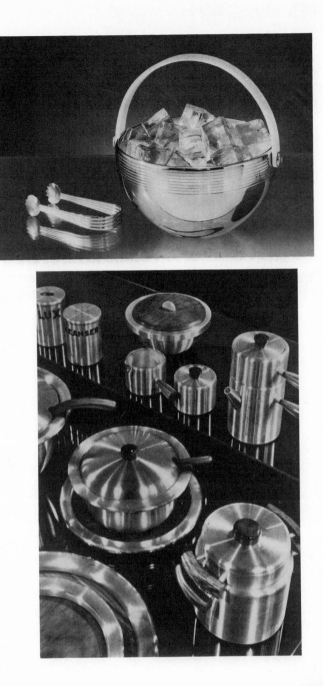

Home accessories by Russel Wright. Handmade silver flatware (*opposite*), c. 1930. Ice bucket and tongs (*above*), 1933. Spun aluminum stove-to-table wear (*center*), 1933. Bun warmer (*right*), c. 1933.

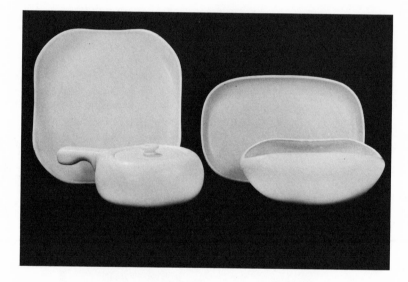

Russel Wright's "American Modern" dinnerware (1937) was in its time immensely popular, favored in particular by young couples starting married life in the final years of the Depression. Its graceful, flowing lines owe as much to the influence of Surrealism's amorphous shapes as to Wright's desire to break away from the geometric forms of the early '30s.

In 1934 Lurelle Guild designed a line of aluminum utensils for Wear-Ever that were so forward-looking for their day that they were displayed in the Philadelphia Art Alliance's Dynamic Design show. *Opposite:* Whistling tea kettle with Bakelite handle and knob (*above*). Contrast (*below*) between old-style tea kettle and Guild's streamline model. *Above:* Guild's 1934 adaptation of an early American coffeepot.

Designs by Lurelle Guild for the International Silver Company, 1934, the first time in the company's history in which signed pieces were offered. *Opposite:* The Glory Bowl (*below*) and The Bordeaux Dish (*above*). *Above:* Regency Covered Dish (*top*), The Empire Bowl (*center*), and The Brompton Wine Cooler (*right*).

Streamlined Model 30 Electrolux vacuum cleaner (*above*), 1937. Upright
Montgomery Ward vacuum cleaner (*right*), designed in 1939 by Walter
Dorwin Teague.

General Electric mixer (*left*), designed in 1934 by Lurelle Guild.
Coldspot refrigerator (*below*) by Raymond Loewy, 1938.

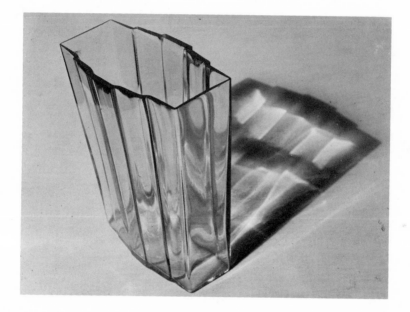

A Depression ideal: creating inexpensive, well-designed objects for the common man. Mass-produced glassware (*opposite and above*), designed for the Fostoria Company by George Sakier, c. 1934.

Depression Modern Steuben glass was probably the best-designed American glass since that produced in the 18th century. *Above:* Table Glass, designed by Frederick Carder, 1934. *Opposite:* Ring Stopper Decanter, 1934.

Unlike the more elaborate and ornate pieces produced before and since, Steuben glass created during the Depression was either starkly plain or simply etched. In the opinion of many, the unadorned pieces are among the most stunningly beautiful designs of the decade. *Above:* Bowl with solid crimped base, designed by Walter Heintze, 1938. *Center:* Mariner's Bowl, designed by Sidney Waugh, 1935. *Opposite, above:* Gazelle Bowl, designed by Sidney Waugh, 1935. *Opposite, below:* Teardrop Candlesticks, designed by F. B. Sellew, 1937.

This 1939 RCA-Victor console cost $450 and was America's first popular-priced television receiver. Its cabinet, bulky and clumsy, displayed the curves favored by contemporary consumers.

The first table model radio and the first practical portable radio (*opposite, inset*), designed by Russel Wright for Wurlitzer, c. 1933. RCA-Victor radio-phonograph (*below*), featuring controls inspired by aeronautics, 1935.

Wallace K. Harrison and J. André Fouilhoux's Trylon and Perisphere, 1939. The symbol of the New York World's Fair represented the final distillation of more than one thousand preliminary sketches—the use of the sphere and triangle (geometry's simplest and most fundamental forms) resulting from a determination to strike a new note in design, yet one simple in form and structurally sound. A streamlined phoenix emerging triumphant from the devastation of the Great Depression—the very essence of the Depression Modern style.

CREDITS

In this list of photographic credits, the following abbreviations are used: a (above), b (below), c (center), l (left), and r (right).

Jacket: Edward Durell Stone Associates, an Ezra Stoller photograph. *Frontispiece:* Republic Steel Corporation.

Preface: p. 17 (counterclockwise, l. to r.), Dunbar Furniture, Pan American World Airways, Halle's, Raymond Loewy International, Inc.

Depression Modern: An Appreciation: Evolutionary charts, Raymond Loewy International, Inc.; p. 24, author; p. 25, New York Public Library Picture Collection; p. 29, Republic Steel Corporation; p. 31, The Austin Company; p. 35, Raymond Loewy International, Inc.; p. 44, Russel Wright.

The Thirties Style in America: An Album: pp. 50-51, The Austin Company; p. 52, The Hecht Company (a), The Campana Corporation (c); p. 53, The Austin Company; p. 54, Johnson & Johnson (a), Arizona Historical Society (c), U. S. Forest Products Laboratory (b); p. 55, *Shreveport Times,* a Langston McEachern photograph (a), Hedrich-Blessing (b); p. 56, The Austin Company; p. 57, CBS; p. 58, Steuben Glass (a), Wallace K. Harrison (b); p. 59, Wallace K. Harrison.

P. 60, Aluminum Company of America (a), Raymond Loewy International, Inc. (b); p. 61, Northwest Architectural Archives (a), The Chase Manhattan Bank (b); pp. 62-63, The Meyercord Company, Hedrich-Blessing photographs; p. 64, Russel Wright; p. 65, Russel Wright (a), Raymond Loewy International, Inc. (b); pp. 66-67, Hedrich-Blessing; pp. 68-69, Time Incorporated.

Pp. 70-71, Northwest Architectural Archives; pp. 72-73, Johnson Wax photographs; p. 74, Herman Miller, Inc., p. 75, Edward Durell Stone Associates; pp. 76-77, Dictaphone Corporation (a), Raymond Loewy International, Inc. (b); p. 78, Burroughs Corporation, Business Forms and Supplies Group; p. 79, Raymond Loewy International, Inc. (a), A. T. & T. (b).

P. 80, Southern California Gas Company (a), Raymond Loewy International, Inc. (b); p. 81, Republic Steel Corporation (a), F. W. Woolworth Co. (b); p. 82, Star Electrical Supply Co.; p. 83, NCR Corporation; p. 84, Raymond Loewy International, Inc.; p. 85, Wm. H. Block Co. (a), The Emporium (b); p. 86, The Archives, The Coca-Cola Company (a.l.), The Great Atlantic and Pacific Tea Company (a.c.), Russel Wright (a.r.), Raymond Loewy International, Inc. (b); pp. 87-89, Raymond Loewy International, Inc.

P. 90, Republic Steel Corporation; pp. 91-96 (a), Raymond Loewy International, Inc.; p. 96 (b), Hedrich-Blessing; pp. 98-99, Pan American World Airways.

P. 100, author (a), Pan American World Airways (b); p. 101, Pan American World Airways; pp. 102-5, Raymond Loewy International, Inc.; pp. 106-7, New York Public Library Picture Collection; p. 108, Triborough Bridge & Tunnel Authority, a Richard Averill Smith photograph; p. 109, The Museum of the City of New York, a Berenice Abbott photograph.

Pp. 110-11, The Spitznagel Partners; p. 112, Alpena County Clerk (a), Ector County Clerk (c), Holabird & Root (b); p. 113, Oregon State Highway Division; p. 114, E. H. Daws; p. 115, Houston First Savings (a), First Federal Savings and Loan Association of New York (b); pp. 116-17, A. L. McCormick (a), Cranbrook Educational Community (c), Columbia

Public Schools (b); p. 118, Wadsworth Atheneum (a), Colorado Springs Fine Arts Center (b); p. 119, Edward Durell Stone Associates.

Pp. 120-21, Walter Dorwin Teague Associates, Inc., Robert Damora photographs; pp. 122-23, Trans-Lux (a), Northwest Architectural Archives (c), Republic Steel Corporation (b); 124-25, Hedrich-Blessing; p. 126, Donald Deskey; p. 127, Northwest Architectural Archives; pp. 128-29, Edward Durell Stone Associates.

Pp. 130-31, Edward Durell Stone Associates, Ezra Stoller photographs (l. and r.a.), a Louis Checkman photograph (r.b.); pp. 132-34, George Fred Keck, Hedrich-Blessing photographs; p. 135, Edward Durell Stone Associates, a Gottscho-Schleisner photograph (a), an Ezra Stoller photograph (b); pp. 136-37, Hedrich-Blessing; pp. 138-39, George Fred Keck, Hedrich-Blessing photographs.

Pp. 140-43 (a, c), Edward Durell Stone Associates, Ezra Stoller photographs; p. 143 (b), Wallace K. Harrison; pp. 144-145, Robert Damora; pp. 146-47, T. Trip Russell; p. 148, The Museum of the City of New York; p. 149, Hedrich-Blessing.

P. 150, Wallace K. Harrison; p. 151-53, Hedrich-Blessing; pp. 154-55, Russel Wright; pp. 156-58, Herman Miller, Inc.; p. 159, Simmons Company.

P. 160, Walter Dorwin Teague Associates, Inc. (a), Russel Wright (b); p. 161, B. Altman & Co.; pp. 162-63, Lillian Kiesler, Lenny Di Caro photographs; p. 164, Armstrong Cork Company; p. 165, author; pp. 166-67 (a), Edward Durell Stone Associates, Ezra Stoller photographs; p. 167 (b), George Sakier; pp. 168-69, Russel Wright.

Pp. 170-73, Russel Wright; pp. 174-75, Wear-Ever Aluminum, Inc.; pp. 176-77, author; p. 178, Electrolux Corporation (a), Walter Dorwin Teague Associates, Inc. (b); p. 179, author (a), Raymond Loewy International, Inc. (b).

Pp. 180-81, George Sakier; pp. 182-85, Steuben Glass; p. 186, RCA (a), Russel Wright (b); p. 187, RCA; p. 188, Wallace K. Harrison.

INDEX